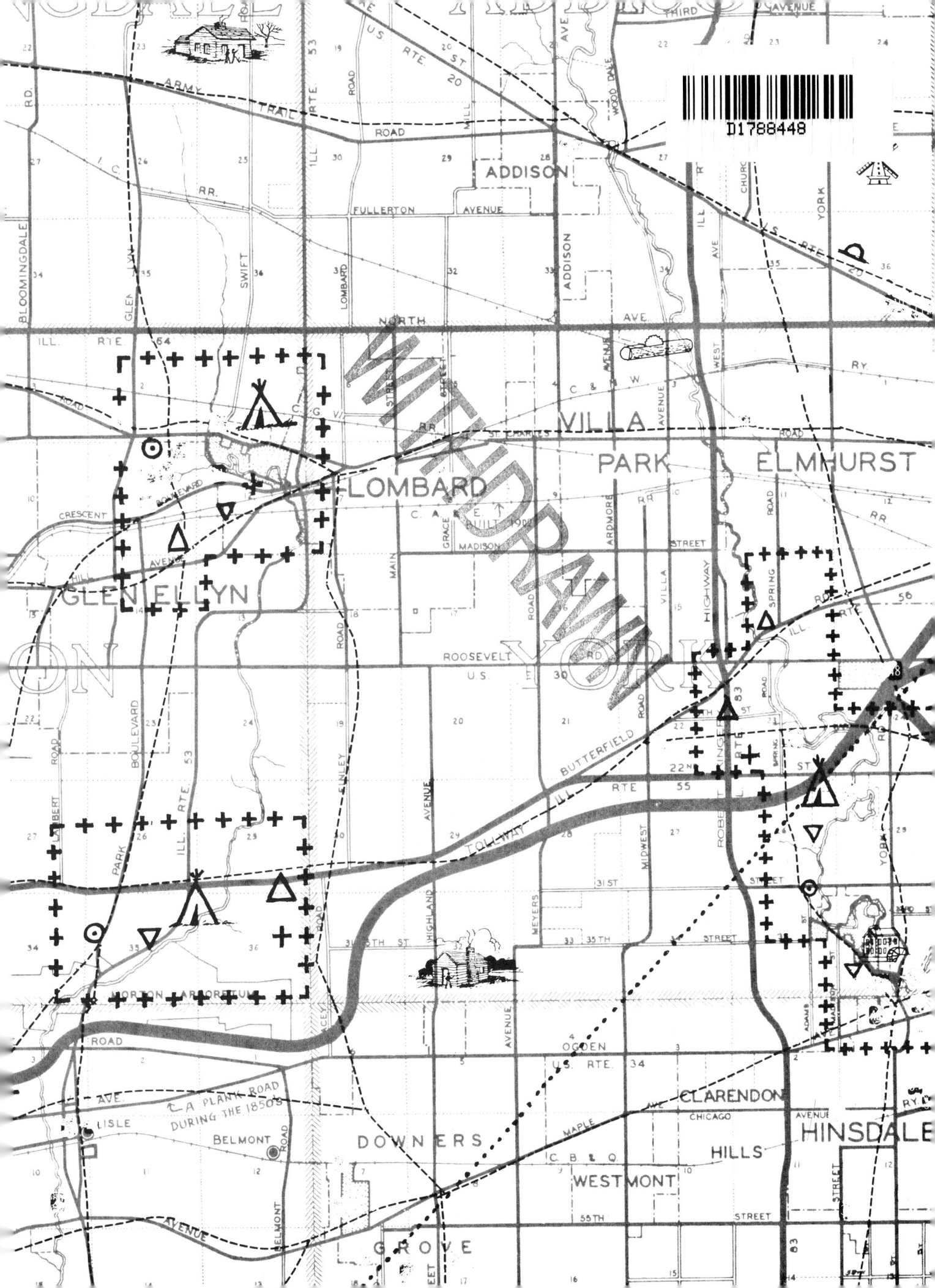

ELMHURST: Trails From Yesterday

by

Don Russell

Published by the Heritage Committee of the Elmhurst Bicentennial Commission on the authority of the City of Elmhurst, Illinois

Copyright © 1977
by the City of Elmhurst - DuPage County, Illinois

ISBN #0-912868-01-5

printed in Wheaton, Illinois
by Kjellberg & Sons, Inc.

FOREWORD

The Bicentennial History of Elmhurst began as a life-long dream of Robert C. Stanger who shared with Carl Sandburg this sentiment: "If we have no regard for our past, we will have little future worth remembering."

When the Elmhurst Bicentennial Commission was established December 16, 1974, and was considering projects, Dr. Stanger strongly recommended the publication of a complete history of the city of Elmhurst. The Bicentennial Commission accepted the project and budgeted money for a small paperback booklet. The Heritage Committee was assigned the project. A research committee of twenty selected volunteers was formed and Don Russell was later selected as the author.

Once undertaken, the writing of a new Elmhurst history proved to be a much greater project than originally conceived. The Research Committee had begun to sift through countless facts and fictions and soon found gaps in available resource materials. The original framework for the writing of the history proved to have its limitations. The Heritage Committee recognized the need for expanded project conception and enlarged financial support.

Again the committee called on Dr. Stanger. He appeared before the City Council and strongly urged that a "more suitable" book should be produced. As a result of Dr. Stanger's personal commitment and sustained vision, the City Council voted its support of the history project.

After Dr. Stanger's death, all involved in the project felt the loss of his guidance. But his inspiration and the concerted efforts of many people have brought this book to fruition.

The author and the research committee have placed emphasis on the origins of organizations and institutions of social and commercial development. The constraints of time and space have limited "completeness" in many areas and have left opportunities for further research and reporting for future historians.

Norman P. Smalley
Chairman
Elmhurst Bicentennial Commission

DEDICATION

Dedicated to
Dr. Robert C. Stanger

"He was a man whose devotion and commitment to what is honorable and excellent were revealed in his life as a pastor, as a teacher, as an academic administrator, and as a civic leader. Faith in God, and hope in man symbolized his perspectives. He was esteemed by all who had personal and professional relationships with him."

Prof. Emeritus Rudolf Schade at
Nov. 5, 1976 Memorial
Service for Dr. Robert C. Stanger

CONTENTS

Foreword III
Dedication IV
Bicentennial Commission VI
Research Committee VI
Acknowledgments VI
The Land and its Earliest Peoples 2
Territories, Counties, and Townships 8
The Early Settlers 12
Cottage Hill Days 25
Cottage Hill in the 1860s 31
Elmhurst After the Chicago Fire 36
Incorporation as a Village 43
Growth as a Village 47
Elmhurst in the 1890s 58
Turn of the Century 66
Elmhurst Becomes a City 72
Sports in Elmhurst 86
World War I Changes 94
Years of Suburban Expansion 99
Decade of Standing Still 109
Elmhurst and the Arts 115
Years of War and Recovery 129
The Booming 1950s 135
The Turbulent 1960s 140
City of the 1970s 143
Elmhurst Chronology 146
Elmhurst - Village and City Officials 149
Bibliography 168
Index 170

ACKNOWLEDGMENTS

The Heritage Committee of the Bicentennial Commission wishes to thank the many friends and colleagues who have given their support and advice during the preparation of this book, especially those of the Elmhurst Bicentennial Commission, the Elmhurst City Council, the Elmhurst Historical Museum, the Elmhurst Historical Society and the Elmhurst Historical Research Committee.

ELMHURST BICENTENNIAL COMMISSION

Deborah Ames
Alben F. Bates, Jr.
Donald Bjork
Phyllis Carroll
Margaret Cooper
Edward DePasque
Jackie Haddad
Eleanor Hookham
Elmer Jacobs
John Jordan
Janice Ladd
Frank Mushow
Norman Smalley
Robert Stanger
Ruth Strand
Donald Stoner
Russell Weigand

HISTORICAL RESEARCH COMMITTEE

Donald Cooper
Margaret Cooper
Jean Costigan
Eleanor Davis
Edward DePasque
Stanley Dziedic
Walter Huxmann
Stacey Irmiter
Theodore Kross
Ralph Mahon
Joan Marella
Daniel Nixon
Rudolph Schade
Marilyn Scheahan
Robert Stanger
Nellie Stickle
Ruth Strand
Joyce Van Norman

Editor, Joan Marella

Historical Consultant, Ruth Strand

The Heritage Committee is also gratefully indebted to Alben Bates, Jr., Donald Cooper, Lillian Harlan, Roger Harrington, Alvin Kraft, Theodore Kross, Langdon Longwell, Finley McGrew, Walter Purdy, Norman Smalley, Nellie Stickle, Ruth Stickle, Donald Stoner, Nancy Wilson, and Dorothy Ziegler. The Committee also thanks The Alben F. Bates and Clara G. Bates Foundation.

The Heritage Committee on behalf of the Elmhurst community acknowledges with deep gratitude the perseverance and constant personal concern with which Ruth Strand as Chairman of The Heritage Committee, succeeding Dr. Stanger, has carried this project, *Elmhurst; Trails from Yesterday* to Completion.

INTRODUCTION

"The early settlers of Elmhurst were tree lovers. In hundreds of day or night walks I took in Elmhurst, I was grateful to those old timers for the noble elms, oaks, maples and pines they bequeathed to us. I would salute those of the present generation who have the spirit of the early tree lovers." So wrote Carl Sandburg to Elmhurst historian Helmut Berens.

It is paradoxical that a community should be called an elm forest or "tree town" when most of its original area had been treeless prairie land and all of its elm trees planted by such pioneers as Lathrop, Bryan, and Wadhams. The foresight of these men is the more remarkable when it is recalled that to pioneers in the great forest to the eastward, trees had been a nuisance, and planting a tree - other than a fruit tree - was unheard of. There had been obvious change from the open prairie of the 1840s to the tree-lined streets of 1869. The trees made Elmhurst a suburb at a time when a suburb was a retreat to the country from the booming and noisy city of Chicago.

It was the growth of these trees and others planted soon afterward which inspired Thomas Barbour Bryan to suggest changing the name of Cottage Hill to Elmhurst. At a citizens meeting in Byrd's Nest Chapel in 1869, other townsmen agreed with Mr. Bryan and voted to accept the new name which was a compound of the tree name *elm* and a German cognate for the word *forest*. By their action, the history of Cottage Hill became from that moment, the history of Elmhurst.

THE LAND AND ITS EARLIEST PEOPLES

Elmhurst is the largest city in DuPage County. It is also one of fifty Illinois cities of more than 20,000 population within the Chicago metropolitan area. Elmhurst is older than most of the fifty cities and in its origin was not suburban; it was a growing community when Chicago was still a small village. It is not to be supposed that the two, even when not far apart in population, had any possibility of rivalry. Chicago, even as a tiny hamlet, was important. It had been a place name on maps for a century and a half before it acquired permanent population. Its geographical advantages were evident; those of Elmhurst, though less impressive, were important enough that some kind of settlement in the area was inevitable.

Most early American cities were built on streams, primarily because water is necessary to human life, but also because water transportation was the most practicable through the wilderness of the eastern woodlands. Even if a stream were too small to navigate, it might offer waterpower for the necessary grist mill. Elmhurst's only stream is Salt Creek, too small for navigation, and its most practicable mill, Graue's, was built downstream at Fullersburg. There must be other reasons for Elmhurst's early existence, and those reasons are to be found in the geologic changes of the immediate area.

GEOLOGY

The cooled volcanic rocks of the Pre-Cambrian Era concern us little, for they are buried deep beneath Elmhurst. However, during the Paleozoic Era that followed, the entire Great Lakes region was covered with inland seas that for more than a quarter of a billion years deposited sediments, some of which became limestone such as has been quarried since 1883 by the Elmhurst-Chicago Stone Company at the west end of First Street. The seas drained away during the Mesozoic Era, at which time erosion began to shape the region into some resemblance of its present status. This process was interrupted a mere million years ago by the four ice ages of the Pleistocene Epoch. The four glaciers that crept down from the north are known to geologists as the Nebraskan, Kansan, Illinoian, and Wisconsin. The heavy weight of ice leveled hills, ground rock to gravel and sand, and gouged out the hollows that became the Great Lakes. The Illinoian was so named because it covered most of Illinois. The Wisconsin, of 50,000 years ago, covered only the northeast quarter of Illinois, but because it was most recent, its effects are visible from Chicago through DuPage County.

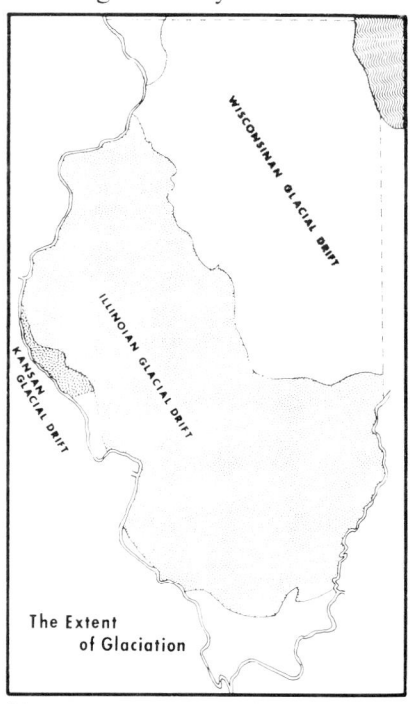

The Extent of Glaciation

Robert P. Howard: Illinois: A History of the Prairie State 1972

The last glacier, the Wisconsin, began to melt some 25,000 years ago, its waters forming the Great Lakes, but a much greater Great Lakes than we know today. The much larger Lake

The Land And Its Earliest Peoples

Michigan is called by geologists Lake Chicago and one of its banks can be traced about two miles east of Elmhurst. Lake Chicago spilled its excess water southward, roughly by way of the Des Plaines River, the Illinois River, and the Mississippi. All of these rivers were immensely large in the post-glacial period.

Somewhere between Elmhurst and Chicago's Loop and between the Des Plaines and Chicago Rivers, there is a continental divide, a height of land, that theoretically separates the waters that flow into Lake Michigan and eventually into the Atlantic Ocean by way of the other lakes and the St. Lawrence River, from the waters that flow from the Des Plaines River, Salt Creek, and the DuPage River, by way of the Illinois River and the Mississippi into the Gulf of Mexico. Many thousands of Elmhurst commuters for many years have passed over that great divide daily, yet it is doubtful if any one of them could tell where it is. It was never a readily observable height, and land development has helped to obscure it.

In the early days of settlement, Chicago was mostly swamp. Describing it in 1831 Mrs. John H. Kinzie said: "The land was a low wet prairie, scarcely affording good walking in the driest summer weather, while at other seasons it was absolutely impassable." Melting snows of spring or a heavy rain at any time transformed the prairie into a shallow lake that also ignored the divide. Milo M. Quaife summed it up: "During much of the year Chicago presented all of the attributes of a first-class marsh."

Dr. Frederick H. Bates, of a pioneer Elmhurst family, once noted that in 1850, anyone standing at the intersection of St. Charles Road and Cottage Hill Avenue would have had an unobstructed view for several miles in all directions. "Elmhurst dominates the entire section by reason of its superior elevation," he wrote. "It is not generally known that we (Elmhurst) are seventy feet higher than the Des Plaines River because the rise is so gradual.....there is a fall towards the (Salt) creek, of over twenty feet, a mile west, so that Elmhurst is on a ridge, with drainage both east and west." In the area along Salt Creek and other small water ways, the native trees were willow, ash, cottonwood, box elder, maple, and butternut. Of course, the elm, too, was native to northern Illinois.

Wild roses and wild grapes were common in the earlier days. Somewhat later the daughter of another pioneer family, Carlotta Koch, named dog-tooth violets, anemone, Dutchman's breeches, trillium, bloodroot, and jack-in-the-pulpit as wild flowers common in the area known as Graue's Woods. That too was along Salt Creek. Travelers who had toiled through Chicago's swamps and marshes would have seen Elmhurst's advantages.

COMING OF THE INDIANS

The earliest travelers in DuPage County watched the ice go out at the end of the glacial ages. Excavations on both branches of the DuPage River have uncovered flint weapons dated from 11,000 B.C. to 7,500 B.C., known as the Middle Archaic Period. In 1974 Lois Braverman, surveyor for the Illinois Foundation of Archaeology, found artifacts dated from the same period in the town of Oak Brook. It is aptly observed by Harriet Smith that "All Americans, starting with the earliest Indians, are descendants of immigrants." It is generally accepted that the Americas were peopled by hunting bands crossing a land bridge formed during the ice ages from Siberia to Alaska. It is logical to assume that the immense amount of glacial ice covering the land would have lowered the sea level to make this possible. Some scientists place the beginning of this movement as far back as 50,000 years ago.

Primitive as these people must have been, their hunting parties had sufficient organization and leadership to attack the mammoth, an elephant-like animal much larger than the present-day African or Asiatic elephants. Successive bands of hunters of several kinds of Asiatic peoples followed the mammoth, woolly rhinoceros, and a prehistoric bison into America during tens of thousands of years. By 8000 B.C. some of them reached Illinois, as determined since 1956 by excavations at the Modoc Rock Shelter in Randolph County, the Koster site in Calhoun County, and the Oak Brook sites. During the 5,000 or more years the earliest or Archaic man lived in Illinois, he had changed. He had hunted the mastodon, another elephant-like relative of the mammoth. (Wheaton College has mounted a mastodon skeleton found in this area.) But the mastodon, musk-ox, ground sloth, and giant beaver moved west and north, and the earliest DuPage County resident learned to hunt deer, elk, bear, and raccoon. He chipped spear points from flint and used an atlatl, a throwing stick, to hurl his spear but had not yet invented the bow and arrow.

It may well be that some of these ancient people passed through the site of Elmhurst on their way to the shore of Lake Chicago in search of mussels and snails. These early peoples had to keep moving in their search for food, obtained by hunting, and by finding and gathering. By 500 A.D. corn reached Illinois and farming was begun. They made pottery in which food could be stored, but rarely stored enough to last through an Illinois winter. There would have been many more of these peoples had not so many starved to death. The survivors are those we call Indians for no better reason than that Columbus assumed he had reached India or the "Indies" on his first voyage. Giving them this misapplied name has resulted in regarding all of them as a race and body politic whereas their tribes and nations were diverse in cultures, physical characteristics, and languages. Indians spoke hundreds of languages which ethnologists classify into fifty or more linguistic families for the area north of Mexico. Most of the Indians in Illinois belonged to the Algonquian language family, found from Virginia northward along the Atlantic Coast, westward to the Mississippi, and north and west of the Great Lakes.

The biennial *Blue Book of the State of Illinois* in presenting the state's chain of title, names only the Illinois or Illini Indians, a confederacy sometimes called Illiniwek including the Michigami, Kaskaskia, Peoria, Cahokia, and Tamaroa. A sixth tribe, the Moingwena, is sometimes added. Father Jacques Marquette and Louis Jolliet in 1673 followed the Wisconsin River to the Mississippi and descended the Mississippi to the mouth of the Arkansas. On their return, the Illini told them of a short cut up the Illinois River to the Des Plaines and the Chicago Portage. This was the first exploration of the "Illinois Country," which came to mean much more country than the Illini knew about. Although Marquette called Lake Michigan the Lac des Ilinois, it is not known that the Illini ever came much further east than the vicinity of Starved Rock, where Marquette preached to them.

Closely related to the Illini were the Miami, with their allies, the Wea and the Piankeshaw. A French mission to a Miami village is subject of a marker at Swedish Covenent Hospital, Foster and California avenues, Chicago, and other Miami or Wea village sites were just north of the Loop, and along the south branch of the Chicago River. Later the Miamis moved eastward, to the upper Wabash River in Indiana, and the Maumee River in Ohio. Miamis may have visited the site of Elmhurst, as may have other tribes that passed through or lived for a time in northern Illinois - Kickapoo, Sauk, Fox, Menominee, Winnebago and other Siouan tribes, and the Iroquois.

Not far northwest of Elmhurst, at Lawrence Avenue and East River Road, is the grave of Alexander Robinson, or Che-Che-Pin-Qua, called chief of the Potawatomi, Ottawa, and Chippewa. To interpret this as meaning that Robinson was top man for all Indians of these three tribes would be a gross exaggeration. His influence extended only to a small mixed group in the Chicago region. The Chippewa, or Ojibway, constitute one of the largest tribes of the Algonquian stock, perhaps 60,000. They lived, and still live in about the same numbers, on both sides of Lake Superior and north of Lake Huron. Only a small band of Chippewas wandered as far south as Chicago. The great chief of the Ottawas was Pontiac, who led warfare against the English in 1763. Later scattered bands of Ottawas came to Illinois.

The Potawatomi may never have numbered more than 2,500 persons, living in widely scattered villages with little unity of action. Potawatomis were largely responsible for the Fort Dearborn massacre in 1812, but other bands of Potawatomi remained friendly to Americans.

Robinson had a prominent part in negotiating the Treaty of Chicago in 1833, by which the combined tribes agreed to give up their claims to Illinois lands and move west.

POTAWATOMI VILLAGES

The Potawatomi are the only Indians definitely known to have lived in the immediate vicinity of Elmhurst. A major village called Sauganakka was on the bend of Salt Creek at Oak Brook, south of Elmhurst. North of that village have been identified two camps, a signal station, two chipping stations, and a mound. Other Potawatomi sites are near the old spring north of Harger Road, in Churchill Forest Preserve, at Butterfield Road and U.S. 53 south of Lombard and Glen Ellyn, at Naperville, Warrenville, and West Chicago.

Villages might consist of forty to sixty lodges, arranged in a semicircle facing a river. The traditional Potawatomi lodge was a circular, domed wigwam of bent-over poles, covered with bark or mats. After contact with the Hurons, an Iroquoian people, some Potawatomis built squared long-houses, especially in winter. And some had tipis (tepees) of interlocked poles, covered with bark or buffalo hide.

George Quimby *Indian Life in the Upper Great Lakes* 1961
Mat-covered domed wigwam - Potawatomi.

Near their villages, the Potawatomis raised corn, beans, squash, melons and tobacco. They tapped maple trees for syrup and gathered wild rice, beech nuts, wild plums, and other nuts and berries. They did some fishing with spears and nets. It was common for observers to say that "the women do all the work," and they did most of the farming and gathering, while the men's "entire occupation is hunting." This reflects a common European idea that hunting was a sport of the aristocracy. For the Indian, especially when armed only with bow and arrow which he laboriously made himself, it must have been the hardest kind of work.

Marquette and Jolliet reported large herds of buffalo along the Illinois River, and buffalo were numerous in Illinois until the "Winter of the Deep Snow," 1830-1831, which covered most of Illinois and destroyed much wild life. Before that the Potawatomis had annual buffalo hunts, directed by leaders chosen from the buffalo clan. The keeper of the sacred bundle of the clan held ceremonies to attract the buffalo. Guards named by the clan used elkhorn-handled whips to control the hunters, preventing them from going it alone and stampeding the herd. When the herd was sighted, the hunters were divided into two parties to attempt to surround the buffalo. The method was similar to that used later by the Plains Indians, but it is to be remembered that Potawatomis had few, if any, horses, and hunting buffalo on foot was highly dangerous. If the "surround" was successful in bringing down enough meat to supply the village, the hunters were turned loose for such individual exploits as they desired to attempt. After they returned to the village, feasts were held with ceremonies naming children born while the hunt was on. This might be a considerable number, for buffalo herds were not always found when wanted, and the hunt might last for an extended period of time.

Aside from the limited number of buffalo, the only large game animal in this region was the deer; and the deer could be speedy and elusive. An occasional black bear was taken, usually when sluggish in his winter den. The Potawatomis ate beaver, otter, mink, muskrat, squirrel, and rabbit; woodhen and a few other birds, including migrating ducks and geese. It took a large number of any of these to feed an Indian family band. A few hundred hungry Indians could clean out all the game, large and small, within a considerable distance from their villages. That is one reason 2,500 Potawatomis (the highest estimate seems to be less than 6,000) spread themselves thin all the way from Lake Erie to the Mississippi River as they sought areas where there was still something to hunt.

The Potawatomi, like other Indians, were a noisy people. One observer noted that the women and girls danced at night to the sound of a drum and a gourd rattle containing shot or pebbles. The old men danced the medicine dance, resembling a set of demons, and all of this takes place during the night. The young men danced the war dance, striking a post with a tomahawk, while they recounted their achievements. Everyone danced, and all of it was punctuated with songs, shouts, and war whoops. In the daytime, they played la crosse with a little racket and a wooden ball.

Potawatomi women were noted for their decorative work with porcupine quills, but from earliest contacts, they adapted to European dress, a white chemise being characteristic. However, they used Indian designs in their work with beads and ribbons.

The Potawatomi were called good friends and

bad enemies and one gets the impression that they were a people who adapted themselves to life as they found it and were more easy going than combative. Chiefs of Potawatomi bands signed their names, or marks, to 53 treaties.

Potawatomi costumes of the type worn about 1800.

FIRST SETTLERS

Bailey Hobson was the first settler in DuPage County, arriving in March, 1831. He built a grist mill on the west branch of the DuPage River in 1834. Hobson was soon joined by Christopher Paine, Captain Joseph Naper, captain of the schooner *Telegraph* which he had sailed to Chicago; Joseph's brother, John Naper; and others to the number of twenty or more families. By the spring of 1832 there were perhaps 180 persons living in or near Naper's Settlement which eventually became Naperville. Captain Naper built a grist mill and a trading post and soon had friendly relations with the Potawatomi living nearby. One of them (named Shata according to *A History of the County of DuPage*, by C.W. Richmond and H.F. Valette and according to others, a son of Shabbona or a son of Half Day) brought warning of the outbreak of the Black Hawk War, along with a rumor, later proved false, that the Sauks were raiding along the Fox River. Many residents fled to Fort Dearborn (Chicago); others took their chances in the fort built by Naper (now captain of the militia). Actually, the war came no nearer DuPage County than Indian Creek, north of Ottawa, where fifteen settlers were massacred, probably by a Potawatomi band not allied with Black Hawk's following.

Black Hawk, who had fought with the British in the War of 1812, had ambitions to head a confederacy like that of Tecumseh, but he failed to sell the Potawatomis on his idea. Most of them helped the settlers as scouts against Black Hawk's following, and one leader, Shabbona, became an Illinois hero for warning settlers of hostile bands.

By the Treaty of Chicago in 1833 the Potawatomis, along with Ottawas and Chippewas, agreed to move beyond the Mississippi. By 1840 most of them had gone. Although some stayed behind, it is not known if any remained in DuPage County.

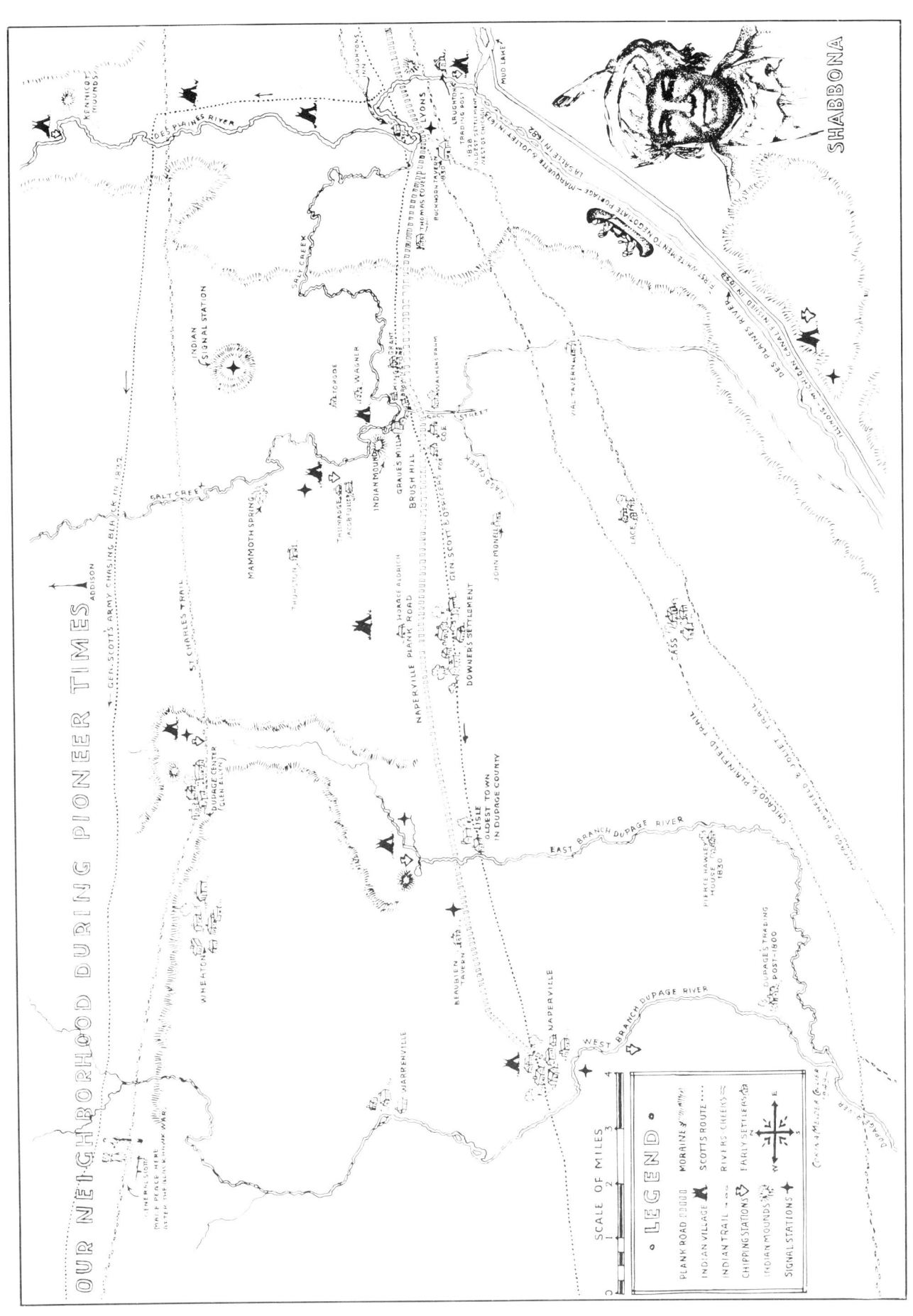

TERRITORIES, COUNTIES, AND TOWNSHIPS

Even while only Potawatomi Indians lived in the area now designated as Elmhurst, it was mapped as lying within a successively large number of often conflicting political and governmental jurisdictions. From the time of the exploration of Marquette and Jolliet in 1673, the "Illinois Country" was claimed as a part of New France. Missionaries and fur trappers, who had been active around Green Bay, pushed south to meet the Illini along the Illinois River. Rene Robert Cavelier Sieur de La Salle came in 1679 and built Fort St. Louis at Starved Rock and Fort Crevecoeur at Peoria Lake. LaSalle is said to have been the first to name "Checagou" as the site of future Chicago, but it was a place name only and no one lived there permanently for another century. French interest shifted to Kaskaskia and Cahokia and the first governmental recognition of the Illinois Country was the building of Fort de Chartres, near Kaskaskia, 1718-1720. New Orleans got its start in 1718 in the midst of John Law's ill-fated Mississippi Bubble, and the Illinois Country was made part of Louisiana, to the dismay of the fur traders of Quebec. Those disturbances, aptly named by the English colonists King William's War, Queen Anne's War, and King George's War, and the final French and Indian War that followed, had little effect on the scant population of Illinois except for some fighting among Indian tribes that reflected their shifting alliances and interests in the fur trade. In 1762, feeling guilty about dragging Spain into a losing war, France ceded Louisiana to Spain, leaving the Illinois Country as part of New France. The following year France surrendered all of New France to England.

Of course England had given no recognition to these boundaries of French jurisdiction, England having its own set of conflicting political entities that were of no concern to residents of the Illinois Country. Charters granted by the crown to several colonies extended their boundaries to the Pacific Ocean, which in the early 17th century was assumed to be only a few hundred miles from the Atlantic. Thus, according to the charter of 1662 our address would have been Elmhurst, Connecticut, for that colony's boundaries cut straight across what became northern Illinois. However, a letter would have had to be directed to Elmhurst, Virginia, to get any attention from a Virginia postmaster, for Virginia's 1609 charter was interpreted to include the areas that became Kentucky and the five states formed from the Northwest Territory, including Illinois. New York also had a claim, derived from a treaty with the Iroquois confederacy.

England ignored all this in taking over the fallen French empire. By a proclamation of 1763, it was ordered that "lands beyond the heads of sources of any of the rivers which fall into the Atlantic Ocean from the west or north west" should be reserved to "the several nations or tribes of Indians with whom we are connected." This left the residents of Illinois without any government whatever, to the embarrassment of the British, who even proposed to deport the Kaskaskia and Cahokia French to Quebec, but nothing came of this idea. The English colonists, who had already crossed the mountains at several points (notably Pittsburgh) whose waters did not fall into the Atlantic, gave little heed to this proclamation enjoining them not to molest or disturb the Indians. However, when the British Parliament, still worried about the isolated residents of Illinois, passed the Quebec Act of 1774, making all the western country "part and parcel of the Province of Quebec," a great howl went up from the colonists over this curb to western expansion. At this time a letter might have been addressed to Elmhurst, Quebec.

Virginia was active in backing its western claims, and during the American Revolution commissioned George Rogers Clark to take

Territories, Counties, and Townships

over the British posts in the Illinois Country. Clark's capture of Kaskaskia and Cahokia, and especially of Vincennes, is one of the heroic sagas of Western expansion. The Virginia legislature, which had previously set up Kentucky as a county, established the County of Illinois, December 9, 1778, to include all Virginia-claimed territory north of the Ohio River. Kaskaskia was the county seat.

At the close of the Revolution, seven states had western land claims, some of them disputed, while six had no such claims. After much argument, it was agreed that the western lands should be devoted to the upkeep of the general government. New York ceded its claims in 1781, Virginia in 1784, Massachusetts in 1785, and Connecticut in 1786. This cleared the way for the Ordinance of 1787 to establish the Territory Northwest of the Ohio River, commonly called Northwest Territory, and including the future states of Ohio, Indiana, Illinois, Michigan, and Wisconsin. In 1800, anticipating

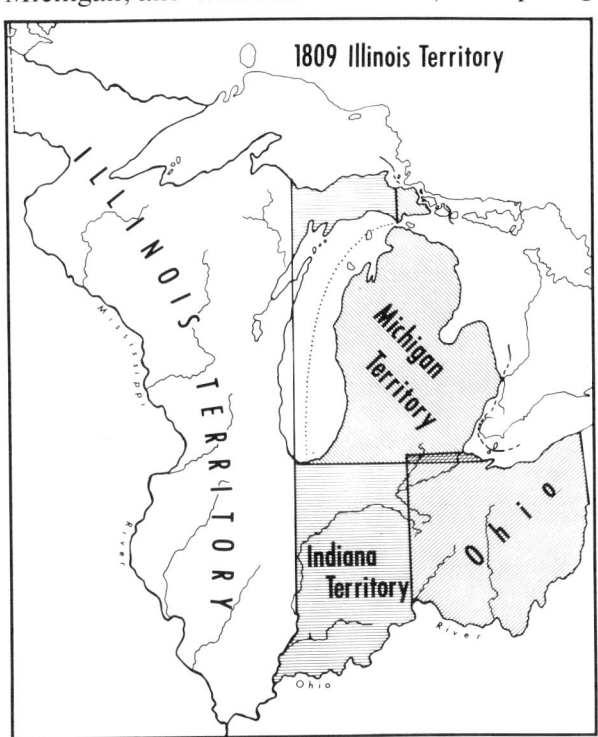

Robert P. Howard, Illinois: A History of the Prairie State 1972.

the admission of Ohio as a state, Northwest Territory was reduced to its eastern part and the rest of it became Indiana Territory. In 1809 Illinois Territory was set up to include the future states of Illinois and Wisconsin, and parts of Michigan and Minnesota. In 1818 Illinois was admitted as a state with its present boundaries.

Thus the site of Elmhurst was successively in Northwest Territory, Indiana Territory, and Illinois Territory before its final status as part of Illinois. It narrowly missed being in Wisconsin. When Illinois statehood was proposed, the northern boundary was to be a line running east and west through the southern tip of Lake Michigan. At the insistance of Delegate Nathaniel Pope, the line was moved 51 miles north, to north latitude forty-two degrees, thirty minutes, "giving to the proposed state the port of Chicago" and of course, Elmhurst and DuPage County.

RUNNING COUNTY LINES

In the early years local government was principally county government and the founding fathers were not inclined to leave any part of the public domain without law and order, whether or not anyone lived there. What is now Illinois was still a part of the Northwest Territory when its first county, St. Clair, was established in 1790. It extended from the Ohio River to the Illinois and eastward to a diagonal line almost bisecting the future state. East of that was Knox County, eventually to retreat into Indiana. Knox County was bounded on the north by the Illinois River to the forks of the DesPlaines and Kankakee Rivers. From the forks a line was drawn due north to the border of the British Possessions now known as Canada. This line ran a few miles west of the present western boundaries of DuPage and Cook counties, including both in Knox County.

In 1801 Indiana Territory amended county boundaries, shoving Knox County toward Indiana, and giving St. Clair County all of the area to the north, including all of present Wisconsin, part of the northern peninsula of Michigan, and Minnesota to the Mississippi River. The DuPage County area remained part of this huge St. Clair county until 1812 when St. Clair was cut back closer to its present boundaries and Madison County was organized and given jurisdiction northward. As settlement moved northward in Illinois, this pattern was continued with new counties crawling up the map and a northern county taking over the unsettled areas - cut back to the Illinois boundary when the state was admitted in 1818. Thus the DuPage County area was in Madison County, 1812-1814; Edwards County, 1814-1816; Crawford County,

THE ORIGIN OF DUPAGE COUNTY

Counties of Illinois: Their Origin and Evolution, n.d.

Territories, Counties, And Townships

1816-1819; Clark County, 1819-1821; Pike County, 1821-1823; attached to Fulton County, 1823-1825; Putnam County, 1825-1831; and Cook County, 1821-1839. DuPage County was established February 9, 1839.

Very little is known of DuPage, or DuPazhe, for whom the river and county were named. He is said to have had a trading post at the forks of the DuPage River (south of Naperville) about 1800, or near Plainfield about 1790 or both. However, a Lake DuPage, apparently a wide place in the Des Plaines River near its junction with the Illinois, is marked as early as 1778 on a map by Captain Thomas Hutchins of the 60th Regiment of Foot, and as Hutchins made his surveys between 1764 and 1775, that puts the name DuPage back a quarter century. Lake DuPage also appears on maps by John Andrews, 1782, and John Melish, 1818. The use of the name DuPage was probably extended from the lake to the river that emptied there or nearby. If DuPage flourished in 1775 and earlier, he had no employment by latter-day fur companies with which his name has been associated. About all we know is that he was a French fur trader, a long way from Kaskaskia, Prairie du Chien, or Michilimackinac, but probably had connections with Quebec. There was a prominent Kaskaskia family named Pagé.

TOWNS AND TOWNSHIPS

Quite as important in Westward expansion as the Ordinance of 1787 establishing Northwest Territory, was the Ordinance of 1785, providing for the survey of public lands. It ordered that surveyors "shall proceed to divide the said territory into townships of six miles square by lines running due north and south, and others crossing these at right angles, as near as may be....The parts of the subdivisions respectively shall be marked by subdivisions into lots of one mile square, or 640 acres, in the same directions as the external lines, and numbered from 1 to 36." There was one other important provision: "There shall be reserved the lot N.16, of every township, for the maintenance of public schools within the said township."

This ordinance established a land policy that ever afterward governed all land acquired by the United States. It provided for the orderly sale of lands at not less than one dollar an acre. The survey made possible valid titles, avoiding the disputes that had marked the haphazard settlement of other states, notably Kentucky. And by reserving a section for public schools, it made the township a unit of government, at least as a school district.

Northern Illinois was settled largely from the east where the New England *town* was familiar as a unit of local government with its town meeting. The early settlers identified the town with the congressional township as laid out by the surveyors although the boundaries did not necessarily coincide. Southern Illinois was settled largely from the South, where the ancient English township had been generally ignored. Under the Illinois Constitution of 1818, counties were divided into precincts which were largely voting districts. The Constitution of 1848 provided that the people of any county might adopt the township form of government if approved by a majority of the voters. Of the state's 102 counties, 85 adopted the township idea. DuPage County's nine townships, are Addison, York, Downers Grove, Bloomingdale, Milton, Lisle, Wayne, Winfield, and Naperville. Elmhurst, largely in York, extends into Addison. York Township is commonly and officially called Town of York. Town of Addison is less commonly used for Addison Township because of confusion with the village of Addison. DuPage County adopted the township form of government in 1850. York Township was so named because many of its early settlers came from the state of New York.

THE EARLY SETTLERS

Although Bailey Hobson, the Napers, and some 180 others were living in the Naperville area at the time of the Black Hawk War of 1832, neither of the townships in which Elmhurst is located had any settlers before 1834. It may seem strange that the western extremity of the county was occupied before the eastern fringe. One reason was routes of travel. Bailey Hobson had followed Stephen J. Scott, who settled at the forks of the DuPage River in 1830. Hobson had followed river routes such as those which had dictated that southern Illinois should be settled first, but the Napers came overland from Chicago.

The opening of the Erie Canal greatly stimulated travel and settlement in the north. The Pre-emption Law of 1830 provided that squatters who had cultivated public lands should have the first right to purchase them; this was spelled out in greater detail in an 1842 act. Squatters had formed the Big Woods Claim Society in 1836, followed by the DuPage County Society for Mutual Protection in 1839. This organization enforced squatters' rights by vigilante methods. In one incident, the cabin of a claim jumper in Milton Township was burned. Most of the activity centered in Naperville. So highly regarded was the Pre-emption Act that a tavern erected in Naperville in 1834 was named the Pre-emption House. It continued in use as a hotel for more than a century, but was recently demolished.

The defeat of Black Hawk in 1832 ended fear of Indian hostilities, and the Treaty of Chicago in 1833 opened to settlement the lands of the Potawatomi, Ottawa, and Chippewa. Also in 1833, a government project provided for the dredging of a sand bar from the mouth of the Chicago River, opening the Port of Chicago. Furthermore, in 1833 Chicago was incorporated as a village. There was much to stimulate settlement in northern Illinois.

However, there was one geographical feature in this new country that made settlement spotty and irregular. That was the prairie. Grass growing on the prairie for countless ages left masses of roots that could not be cut by the crude iron plows of the pioneers. A steel plow that would cut through the prairie sod was invented in 1837 by John Deere of Grand Detour, Illinois, but it was some years before his plow was widely distributed. Pioneers sought out wooded tracts, as is reflected in such names as Big Woods, Downer's Grove, and Babcock's Grove. Pioneers in the big woods to the east had cleared trees from every foot of land they planted, and felling trees with an ax and eventually grubbing up the stump was exceedingly hard work. It might be supposed then that the settlers would welcome good land that was treeless. However, from the few trees in the area were built the log cabins in which they lived and most or all of their furniture, and there was a constant need for firewood.

The first settler in the Town of York was Elisha Fish, who took up the southeast quarter of section 35 in 1834. He was joined the following year by Henry Reader, Luther Morton, Benjamin Fuller, and Nicholas Torode, Sr. Mr. Torode was a native of Guernsey, one of the Channel Islands, which are French although ruled by England since the time of William the Conqueror. The name Frenchman's Woods was used in years past to refer to the Torode property where many generations of Elmhurst residents picnicked. Mr. Torode was the first to make use of the area's limestone, building a stone house at York and Roosevelt roads. Torode also established a sawmill on Salt Creek which was the predecessor of the Graue grist mill. Addison Township was first settled in 1834 by Hezekiah Duncklee and Mason Smith.

York Township settlers of 1836 included John Talmadge, a veteran of the War of 1812, David Talmadge, Jesse Atwater, Edward Eldridge, Jacob W. Fuller, David Thurston, and

The Early Settlers

John Glos, sometimes regarded as Elmhurst's first settler. In 1837 they were joined by Sheldon Peck, W. Churchill, Zerais Cobb, John Bohlander, and John Thrasher.

GLOS

John Glos, Jr. came to the United States from Bavaria in 1832 at the age of 20 and spent some

John Glos, Jr. (1812-1888) brought his parents and family to Cottage Hill.

time in New England but found little there to encourage him in his search for farmland. However, he heard glowing reports of possibilities in Illinois, so he returned to Germany to tell his father, John Glos, Sr. The story was reported in the *Fox Valley Chronicle*, St. Charles, Illinois on January 6, 1882.

> The old gentleman was greatly dissatisfied with German politics of the day; upon hearing his son's favorable reports, he sold his farm and other properties and embarked with his family for America.
>
> When the family arrived in Boston, John Jr. showed his father over many parts of Massachusetts, but Glos Sr. did not like the stony ground of New England. His son then told him he could take him to a part of the country where he could plow a furrow 3 miles long without a break or stones. This idea suited the elder Glos, and with a large amount of money to spend on new land, he decided to come to Illinois. John Jr. made the arrangements in the Spring of 1837 for transporting about 80 Germans and their baggage. The colony went from Boston to Providence by railway, and thence to New York and Albany by water. At Albany, they took the "raging canawl" and came to Buffalo, where they embarked on a lake steamer.
>
> The group had great experiences on the Erie Canal, much time was devoted to guarding life, limb, and luggage from low bridges on the canal and other hazards. As it was, a great deal of baggage was damaged.
>
> The Great Lakes were a wonder to the whole party, for they (the lakes) were apparently as extensive as the ocean, and their tempests were worse, if possible, than those on the "vasty deep."
>
> At Chicago, the Glos family purchased ox teams and started westward. While the family was camping at Oak Ridge, the flies troubled the old gentleman's steers so badly that they all ran away and when found after several days search, they had turned the yoke (a type of wooden bar across the necks of the oxen which joined them in pairs) and Mr. Glos Sr. thought the animals were bewitched. He had never seen such an occurrence in Germany or France where cattle were yoked by the horns. (During this time, the family was offered land on the Chicago River between Madison and Washington streets which the elder Glos rejected as too swampy. He also rejected a tract of land in present day Oak Park as too sandy.)
>
> Finally, when the party reached the beautiful prairie about what was long-known as Cottage Hill, the father said it was good enough, and there he set his stakes, and dwelt among his children for more than 44 years.

In Cottage Hill, they settled along St. Charles road between the county line and Poplar Avenue. Their first farmhouse was about where Sandburg Junior High School now stands; later they built south of the road in the area now known as Crescent Park. The Glos farm was not within Elmhurst city limits for many decades. John Glos, Sr. died in Elmhurst at the age of 93.

John Glos, Jr., moved to the village of St.

Charles and later he and his son Adam M. Glos pioneered in Wayne Township, DuPage County. John Glos, Sr. and his son Adam (no initial) founded the Elmhurst branch of the family. Adam Glos had five children, Adam S., Catherine (Mrs. August Timke), Henry L., Jacob, and Mary (Mrs. Gustave Fischer).

Two other families that settled in this area slightly before the Gloses were the Franzens and the Graues. John Henry Franzen was born in Schale, Prussia. In 1834, his parents decided to emigrate to America. However, when the Franzen family arrived at Bremen, Germany, their port of embarkation, they discovered they were five dollars short of the sum needed for transport for the two adults and five children, among them John. After some distress, a kind fellow emigré loaned the needed five dollars. Several weeks later, the Franzen family arrived in Baltimore, Maryland. Having tried several eastern settlements, the Franzens decided to come to Chicago. After two years, they moved eighteen miles further west to Addison, DuPage County. Here they established a brick factory and linseed presses. Their determination had paid off only three years after their decision to emigrate.

GRAUE

The Graue family's journey was more direct than that of the Franzen's. In 1833 Frederick Graue, his wife Lucie, and six children arrived from Hanover, Germany and settled in Albany Township, New York. Within a year Graue

Fredrick Graue, second son of Fredrick Graue, was born in 1819.

decided to move further west and in May of 1834 settled in an area of the prairie which was to become part of Cottage Hill. Frederick had five sons and one daughter - Diedrich, Frederick, August, Henry, Ludwig, and Wilhelmina. Three years after the father Frederick had staked his claim in what became known as the Graue Woods area, he was killed by a falling log. Diedrich, the oldest son, born in 1814, took over the homestead. He received in addition to the original claim two land grants of 160 acres each - one signed by President John Tyler in 1843 and other by President James K. Polk in 1845. Together these grants comprised much of what is now the north side of Elmhurst.

In 1854 Ludwig, who had been operating a small stone quarry on part of the Graue property, decided to go into the merchandising business and established Graue General Store. The son Frederick was operating a small sawmill on the north edge of Cottage Hill. Henry and August, five years old when the Graues came to Cottage Hill, were farming, but in 1881 August took over the operation of the Graue Store. After his death his sons William and Julius continued the business. William became postmaster in 1898; he was an organizer of the First National Bank of Elmhurst and of Elmhurst State Bank.

Albert Graue, son of Diedrich, born in 1862 was a pioneer real estate broker in Elmhurst. It was he and his son, Fremont, who eventually subdivided all the land held by his father. The number of homes built or financed by Albert during his 38 years of activity in real estate probably runs into the thousands. Much of the area north of North Avenue and west of York Street was opened by him.

The Otto Ahrens family came to America by sailing ship to New Orleans and came up the Mississippi and Illinois rivers to DuPage County in 1849. The family purchased 160 acres in Sections 13 and 14. A part of their farm land is occupied by the store of Marshall Field & Company in Oak Brook.

Most of the settlers of this period were attracted by Salt Creek. Water was a necessity, and so were the trees that grew along its banks. Helmut Berens recorded an Indian legend that this stream was known as Lovely Little River when it was the scene of romance between Pypegee, son of Shabbonah of the Potawatomis, and the fair maiden Winnewalla. Prosaic pioneers renamed it Salt Creek, of which there must be hundreds in the United States, each one so named because some wagoner lost a load of salt in its waters. Our legend dates at least to the 1857 *History of the County of DuPage, Illinois*, by C.W. Richmond and H.F. Vallette, who state, "The stream received its name from this circumstance: A hoosier team, loaded with salt, be-

The Early Settlers

came 'stalled' while fording it, and the driver was obliged to lighten his load by rolling several barrels into the water." As we also have the name of the driver, John Reid, and his destination, Galena, the story seems well authenticated.

BATES

Elmhurst had its immediate origin with Gerry Bates, who came here in 1842. He was named for Elbridge Gerry, a signer of the Declaration of Independence, a vice-president of the United

Gerry Bates
(1800-1878)

Georgia Smith Bates (1824-1903) First school teacher in Cottage Hill and second wife of Gerry Bates.

States, and immortalized by the term gerrymander, meaning to lay out a legislative district for the advantage of a political party. His grandfather, Captain Benjamin Bates, had been forced to contribute his ship to the cause of the Continental Navy, and in compensation was granted 8,000 acres of the national domain, and at the age of 84 led a train of a hundred wagons from Massachusetts to Ohio, settling near Painesville. Here Gerry Bates, born in Chesterfield, Massachusetts, August 18, 1800, grew up. Hearing of the Illinois prairies that needed not to be cleared of forests before cultivation (perhaps he had also heard of Deere's plow), Gerry Bates decided to pioneer further west. Leaving Ohio in March, 1842, in a light one-horse cutter, he expected to reach Chicago in three weeks, but storms and huge snowdrifts delayed him until May.

After getting information at the land office, he drove over the old plank road, later called Butterfield Road (for Lyman Butterfield, pioneer settler of Milton Township) and conferred with Nicholas Torode and John Talmadge. By this time, lands along Salt Creek were taken up, and Bates decided on the vacant prairie on the east half of section 2, between St. Charles Road and North Avenue, and from York Street west one-half mile. Completing his purchase at $1.25 an acre, he returned to Ohio to dispose of his interests there and he did not return until 1845. Meanwhile, in the spring of 1843, he sent his brother-in-law, John L. Hovey, to take possession of the property.

Hovey built a tavern, opened in 1843 at the present intersection of St. Charles Road and Cottage Hill Avenue. He named his structure Hill Cottage Tavern for Hill House, the Bates home in Ohio. It became a stage stop for the Frink and Walker stage coach line from Chicago to the Fox River Valley. *Tavern* is a word that has changed meaning over the decades. In the early nineteenth century it was an inn - later hotel and in our day motel - where the traveler could stop for food and drink and for a night's lodging. Horses could also be fed and sheltered. After repeal of Prohibition in 1933, "tavern" was revived to mean "a house where liquors are sold to be drunk on the premises," replacing "saloon," which had gained a bad

Hill Cottage, originally a simple building standing in the middle of a treeless prairie, appeared as shown when used as a residence of the G.P.A. Healy's in 1857 and the Henry W. Kings in 1867.

Hill Cottage, as it appears in the 1970s, was remodeled and enlarged by Mahlon Ogden some time during 1873-1883 before it was moved to its present location on South York Street.

name during the Prohibition agitation. The tavern of the 1840s was also a house where liquors were drunk on the premises and a gathering place for residents of the surrounding community. As the number of residents increased, there arose demand for a post office, with the tavern the obvious location.

Rufus Blanchard in his *History of DuPage County, Illinois,* 1882, records: "John Wentworth was then the district representative in Congress and to him the inhabitants (of Hill Cottage) sent their petition. The Postmaster General objected to the name on the grounds that there were already towns with names of ''hill'' something, and suggested a transposition of the name, making it Cottage Hill. This was accepted by the petitioners and the village was 'baptised' accordingly.'' The post office was established December 9, 1845, with Hovey as postmaster.

The house that Hovey built retained the name *Hill Cottage Tavern*, and a part of it still exists, although moved from its original site. Through the years it has been occupied by many persons of local and even of national fame. James Lusk bought it in 1851 from Gerry Bates and sold it in 1856 to Thomas B. Bryan, often called "the father of Elmhurst." Bryan turned it over to G.P.A. Healy, famous portrait painter who lived there from 1857 to 1864 and renamed the estate *Clover Lawn*. George M. Wheeler, real estate broker was occupant until 1867, selling to Henry W. King, Chicago merchant, who opened the house to refugees from the Chicago fire. Other residents were George F. Rumsey, grain commission operator; and Mahlon D. Ogden, brother of Chicago's first mayor. Ogden added a three-story wing to the house.

James L. Houghteling, banker, was followed by Brigadier General Alexander Caldwell McClurg, Civil War veteran who founded A.C. McClurg Co., Chicago book publisher of great prestige at the turn of the century. General McClurg died in 1901. His company survives as a wholesale book distributor. Owen Aldis was another resident and in 1891, John R. Case, Jr., bought the house from Frank Sturges, manufacturer. Sturges wanted *Hill Cottage* off his land to make room for a house he was building, so Case moved it to 413 South York Street, where it still stands. Case called the estate *Orchard Place* because of the many fruit trees planted on the land by his father. Case rented the house and during this period it was occupied by the Skeele family, by Charles Howe, by Francis King, and by Mrs. Emmons Blaine, philanthropist, founder of the School of Education of the University of Chicago, and daughter of Cyrus H. McCormick, inventor of the reaper. The Robert P. Durhams lived in *Orchard Place* from 1916 to 1946. In 1948 Mr. and Mrs. Joe Reilly bought the house, renovated and refurnished it in accordance with its historic origins, and renamed it *Hill Cottage*. It was bought by Mr. and Mrs. Theodore Wilson in 1963, and subsequently by Mr. and Mrs. Thomas L. Collins.

STAGE STATION AND POST OFFICE

A letter written by William Beckman dated April 30, 1913, contains the only existing information on stage coach days at Hill Cottage Tavern. Beckman was the brother of Mrs. Henry Bucholz, member of a pioneer farming family whose farm is now East End Park. William relates his experiences as a stage coach driver. As a boy of sixteen, he was at Hill Cot-

Courtesy of Chicago Historical Society

The Chicago stage office of Frink and Walker. In 1838 Frink and Walker bought out the first stage company run by Templeton and operated through DuPage County along St. Charles Road connecting Chicago and Galena.

tage Tavern waiting for the mail one day when the stage coach came in from St. Charles with the driver so ill with chills that he could hardly get off the coach. The hotel man, possibly Hovey, had seen the boy driving a four-horse team at the farm, and asked if he could drive the stage coach to Chicago. He said he would be glad to do so. When he reached the Chicago stage office, he was met by John Frink, one of the owners. Having heard the story, Frink climbed to the seat beside the boy and directed him to the post office, where William unloaded the mail, then they drove to the barn. Satisfied, Frink offered the boy a regular job as driver,

The Early Settlers

starting with the return trip to St. Charles the next day. He kept the job more than four years and before he quit was advanced to superintendent of the Illinois division of the stage line.

Beckman tells of the decline of the stage line. The Galena and Chicago Union Railroad started building in 1847, and when it reached O'Plane, now Maywood, in 1848, the stage would meet passengers there and take them and the mail to points farther west. (O'Plane is a corruption of AuxPlaines, a variant of Des Plaines River.) When the railroad reached Cottage Hill in 1849, stage coaches and horses were kept at the tavern to meet trains there. "The next stopping place was at the junction some six miles east of St. Charles, and the next were Elgin, Marengo, and Belvidere. When the railroad got as far as Belvidere, I drove for a while from Belvidere to Freeport, but concluded that my occupation was gone so in December, 1851, I packed up my grip and came to California.....I have lived in California ever since, and have for the last thirty-five years been president and manager of the People's Savings Bank (Sacramento) which I organized."

This early home town boy who made good tells of playing checkers with Elmhurst's first literary figure, Edward Bonney, who is said to have written *The Banditti of the Prairies; or The Murderer's Doom! A Tale of the Mississippi Valley* while living at the southwest corner of York and Arthur streets between 1847 and 1857. There are those who deny that he wrote the book, but early drafts of the manuscript turned up by a granddaughter, Miss Jessamine Hoagland, are now at Indiana University; these seem to indicate his authorship, however much the book may have been improved by its publisher. Bonney, an amateur detective, perhaps interested in reward money, ran down the murderers of John Miller and his son-in-law Henry Leicy or Leiza, in Lee County, and they were hanged. Bonney also helped in solving the murder of Colonel George Davenport at Rock Island in 1845. The book, originally published in 1850 by W.W. Danenhower, a Chicago book dealer, became a frontier classic and was many times reprinted, including a 1963 edition by University of Oklahoma Press, which is still available. The book was so widely known that when A.S. Mercer came to write the story of Wyoming's Johnson County War, he imitated Bonney's title with *The Banditti of the Plains*.

Beckman said Bonney's home "had wooden shutters at all the windows, which were closed as soon as night came and he would not go out of the house after dark. The way I remember it was that when he captured those fellows he had to go among them and commit some depredations also, and after he exposed them and sent them to state prison, their friends swore vengeance against Bonney."

Bonney sold his house in 1857 to the Lucian Hagans family. Its last occupant was Miss Carolyn Wade, artist and instructor at the Art Institute of Chicago. It was demolished to make way for Immaculate Conception Center.

THE FIRST RAILROAD
The Pioneer

The Galena and Chicago Union was chartered in 1836, but construction was delayed by the panic of 1837 and building was not started until 1847. During the same period, Gerry Bates had built a new home on Park Avenue and gave the railroad its right-of-way on condition that

Courtesy of Chicago Historical Society
The Pioneer

the station would be built opposite his home. The railroad accepted the agreement and established the station called Cottage Hill. It quickly became a busy place. A well was dug alongside the station to supply water for the new locomotive, which was a woodburner. The locomotive, The Pioneer, had been purchased in the East and was sent by boat across Lake Michigan from Michigan City to Chicago. (The Pioneer is now on exhibit at the Chicago Historical Society.)

When the rails reached Elmhurst, the first passenger car was put into service. John R. Case, Jr., recalled his mother's story of the original run of the Galena and Chicago Union on July 4, 1849: People had received special invitations for the first trip from Chicago, among them Mrs. Case. When the train reached

Cottage Hill, the lunch break was taken in the shadow of The Pioneer because it was the only shaded spot in the treeless area.

In 1849, Gerry Bates took over as postmaster from Edward Bonney, who had succeeded John Hovey in 1847. Bates continued as postmaster, with two interruptions until his death on July 29, 1878.

ORIGINAL COTTAGE HILL

York Township was organized in 1850, with Edward Eldridge as first supervisor. He was soon succeeded by Gerry Bates who served through 1852. In 1854, Gerry Bates platted the "original Cottage Hill" subdivision between the railroad and North Avenue and from York Street to Addison Avenue. The south half of the east half of Section 2 was later platted by Bates as the Summit Addition to Cottage Hill. Pur-

Thomas Barbour Bryan (1828-1906). In 1868 he proposed the name *Elmhurst* for then Cottage Hill.

chaser of the first lot in "original Cottage Hill" was Louis (Ludwig) Graue who opened a general store with the agreement that Bates would discontinue his store south of the tracks. As mentioned Frederick Graue had been operating a small saw mill. In 1838, finding the water power unsatisfactory, he relocated the mill on Salt Creek at Brush Hill (present day Hinsdale). When the mill was destroyed by fire, he built a brick grist mill. The construction took him from 1847 to 1852. Today the mill is operated as a museum by the Graue Mill Corporation.

In 1856, Thomas Barbour Bryan, who was to become one of Elmhurst's most eminent citizens, bought a thousand acres in Cottage Hill, including the Hill Cottage Tavern. He sold *Hill Cottage* the following year to George Peter Alexander Healy.

G.P.A. HEALY

Healy has been called the best American portrait painter of the nineteenth century. Probably more presidents sat for Healy than for any other artist; these include John Quincy Adams, Jackson, Van Buren, Tyler, Polk, Fillmore, Pierce, Buchanan, Lincoln, Grant, and Arthur. Other portraits are of Webster, Clay, Calhoun, Seward, and General Sherman. His "Webster's Reply to Hayne" in Faneuil Hall, Boston, contains 130 figure portraits. During his years in Chicago and Cottage Hill, he painted portraits of 500 Chicagoans. Many of these portraits are owned by the Chicago Historical Society.

G.P.A. Healy was born in Boston in 1808. He studied in Paris and was awarded a medal at

G.P.A. Healey (1813-1894). Nineteenth century American portrait painter.

Inset - 1-cent postage stamp taken from one of the Healey portraits of Lincoln.

the Paris Exposition of 1855. He lived at Hill Cottage from 1857 to 1864, renaming it *Clover Lawn*. His family included six daughters and one son.

During his residence in Elmhurst, Healy painted portraits of several prominent local families, among them the Bryans, with whom the Healy family had a close friendship, and the Elisha Hagans.

He painted the Thomas B. Bryan family in 1857. Nearly twenty years later, in 1874, long after Healy had left Elmhurst, he painted the Bryan's daughter, Jenny. Both Bryan portraits hang in the Virginia Museum of Fine Arts in Richmond. It was Bryan who arranged through a personal letter for Healy to paint Lincoln in

Springfield shortly after he was elected President. This portrait, known as the "beardless Lincoln," is the only one existing of President Lincoln without a beard. The portrait was chosen in 1959 for the 1-cent Lincoln sesquicentennial postage stamp.

Healy painted the Hagans portraits because of the friendship which had grown between the two families. The portraits of both Elisha Hagans and Anne, his wife, are signed by Healy and have remained in the Hagans family. A

Elisha Hagans (1796-1864)   Anne Hagans (1807-1881)

letter from Wilbur Hagans, Elisha's grandson, makes Healy's considerable talent quite apparent. Wilbur wrote June 22, 1939, "Mr. Healy and my grandfather were very great friends and he (Healy) was able to get a most satisfactory likeness although the portrait was really painted after my grandfather's death in 1864."

Wilbur also remarked in an April, 1937 letter, "Men with the charm of Mr. Healy are no more. We shall never look upon his like again."

In 1867, G.P.A. Healy left Chicago for Rome, maintained a studio in Paris from 1885 to 1892, and then returned to Chicago where he died June 24, 1892. His work is on view at the White House and Corcoran Gallery in Washington, D.C., at the Newberry Library, Chicago, and at the Art Institute, Chicago.

THE EARLIEST SCHOOLS

The earliest schools were set up and financed by parents. In 1838 Miss Fuller taught in a log cabin owned by Elias Brown. Later Miss C. Barnes taught classes in the home of John Talmadge in Frenchman's Woods.

In 1850, School District No. 1 was organized at a meeting in Gerry Bates' parlor. The Town of York sold its school section for $5 an acre (it may be recalled that Bates paid only $1.25 an acre for the first land purchased in Cottage Hill),

Peter Torode home showing small section at the back of building which housed the first school in the village. When the school originally located on St. Charles Road became too small, it was purchased by Torode for use as a summer kitchen, and moved to his lot at 331 South York Street where it was attached to the back of his house.

The first two room school house, originally located on Church Street, was built in 1857. Later moved to Schiller Street and served as the August Fiebrandt home.

giving it the largest school fund in the county, $3,200 increased to $3,500 by 1857. There were eight public schools in the township, attended by about 400 pupils. The budget for teachers' pay was $800 a year with top pay $25 a month and minimum pay $10 monthly. School was in session eight months of the year.

A frame building, 20 by 24 feet, was put up on St. Charles Road west of Cottage Hill Avenue. Miss Georgia Smith taught 187 pupils there in 1853 and 1854. By 1857 a second school was needed, and a two-story frame building was erected on Church Street near the present site of St. Peter's Church. Among the first teachers were Elvira Bates, Henry Glos, who taught German, and Samantha Morey. Listed as expenses by this second public school were one pound of candles, three candlesticks, a lightning rod, fire wood, a lamp, and lamp stove pipes - a very small list of school supplies when compared to today's complicated school budgets.

Wilbur Hagans recalls this second public school as he knew it when he attended the German section in 1861-62:

> There were no fences except to the north and east of the building. All was prairie on Cottage Hill Avenue between the railroad and St. Charles Road. There were only a few apple trees on the Healy property, no other trees or shrubs.
>
> The upper room of the building was where English was taught, presided over by Miss Electra Snow; the lower room was devoted to teaching German under the competent Mr. Luessenhop. There were about 25 scholars in each section.

Dr. Bates gives the closing history of Elmhurst's second school house: The school house was used for 31 years until the first Hawthorne School was erected in 1888. Diedrich Brandt bought the old school house and moved it across the North Western Railroad tracks to Schiller Street next to Fiebrandt's hardware store and became the August Fiebrandt residence.

GERMAN INFLUENCES

Large numbers of the early settlers in the area that became Elmhurst were German-speaking. Many Germans came to America in organized groups or colonies, usually centering about a religious or communal idea, but those coming to DuPage County arrived individually, at different times and from different parts of Germany. Economic hardship and autocratic government in the German states from the close of the Napoleonic wars through the unsuccessful social revolutions of 1830 and 1848 to the militaristic unification of the German Empire in 1871 caused many to seek a more peaceful home. Travel narratives such as the book of Gottfried Duden, first published in 1829, painted a rose-colored picture of life in the Middle West. Something of this kind led John Glos, Jr., to bring his father and family from Bavaria to York Township. The Graues came from Hanover; others were from Mecklenburg, Holstein, and the Rheinland, speaking Plattdeutsch, or Low German - colloquially "Low Dutch" - "low" because it was the language of the low countries at the mouths of the rivers of north Germany. However, High German of the highlands became the language of literature, of Luther, Goethe, and Schiller, and of the Evangelical and Lutheran pastors who came to minister to settlers in DuPage County.

To add to the German mixture, many came from earlier German migrations to New England and the eastern seaboard, and especially from western Pennsylvania, which had a large German population before the Revolution. The first settlers in Addison Township were Ebenezer Duncklee from Hillsborough, New Hampshire, and Mason Smith from Potsdam, New York, in 1834. The next year Ebenezer Duncklee was joined by his brother Hezekiah and their families. Their settlement along Salt Creek was called Duncklee's Grove. It is now known as Churchville. The Duncklees planted three barrels of frozen apples, resulting in an orchard that supplied the entire region. They put up hay from the prairie grass but also raised clover, timothy, and herdsgrass. Other crops were spring wheat, oats, corn, and potatoes. A list of 30 of the earliest settlers in Addison Township shows 16 who came from Germany, and others of German descent, among them nine from New York, three from New Hampshire (including the Duncklees), one from Massachusetts and one from Vermont.

FRANCIS ARNOLD HOFFMANN

Francis Arnold Hoffmann, christened Franz, was born in Herford, Prussia, in 1822. His father was a bookbinder and book seller. Franz

Francis Hoffmann (1822-1903)

was bookish and an experimentor in botany. After graduating from the gymnasium he decided, with his father's consent, to run off to America to escape Prussian compulsory military service. He arrived in New York in 1839 and worked his way to Chicago on Hudson River freight boats, Erie Canal barges, and a Great Lakes schooner. Penniless, he worked as a boot black in the Lake House and also as a printer's helper. He was then recruited to go to Duncklee's Grove as a teacher. Franz was paid $40 a year and boarded around among the parents. The log schoolhouse was also used for church services and Zion Lutheran Church was founded here in 1838 with the Rev. L.C. Ervendberg as pastor. In the absence of a regular pastor, Hoffmann read sermons at Sunday services, and after a year of study at Ann Arbor, Michigan, he served as pastor from 1843 to 1847. Franz also served as postmaster, and as school trustee, and was editor for a time of *Illinois Staatszeitung*, German newspaper in Chicago. It is said he often walked sixteen miles from Duncklee's Grove to Chicago to deliver his manuscript.

Hoffmann became a leader of German Americans in Illinois. After serving as pastor in Schaumburg from 1847 until 1851, he gave up the ministry and moved to Chicago to study law. He was admitted to the bar in 1852 and in the same year was elected alderman from Chicago's Eighth Ward. He was prominent in the anti-slavery movement and was nominated for lieutenant governor by the newly formed Republican Party in 1856, but did not qualify because he was not yet a citizen. He was nominated again in 1860 from Cottage Hill and served as lieutenant governor during the Civil War years under Governor Richard Yates.

Republikanische Nominationen.

Als Präsident:
Abraham Lincoln
von Illinois.

Als Vice-Präsident:
Hannibal Hamlin
von Maine.

Für Gouverneur:
Richard Yates, von Morgan.

Für Lieutenant Gouverneur:
F. A. Hoffmann, von Dupage.

Für Auditor:
Jesse K. Dubois, von Lawrence.

Für Staats Sekretär:
Ozias M. Hatch, von Pike.

Für Staats-Schatzmeister:
William Butler, von Sangamon.

Für Superintendent des öffentlichen Unterrichts:
Newton Bateman, von Morgan.

Für Congreß.
Erster	District	E. B. Washburne.
Zweiter	"	Isaac N. Arnold.
Dritter	"	Owen Lovejoy.
Vierter	"	William Kellogg.
Sechster	"	Henry Case.
Siebter	"	J. I. Cunningham.
Achter	"	Joseph Gillespie.

Präsidenten-Electoren.
Für den Staat:
Leonard Swett, von McLean.
John M. Palmer, von Macoupin.

Für die Distrikte:
1. A. C. Fuller, von Boone.
2. Wm. B. Plato, von Kane.
3. Lawrence Weldon, von De Witt.
4. Wm. P. Kellogg, von Fulton.
5. J. Stark, von Hancock.
6. J. C. Confling, von Sangamon.
7. H. P. H. Bromwell, von Coles.
8. I. G. Allen, von Randolph.
9. John Olney, von Gallatin.

Sample Illinois Republican ballot in German showing Lincoln for President and Hoffmann of DuPage for Lieutenant Governor.

Eureka, Hoffmann Summer residence.

While residing on Ohio street, Chicago, in the 1850's he built a summer home at the southeast edge of Addison Township, calling his estate Eureka (now Arlington Cemetery). Carlotta Koch recalled: "while staying there (at the Bucholz farm) Frieda Hoffmann and I became close friends. She lived across the road on the Hoffmann estate where she had a real sure enough playhouse for us to play in." Hoffmann's Chicago home was destroyed in the Chicago fire of 1871, while he aided refugees at his Cottage Hill estate. After the war, he was commissioner of the land department of the Illinois Central Railroad and aided in bringing thousands of Germans to Illinois. In 1875 he moved to Jefferson, Wisconsin, and edited a weekly farm paper, *Haus und Bauernfreund*, using the pen name Hans Buschbauer, which he also used on five agricultural handbooks. He died in 1903 at the age of 81.

More German schools followed the one at which Hoffmann taught. By 1867, there were three German schools and six public schools in Addison Township. Zion Church also expanded. A small frame building was erected in 1842, and was also used by a Reformed and Lutheran group which withdrew in 1848 to form their own church, Evangelical St. Johannes Kirche, near Bensenville.

The German community was centered on the churches and schools of Addison Township during the Civil War years. Expansion of its population southward during the decade following resulted in a demand for German-speaking churches and schools in York Township.

THE EARLIEST CHURCHES
Byrd's Nest Chapel

When Thomas Barbour Bryan bought land in Cottage Hill in 1856, there was no church within the village limits. In 1859, shortly after he moved into his "Byrd's Nest" estate, he

Byrd's Nest Chapel, dedicated 1865.

learned that a Chicago church was being converted into a bowling alley. He decided that he could even the score by converting his basement bowling alley into a chapel. He was licensed as a lay reader by the Episcopal Bishop of Chicago and frequently conducted services, beginning October 5, 1862. Other lay readers were Peter R. Torode and William H. Litchfield. However, Bryan soon erected a separate frame Byrd's Nest Chapel, and opened it for public worship April 23, 1865, with a memorial service for President Lincoln, assassinated nine days before. Bryan was a personal friend of Lincoln, and served as a pall bearer both in Chicago and Springfield. The chapel was also used for village and town meetings; and it was in the chapel in 1869 that Bryan proposed that the village's name be changed from Cottage Hill to Elmhurst. The chapel continued in use until 1914 when Bryan's daughter, Mrs. John Barton Payne, moved to Washington, D.C.

Members of two families tell of attending Byrd's Nest Chapel in early Elmhurst. A Wilbur Hagans letter of 1936 recalls that Byrd's Nest Chapel was never dedicated and hence it was a place of worship for all Protestant denominations. Mr. Bryan in the absence of any minister acted as lay reader.

Phyllis Bates Schwab, in a tape recording gives a personal recollection:

> "I attended (it) as a child and my father and mother were baptized and confirmed there....I was baptized in Byrd's Next Chapel too. Thomas B. Bryan was my godfather....Byrd's Nest Chapel was such a small place - it seated only about 100 people. It was a very small and homey little church...There was a pot-bellied stove at the back of the church and you could smell the burning wood for blocks away....there were chimes in the church, very beautiful chimes."

Mrs. Schwab also remembered two weddings when the church was decorated, "flowers with candles burning. It was very pretty."

Later the Rev. Charles P. Anderson, Rector of Grace Church, Oak Park, officiated for some years, as did the Rev. John Herbert Edwards. The Rev. J.A. Potter, a Methodist minister, served for a time about 1884. The chapel was razed in the early years of the twentieth century.

Old St. Mary's

In the same decade, Roman Catholics in the community shared in the establishment of St. Mary's Church and parish. Father Meinrad Jeggle, a Jesuit priest from Chicago, organized the Cottage Hill Mission in 1862 and purchased one-half acre on the east side of York Street

The Early Settlers

south of present day Church Street for the building of St. Mary's Roman Catholic Church. St. Mary's was the familiar name of the church

Old St. Mary's Catholic Church, second building, parish established 1862.

organized as Immaculate Conception. Until the church was completed, mass was celebrated at the home of Terrence Kenney, one of a few Irishmen in a predominantly German community. At that time there were only forty-nine houses in the village and fewer than twenty Catholic families in the entire area. Redemptorist Fathers took charge of the Mission in 1864. In 1876 the Rev. Charles Becker became the first resident priest, but he stayed only a year, and several successors were in brief residence until 1892 when the Reverend John Zilla took charge. He stayed twenty-four years, during which time he rebuilt Immaculate Conception Church and started its school system. The old church was destroyed by fire in 1898. Instead of rebuilding on the old site, an exchange was made for a larger plot, farther north on York Street.

The Village Minute Record of Elmhurst for December 3, 1898, reads, "whereas the President and Board deeply deplore the destruction of the Catholic Church recently destroyed by fire and whereas said church when rebuilt on the same place would prevent the extension of Center Street....and whereas this is the proper time to take action on the premises...Therefore be it resolved that the Attorney of the Village... is hereby requested to prepare an ordinance for the condemnation of the lands open-

Now a private home, the house at 269 South York Street, built in 1899, was originally the rectory for Old St. Mary's Church and later the home of Edward Steichen, Carl Sandburg's brother-in-law.

ing said Center Street from York Street to Kenilworth Avenue to be the width of 66 feet, the north line of said proposed street to be the south line of the Struckman property." It is also reported that the church land was then sold to the city for $750. W.H. Emery paid the Catholic Church $600 for buildings on the land and Mr. Struckman paid $400 to Father Zilla as "further consideration for said buildings."

In 1899, a church and rectory were built, and also a one-room school with second story living quarters for the Sisters of St. Agnes who staffed it.

St. Peter's Church

When the proseminary that became Elmhurst College was founded in 1871, its students walked three miles to Churchville to attend services. In 1876 adherents of the German Evangelical Synod founded St. Peter's Evangelical Church. Land was purchased on Church Street; the cornerstone was laid September 10; and the church was dedicated December 26, 1876, with Christian Beck as minister. He was succeeded the next year by F.W. Boeber, who served until 1882. Emil Keutchen served from 1882 to 1885. There was always a close connection between St. Peter's Church and the college and in early years students attended services there in a body. Daniel Irion became pastor in 1885 and was named president of Elmhurst College in 1887. He was succeeded as pastor by August Berens.

The Rev. Mr. Berens and his wife Clara were pillars of the church and small community. Both August and Clara had writing interests. Aside

St. Peter's Church, established 1876.

from the publication of his sermons, Mr. Berens was author of a volume of more than fifty poems in German. Mrs. Berens wrote several books of children's stories. These literary works were certainly an influence on their son Helmut who later wrote *Elmhurst: Prairie to Tree Town*.

August Berens served until 1906 and was followed by Alfred Meyer. Among members were Henry Glos, banker and first president of the village of Elmhurst, his brother Adam Glos, pioneer merchant, and Dr. Frederick Fischer, physician in Elmhurst for three decades.

In April, 1887, the church voted to build a parochial school to accommodate 50 to 60 children. The school was paid for by subscription. A small schoolhouse was built for $180. The pastor, the Rev. Frederick Boeber, was also the school teacher until the proseminary supplied one of its graduates as teacher. He was given room and board while he subsisted on the 60

St. Peter's Parochial School (1887-1921).

cents per child per month tuition fee. The teacher also served as organist at $125 per year.

In 1892 the congregation voted to build a new parsonage and a new school house, this time at a cost of $1,200. The school served the German community for several generations. St. Peter's Parochial School closed its doors in 1921.

COTTAGE HILL DAYS

BRYAN

It is time to say something more of Thomas Barbour Bryan, who has been called the "father of Elmhurst" and as he named the infant, his title of paternity would seem well established. He was born in Alexandria, Virginia in 1828. His father Daniel, postmaster and state senator, was descendant of an Irish family that had been in Virginia since 1641. His mother

Thomas Barbour Bryan with his children Charles Page and Jennie. In 1874 G.P.A. Healy painted Jennie's portrait.

Mary was daughter of James Barbour, governor, senator, and brother of Philip Barbour, speaker of the House and Supreme Court justice. Thomas Barbour attended a Virginia preparatory school, then went to Harvard College where he specialized in languages. While an undergraduate he wrote a textbook, *For Germans more easily to learn English*. His knowledge of German was to prove highly useful to him in Elmhurst. Graduated with honors from Harvard Law School in 1848, he practiced law in Newport, Kentucky, then moved across the river to Cincinnati. In 1850 he married Jane Byrd Page, daughter of Charles H. Page, chaplain of Newport Barracks, army post at Newport, Kentucky. Her mother was a member of the Byrd family of Virginia.

The Bryans came to Chicago in 1853, where in addition to law practice, Bryan gave much time to business counselling, real estate investment, and civic projects. He built Bryan Hall on Clark Street, facing the court house. This hall became a center of musical, theatrical, and social events in Chicago. He organized the Graceland Cemetery Association. He was president of the Y.M.C.A. He ran for mayor of Chicago in 1861 and in 1865. Even after building his residence in Cottage Hill, Bryan maintained a Chicago residence.

The completion of *Byrd's Nest* at York Street and St. Charles Road in 1859 may be said to mark the beginning of Elmhurst as a suburb. Although regarded at the time as an outlying summer home, *Byrd's Nest* was often occupied by the Bryans. It was a house of twenty-one rooms: hall, parlor, and drawing room; library, dining room, and billiard room connected by a plant cabinet; art gallery, two kitchens with

Byrd's Nest, the Thomas B. Bryan residence.

pantries, and seven bed chambers with closets; a bathroom (an unusual luxury in that time) and eventually a ballroom on the third floor and a tower or cupola. There was a room for a solar telescope which had been exhibited at the London World's Fair. There were greenhouses, a gymnasium, and the bowling alley which became Byrd's Nest Chapel. Also on the estate grounds were a coach house, gardener's cottage, barns, gardens, and a grape arbor.

The reporter for *The Prairie Farmer* recorded that the house was "surrounded by thousands of newly planted trees." Wilbur Hagans, a family friend, recalled that Bryan had several large elm trees, as large as eighteen inches in diameter, transplanted from the DesPlaines River, but that some of them only lived a few years. There was also an artificial lake known to generations of young skaters as Bryan's Pond. Much of what is known of the interior of the house comes from Wilbur Hagans who lists paintings by G.P.A. Healy, art objects from around the world, tapestries, oriental rugs, and a bed said to have been used by Andrew Jackson in the White House and in which Hagans often slept.

This showplace of the "elegant era" would have seemed a retreat in which the Civil War might have been forgotten, but Bryan was an active supporter of the war effort. He outfitted the company that became known as the "Bryan Blues." After the war, for a Sanitary Fair in Bryan Hall, Chicago, Bryan obtained from President Lincoln the original draft of the Emancipation Proclamation. The Sanitary Fair was for the benefit of the Sanitary Commission which may be regarded as predecessor of the Red Cross. Bryan then bought the Proclamation with a bid of $1,000. Facsimiles of the Proclamation were sold for the benefit of the Chicago Soldier's Home of which Bryan became president in 1867. Eventually, the original draft of the Proclamation was destroyed in the Chicago fire of 1871.

Charles Page Bryan, Thomas Bryan's son, was born in Chicago in 1855, and was brought to Elmhurst as an infant and educated in a private school on the Bryan property. Charles traveled abroad from 1865 until 1867. Then he studied and graduated from the University of Virginia and Columbia Law School and was admitted to the bar in Washington in 1878.

Charles' achievements include the help he gave his father in procuring foreign exhibits for the Chicago's World's Fair in 1891 and 1892 and his term of service as a representative from DuPage County to the Illinois General Assembly beginning in 1892 and continuing through 1897. During his service, he was instrumental in

Charles Page Bryan (1855-1918).

achieving ballot reform for state elections. His diplomatic service included tours in Switzerland, Portugal, Belgium, and Japan. After an accident in Japan, Charles returned to Elmhurst. At home he took an active interest in both the water and the electric light companies, and other civic projects.

HAGANS

Another wartime family was that of Elisha Hagans. Born in Willsboro, New York, on November 23, 1798, Elisha Hagans came from a family which had come to America in 1632 and lived in Preston County, Virginia, since 1817. In 1856, the year the Republican Party was born, Hagans foresaw with William H. Seward the "irrepressible conflict" and wanted no part of it. Hagans started northwest on a land prospecting tour, bought tracts in Minnesota and Iowa, but seemed most attracted by two hundred acres in Cottage Hill he had purchased from Thomas Barbour Bryan. To that acreage he brought his family in 1857 and bought the home of Edward Bonney of the *Banditti of the Prairies* fame. The Hagans family included Elisha and his wife Anne; their daughter Lovela, her husband Lucian Hagans, who was also her cousin, and their son Wilbur, then six years old. Both Elisha and Lucian dealt in real estate in Chicago, but Elisha soon retired to his Cottage Hill home. On his grounds, he kept ten cows and 200 swarms of bees. Elisha died in 1864. Anne survived until 1881.

Lucian Hagans, unlike his father-in-law, was eager to become involved when war came. He

Lucian Hagans (1825-1890).

returned to Preston County and as Secretary of the Commonwealth of Virginia (Federal) under Governor Francis Harrison Pierpoint, was active in the movement that made West Virginia a state in 1863. In 1866 he became owner and editor of the *Wheeling Daily Intelligencer*. He sold it in 1873, purchased an interest in Rand McNally Company and returned to Chicago. In 1874 he built a home at the northwest corner of St. Charles Road and Prospect Street, Elmhurst. He surrounded the house with a half dozen wells, one of them 15 feet in diameter with 14 feet of water, surmounted by a windmill and water tank. Lucian demanded a clock in each of the 15 rooms of the house. Another of his eccentricities was his dislike of neckties. Even his portraits in formal attire show no necktie.

Lovela Hagans, Lucian's wife, was his match and an emancipated woman. Educated at

Madame Lovela Hagans (1829-1917).

Washington Female Seminary in Pennsylvania, she was early active in civic and charitable projects. While in West Virginia, she was one of the founders and first president of the Wheeling Children's Home. In Chicago she was one of the founders of the *Union Signal*, a publication of the Woman's Temperance Publication Association. She was associated with Frances Willard of Evanston and Mrs. T.B. Carse in the Woman's Christian Temperance Union from 1875 to 1916. She was a founder of the Chicago Area Kindergarten Association, a director of Bethesda Day Nursery, and a director of the Woman's Home Missionary Society. Lovela Hagens was also the only woman director of the Elmhurst Spring Water Company. With this background, it is not surprising that when son Wilbur sent wines home from France, she dumped them down the drain as soon as they arrived.

Nevertheless *Hawthorne*, the Lucian Hagans' home, was the scene of much socializ-

Hawthorne, the Lucian Hagans residence

ing. The house was typically Victorian in style with wide porches and cupola. Driveways curved through landscaped gardens and garden paths were bordered with flowering shrubs. Trees included cherry, crabapple, and, of course, hawthorne. Festive occasions were especially scheduled when all these trees were blooming. *Hawthorne* housed many notable guests, among them Senator and Mrs. George Hearst, whose Homestake Mine, still operating in Lead, South Dakota, provided the gold that financed the newspaper empire of their son William Randolph Hearst.

The Hagans and Bryan families were friendly neighbors - when they could get across St. Charles Road. Wilbur Hagans tells of Mrs. Bryan and her sister getting stuck in the mud on their way to Hawthorne for an afternoon call. His father and grandfather brought planks, but the women lost their shoes anyway. However, they made their call and started home "when a drove of cattle arrived and both ladies proved most expert in climbing a friendly fence."

In the "elegant era" afternoon calls were customary. Ladies finished their work, if any, by noon, and were "at home" either every afternoon or on certain days sometimes designated on their engraved calling cards. If a hostess were not at home, one left a card; if she was at home, one also left a card, depositing it on a tray on a stand near the door. There was no excuse for not knowing fellow townsmen by name. These visits were unlike coffee klatches in that everyone dressed up for the occasion.

A long-remembered event at *Hawthorne* was a gymkana for the benefit of the WCTU in the 1880's, the bicycle age. There were bicycle maneuvers, parades, and races and prizes for wheel decorations. The afternoon climaxed in drills and a Maypole quadrille. Tiny Mary Sturges, daughter of the Lee Sturgeses, kept out of everyone's way on her racer decorated with sweetpeas and daisies. She took first prize, a bicycle lamp. Second was Clara Peddle, who had wrapped her bicycle with yellow ribbon, ornamented with black-eyed susans. In the bicycle-built-for-two category, Isabel and W. Brock Greenlee took first on a bicycle decorated in white and gold with yellow daisies, while the ferns and anemones of Harriet Haskell and John Curtiss took second honors. The wheelmen, it may be noted, were all in white flannel or duck, while each girl wore her prettiest lace-trimmed frock.

Those happy days ended as family fortunes declined. Hawthorne estate was subdivided and Madame Hagans moved to a cottage on Mitchell Avenue. She moved to her son's Chicago home a year before her death in 1917.

LATHROP

In 1864 Jedediah H. Lathrop and his wife, a sister of Thomas Barbour Bryan, came from Alexandria, Virginia, and liked what they saw so well that they bought twenty-six acres from Bryan and built a villa at the

Huntington, the Jedediah Lathrop residence. Mr. and Mrs. Jedidiah Lathrop are seated on the veranda (1873).

Lathrop and Field family group (1880s). Bryan Lathrop on ground far left; Jedediah Lathrop seated center; Henry Field standing. Seated to Jedediah Lathrop's left is Florence Lathrop Field.

southwest corner of St. Charles Road and York Street. Their estate was named *Huntington* for Lathrop's mother, Lois Huntington. Their children were Bryan, 20, Barbour, 18, Florence, 6, and Minna who died in 1877 at the age of thirteen. Jedediah Lathrop, a native of Connecticut, had prospered from his interest in the Riggs Bank in Washington and from stock investments. He employed Andrew Nelson and a crew of helpers to landscape his estate. A popular garden idea of that day was arbor vitae hedges clipped into geometrical shapes. Elmhurst was famed for them in the latter days of the century.

In 1868 Jedediah Lathrop planted long rows of elm trees that helped to make Elmhurst the "Tree Town." He also developed a section of Oak Park and River Forest, commemorated in the naming of Lathrop Avenue.

At Jedediah's death his son Bryan, remembering his father's life-long love of trees, had a huge tree moved from Wilmette to Graceland Cemetery where Lathrop was buried. In 1890 the tree moving cost $2,200.

Barbour Lathrop, second son of the family, is credited with having circled the globe

Barbour Lathrop

thirty-eight times between 1866 and 1927. That made him a predecessor of Elmhurst's J. Hart Rosdail, hailed as the world's most traveled man in the 1975 edition of the *Guiness Book of World Records*.

Barbour, born in 1846 in Alexandria, Virginia, took his southern heritage so seriously that at the age of fifteen he ran away and tried to join the Confederate Army as a drummer boy, but his father, staunchly Unionist, jerked him home and slapped him in a New York school, where the noisy little rebel was ostracized by his Yankee schoolmates. He was then sent to the University of Bonn, Germany, and his fluency in German proved an asset when he visited his parents in Cottage Hill. When he dropped out of Harvard law school his father broke with him. Barbour went to San Francisco, entered the newspaper business, and started his travels as correspondent for newspapers and magazines. After his father's death in 1885, Barbour's inheritance enabled him to continue his travels. He had become interested in plants around the world that he believed would be useful in America, an idea not yet adopted by the Department of Agriculture, then in its infancy. In 1893 he met David Fairchild, plant pathologist. They went to Java together, Barbour paying expenses, and continued traveling together for nine years. Dr. Fairchild was appointed special agent and head of the Bureau of Plant Introduction of the Department of Agriculture. Among plants they brought back, some previously unknown in the United States, others in improved varieties, were Egyptian long-staple cotton, nectarines, avocados, mangos, Marrut barley, Durham wheat, broccoli, soybeans, and hops. One monument to Barbour Lathrop's memory is the Lathrop Plant Introduction Garden on the Ogeechee River near Savannah, Georgia.

More closely identified with Elmhurst was Barbour's sister, Florence Lathrop. Certainly

Florence Lathrop Field Page

the social event of the Chicago area for the season of 1879 was the wedding at Byrd's Nest Chapel of Florence and Henry Field, brother of Marshall Field (of Marshall Field & Co.). Neighbors led by Seth Wadhams strung Japanese lanterns on the elm trees (planted by Florence's father) from the Chicago & North Western station along Cottage Hill Avenue to the Lathrop home and the chapel on the estate of her uncle and aunt, the Bryans. Special trains brought wedding guests from Chicago and they were driven down the avenue below the lanterns swinging in the night breeze. For those who have not seen a Japanese lantern, let alone an avenue-full, it might be explained that it was a tissue-paper device, folding accordion-like with a place for a candle at the bottom which when fully extended and lighted displayed colorful Japanese designs. They were a highly popular decoration of the period.

The Fields went to Paris where Florence had been educated and where Henry was European buyer for Marshall Field & Co. Henry Field died in 1890. After his death, Mrs. Field presented a collection of paintings of the Barbizon School to the Art Institute of Chicago. One of the paintings was Jules Breton's "Song of the Lark", which was exhibited at the Chicago World's Fair of 1893. For a generation or two reproductions of it were hung in schoolrooms all over America.

In memory of her husband Henry, Florence Field also presented to the Art Institute the two lions which flank the main entrance. These lions by Edward Kemeys, noted American sculptor, have become a Chicago landmark. (The two lions are not identical; one has tail up; the other, tail down.)

Florence Lathrop Field returned to Elmhurst with her two daughters, Florence and Minna, and lived at the family estate, Huntington. One summer Wilbur Hagans gave the girls a lamb as a playmate. It is not of record whether it ever followed them to school, perhaps because their winters were usually spent at the Field home on Ontario Street, Chicago. As might be guessed, Mrs. Field's friends were literary and artistic, and among those she met was Thomas Nelson Page, a cousin of Mrs. Thomas Barbour Bryan who had been Jane Byrd Page. The result was another brilliant wedding at Byrd's Nest Chapel, June 6, 1893. During their marriage, the Pages spent much of their time in the McKimm Mead House in Washington, and at a summer home in Maine. However, in mentioning the pleasures she found in her fine homes, Mrs. Page always spoke with a single reservation: "The sweetest spot on earth was 'our home' at Elmhurst."

Thomas Nelson Page is probably little read in a less sentimental age, but in the closing years of the nineteenth century he was the voice of the Old South. His short story "Marse Chan" first attracted attention; it was included in an 1887 collection, *In Ole Virginia*. *Two Little Confederates* was a favorite with young readers. His novels included *The Burial of Guns* (1894), *Red Rock* (1895), and *The Old Gentleman of the Black Stock* (1897). He was ambassador to Italy from 1913 until 1918, and died in 1922.

Seth Wadhams, (1812-1888). First owner of residence which became Elmhurst Public Library.

COTTAGE HILL IN THE 1860s

WADHAMS

Seth Wadhams built the house that became the Elmhurst Public Library, and the original Wadhams home is still incorporated in the library's expanded structure. His story is one that makes the rags to riches stories of Horatio Alger, Jr. seem less exaggerated. Born in Goshen, Connecticut, October 29, 1812, at 19 he clerked in a store in Rochester, New York. In 1834, Wadhams went to Vandalia, Illinois, and then to Chicago. He was a harvest hand at 75 cents a day, clerked in a grocery at Dearborn and Lake streets and in the hardware store of Ryerson and Blakely. His diversions included hunting prairie chickens west of Western Avenue and attending the hangings of horse thieves, events assumed to improve public morality. He had a partnership with H.P. Moses in a foundry shop, then founded the Knickerbocker Ice Company which became known as the largest in the west.

White Birch, Seth Wadham's residence, later to become the Elmhurst Public Library.

Wadhams came to Cottage Hill in 1868 and bought a treeless farm called the Burnham Lot, now Wilder Park. The house he built and called *White Birch* was of cream color, or "Milwaukee" brick, square with a central hall, parlor and bedroom on the right, sitting room and dining room on the left, four bedrooms upstairs, kitchen and pantries in an ell with servants' quarters above. Mr. and Mrs. Wadhams had one son, Dana, who died young. Mrs. Wadhams never recovered from the sorrow and became an invalid, seldom leaving the house. However, she so valued the friendship of Mrs. John R. Case that she had a walk cut through the shrubbery to connect their two houses. The Case's cherry farm of 160 acres was at Arlington Avenue and St. Charles Road.

The Wadhams estate was landscaped by Swain Nelson. George Coney, a Cornishman, was gardener and herdsman. There was an enclosure for a herd of Jersey cattle and another for deer. A mirror bordered with antlers from the deer stood for many years at the entrance to the library. There was a legend that a pet deer was buried under the finial urn from the Cook County Court House, which was brought to the estate after the Chicago fire of 1871. There was also a sheep pasture. The entire estate was enclosed by a clipped hedge of arbor vitae. White birch trees were planted to justify the name *White Birch*. Wadhams also joined in planting elm trees along streets and avenues. After his wife died in 1882, he spent his winters in warmer climates and died February 8, 1888, in San Diego, California. He had been accompanied there by the retired Dr. George Heidemann of Elmhurst and Miss Rebecca Richardson, longtime Wadhams housekeeper. She received a legacy with which she built a house at the southwest corner of Church Street and Cottage Hill Avenue. The will was reported to leave the Wadhams estate to three charities and to express the wish that the house should go to Mrs. Henry W. King, daughter of Wadhams' lifelong friend, John R. Case, Sr.

CASE

In 1851, John R. Case, Sr., a resident of Chicago, purchased the west half of a 160 acre section south of St. Charles Road. It was not until near the end of the Civil War that Mr. Case bought the east half of the section. In the early days of Cottage Hill, the Bingham Tavern, used by teamsters and travelers, was located on the east half of this section. The tavern became the Case home when the family moved to the property. The senior Cases lived there until Mr. Case's death.

The Bingham Tavern, the John R. Case, Sr. residence with Case addition at right rear.

Shortly after their arrival, as John Jr. recalls, "My father set out 1,000 cherry trees." It was the only cherry orchard in the area.

"At blossom time it looked like a snow bank. People came from miles to see it. At cherry picking time (Kirschen pfluecken), it was full of German women who came with their children and babies and spent the whole day picking at 50 cents a bushel. All day the orchard resounded with the German vocabulary. At evening the boxes were loaded on hay racks, sometimes one wagon, sometimes two, and we walked the horses to South Water Street, leaving home at midnight and arriving about 5 a.m. in Chicago. This was about 1870 to 1880 when the orchard was in its prime and profitable.

"About the same time (in the early 1860's), my father planted a large apple orchard....this covered all the land from York Street to Kenilworth Avenue and St. Charles Road to May Street."

COTTAGE HILL IN THE CIVIL WAR

Cyrenus Wirt Litchfield of Cottage Hill is credited with being the first Civil War volun-

Cyrenus Litchfield (1803-1876) served as Cottage Hill Justice of Peace beginning in 1852. His son Cyrenus Wirt Litchfield was the first volunteer from Dupage County for the Civil War, and later tutor of Charles Bryan, substitute lay reader at Byrds Nest Chapel, and Justice of the Peace for Elmhurst. A second son William Harvey Litchfield served as Elmhurst village clerk (1887-1890).

teer from DuPage County. He enlisted April 19, 1861, only seven days after the first shot was fired against Fort Sumter, and served in Barker's Dragoons, a cavalry company led by Captain C.W. Barker of Chicago. First to enlist from Addison Township was Frederick Fischer, whose farm home was on Grand Avenue. He was enrolled in June, 1861, and served three years in Company B, 33rd Regiment of Illinois Volunteer Infantry, which took part in the Vicksburg campaign. While he was in the army, his parents had a folding chair made for him by Henry Korthauer, a cabinet maker. Fred carried it strapped to his back throughout his campaigns and it is now on exhibit at the DuPage County Historical Museum. After the war he studied medicine and became one of Elmhurst's most notable physicians, Dr. Frederick John Thomas Fischer. His brother, August H. Fischer of the 105th Illinois Infantry, was killed August 13, 1864, in the Atlanta campaign.

Volunteer regiments were often raised by counties, with companies representing cities or towns, but DuPage County, with an 1860 population of only 15,262, scattered its recruits over many of the 149 regiments of infantry, 17 of cavalry, and two of artillery enrolled by Illinois during the war. An exception was a company raised in York Township and equipped by Thomas Barbour Bryan. Called the "Bryan Blues" it became Company F in the 105th Illinois Infantry.

Illinois had raised six infantry regiments for the Mexican War, so the first to be mustered for the Civil War was numbered the 7th. It included 24 men from DuPage County. Members of this regiment armed themselves, purchasing the 16-shot repeating Henry rifles for $50 apiece. The regiment fought at Fort Donelson and Shiloh, and eventually in the Atlanta campaign, where its heaviest action was in the defense of Allatoona under Brigadier General John M. Corse, the fight that inspired P.P. Bliss to write the gospel hymn, "Hold the Fort, For I Am Coming." The Henry rifles saved the day, but the 7th had 143 casualties.

Muster rolls occasionally show residence of volunteers as Cottage Hill, but more commonly as of York or Addison townships, or even as DuPage County, so that it is difficult to assign local credit. However, a compilation shows that from York Township, with an 1860 population of 1,526 and a vote that year of 237, all male of course, there were 275 enlistments. Addison Township, population, 1,413 and vote 183, had 136 enlistments. Most of them served in the 13th, 33rd, 51st, 52nd, 105th, 141st, 153rd, and 159th Infantry Regiments and in the 8th, 12th, 15th, and 17th Cavalry Regiments.

Bradford Wakeman, of the Wakeman Nursery family, Civil War soldier, 23rd Infantry.

The 13th Infantry had 92 men from DuPage County, most of them in Company K, Captain Walter Blanchard, of Downers Grove. It fought at Pea Ridge, Chickasa Bayou, Vicksburg, Missionary Ridge, and Ringgold, where Capt. Blanchard was killed. Bradford Wakeman of Cottage Hill served in the 23rd Infantry.

The 33rd Infantry enrolled 47 DuPage County men. It fought at Port Gibson, Champion's Hill, Black River Bridge, Vicksburg, Jackson, and Mobile.

The 51st Infantry, with 18 men from DuPage County, was engaged at Island No. 10 and Chickamauga, and in the Battle of Kennesaw Mountain lost three officers killed, four wounded, and 105 enlisted men killed or wounded. Among the casualties were eleven from Cottage Hill: Ansel Bates, Gustav Bleasch, John Foley, Paul Hoffman, Christian Johnson, Philip Kehler, Stephen Keiler, Henry Lapp, John Lauerman, Edgar Snow, and William Welsh. Albert Ugoveck of Cottage Hill served in the 58th Infantry.

The 105th Infantry had the largest enlistment from DuPage County, 403 men in four companies. One of these companies, the "Bryan Blues" from York Township, led by Seth F. Daniels was Company F. Captain Locke of Addison headed Company I. Henry F. Vallette was lieutenant colonel. Cottage Hill men in the 105th included Henry Koxing, Andrew Newman, and Herman Timer. This regiment served through the Atlanta campaign, including the battles of Resaca, Kennesaw Mountain, Peachtree Creek, and Atlanta.

DuPage County men served in several other organizations in the Chattanooga and Atlanta campaigns, including the 19th, 36th, 42nd, 44th, 51st, 72nd, 88th, and 89th Infantry Regiments and the 12th Cavalry. The 141st Infantry was raised in 1864 to serve 100 days guard duty to relieve veteran regiments. There were DuPage County men also in the 153rd and 159th Infantry Regiments, similarly raised for guard duty, to serve for one year.

The 8th Illinois Cavalry was a notable regiment in the Army of the Potomac, and was raised largely in DuPage County. Captain Marcellus Jones of Danby (Glen Ellyn) is credited with firing the first shot at Gettysburg. William Vinton of Cottage Hill served in the 12th Illinois Cavalry, which also served in the eastern theatre of war, including Gettysburg, before joining Sherman's forces in the Atlanta campaign. DuPage County men were in the 15th Cavalry at Vicksburg and Chattanooga. Frederick Boltman and William Stoner of Cottage Hill enlisted in the 17th Cavalry, which served largely in campaigns in Missouri. DuPage County was also represented in the artillery, more in the 2nd Regiment of Light Artillery than in the 1st, and others in separate companies such as Cogswell's Battery and Petit's Battery.

ELMHURST AFTER THE WAR

Elmhurst in 1869 consisted of post office and railway station, and whatever had gathered around them. The post office which had first been located in Hill Cottage Tavern was moved in 1869 to Gerry Bates' property on Park Avenue across from the railway station and was located in a one-story building

Courtesy of Chicago Historical Society
Elmhurst's second Post Office and Gerry Bates' General Store. Old account books from the store reveal that customers charged their postage stamps along with their groceries.

next to Elmhurst City Market. From the time John Hovey was appointed postmaster of Cottage Hill in 1845 until 1869, there were seven postmasters with Gerry Bates serving three times. He served from 1849 until 1859. Ludwig Graue served briefly in 1859 followed by Diedrich Mong. Bates served again from 1861 until 1865. On March 2, 1865, Augustus Palmer was appointed. During his term the name Cottage Hill was officially changed to Elmhurst in the post office records. However, during Bates' third term there must have been some problems about the village's name change, for Bates' appointment was to the post office of Elmhurst from November 20, 1868 to February 25, 1869; to the post office of Cottage Hill from February 25, 1869 to May 26, 1870; and to Elmhurst again beginning May 26, 1870, when the town was once more officially and finally named Elmhurst.

Among those merchants who picked up their mail, as did all residents (there was no mail carrier delivery until 1918), were Otto Dehling whose saloon was at First and York streets and James Ungery who had opened a saloon on First Street, across from the railroad station, on the site of the Union Hotel which had been destroyed by fire.

Diedrich Mong farmed east of York Street, and opened a tavern, later expanded into a general store, on York Street south of the tracks. He also was railway station agent. Ludwig Graue had his store at 136 Park Avenue, the oldest brick building in Elmhurst, erected in 1864 to replace his First Street store built in 1854.

Standing in front of the second Graue general store, 136 Park Avenue, are (L to R) William Asche, August Graue, William Graue, Richard Bourke, and Tom Hagan.

Merchandise offered in the Graue store was typical for general stores of the period, including groceries, dry goods, notions, boots and shoes, turpentine, linseed oil, white lead, kerosene, and the first gasoline to be sold in Elmhurst.

The Elmhurst Historical Museum has some of the Graue Grocery Store sales slips and on the back of them is the store's motto: "Not how Cheap but how Good." If a customer or passerby lingered until closing time, he would see one of the Graues lock the

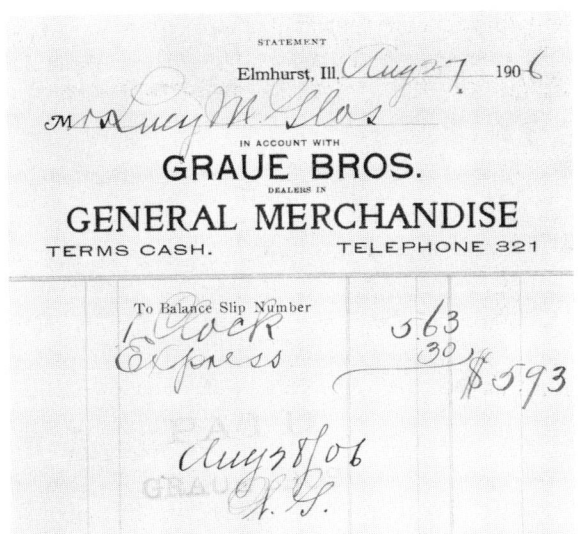

A 1906 sales slip showing a mere three digits for the telephone number.

store with an eight inch long key which weighed eight pounds. Both key and lock were from Germany. The Graue Store like Hill Cottage Tavern has been designated as an Illinois historic landmark.

On the east side of York Street a wooden sidewalk, two feet wide, extended as far south as St. Mary's Church. It was made of planks laid lengthwise, nailed to two-by-fours. On both sides of York Street were ditches two to five feet deep, and near the present Marion Street a low bog, bridged by a stone culvert. When Dr. George Heidemann, who had returned from the Civil War to become Elmhurst's first physician, built his home and office on North York Street near Third, he offered to buy three inch oak planks from the railroad for a sidewalk if his neighbors would build it. The following Sunday a storekeeper donated spikes; section hands, some of whom lived along the route, spiked the planks to railroad ties, a teamster contributed the hauling. John

Dr. George Heidemann (1839-1908) practiced medicine in the village for thirty-five years.

Conrad, a saloon keeper, opened a keg of lager beer for the workers, and the one foot wide sidewalk was built from Moritz Hoelscher's store on First Street, east to York Street, and north to the doctor's residence. It was used for ten years.

ELMHURST AFTER THE CHICAGO FIRE

KINGS

Henry W. King was born in Martinsburg, New York, on December 28, 1828. He attended the State Academy at Lewville, a preparatory school, but at 17 went to work in his father's store. He came to Chicago in 1854 and entered the wholesale clothing business with several partners. Mr. King established the firm of Henry W. King and Company in 1868. He was also a partner in the firm of Browning, King and Company which operated a retail store in Chicago with branches in other cities.

In 1867 Henry W. King and his wife, Aurelia Case King, purchased *Hill Cottage* which had been renamed *Clover Lawn*. by artist Healy. The Kings used *Clover Lawn* as a summer home until their house and business in Chicago were destroyed in the Chicago fire of 1871. Mrs. King tells of the alarm of fire at one o'clock in the night. Mr. King went to his store. A friend put Michigan Central freight cars at his disposal and much goods were loaded before the nearby depot caught fire and it was necessary to move the train out. King rushed home with books and papers. By that time the house was threatened. Loading a few valuables into their carriage, they fled north "into a shower of fire....The wind was like a tornado, and I held fast to my little ones, fearing they would be lifted from my sight." In Lincoln Park "the dry leaves and even the very ground took fire beneath our feet." They fled on, "crossing a bridge on North Avenue and reaching the West Side, where we found a conveyance at noon on Monday which brought us out to Elmhurst....Our house is full....We are more fortunate and feel almost ashamed to be so comfortable."

King estimated his losses at $200,000, but with the goods saved in the freight train, returned from Michigan City within two weeks, he was back in business at Washington and Canal streets. He became president of the Relief and Aid Society and served it as treasurer from 1873 to 1888. By this time he had recovered from his losses, and when Mrs. King inherited the Wadhams estate, he had the house enlarged, renamed it *Lancaster Lodge,* and had the grounds landscaped by

Lancaster Lodge, Henry W. King's second home, showing the remodeling of *White Birch* built by Seth Wadhams. In 1905 this residence became the T.E. Wilder home.

Frederick Law Olmsted who had laid out Central Park in New York City, and the Village of Riverside, Illinois. Henry King died April 16, 1898. After Mrs. King died the estate was sold to Thomas Edward Wilder.

The King's daughter, Elizabeth, was married to Cyrus Bentley. The couple built a large house at Cottage Hill Avenue and Arthur Street. This house was later bought by Frederick B. Snite, and then became the convent for the Sisters of St. Agnes who taught at the Immaculate Conception Parochial School. This house was razed to make room for the I.C. Convent.

Francis King, son of the Henry W. King, was married in 1890 to Louisa Yeomans.

They came to Elmhurst to live, at first in *Hill Cottage,* and after the death of Henry King at *Lancaster Lodge.* Louisa King became interested in the garden of her mother-in-law who was knowledgeable in garden lore and had a library on the subject. The herb garden was based on descriptions by Erasmus; the flower garden modeled on Mount Vernon with its box-hedge borders. The Francis Kings bought the McCormick house at Claremont Avenue and Prospect Street, where Louisa King had her first garden, but

Louisa Yeoman King (1863-1948).

it was not until after they moved to Alma, Michigan, in 1907 that she became an authority on the subject. Her first book, *The Well Considered Garden,* telling of her early experiences, became a guide for amateur gardeners. Her paper "Color in the Flower Garden," written for the Massachusetts Horticultural Society in 1912, discussed an aspect of gardening that became her major contribution. In 1912 she helped organize the Michigan Garden Club and was its first president, serving until 1915. In 1913 she was active in the organization of the Garden Club of America and was elected one of its four vice presidents. The Women's National Farm and Garden Association, organized in Philadelphia in 1914, was largely Louisa King's idea and she was its first president.

Francis King died in 1927, and Louisa King moved to New York state to be near her children. There she dedicated the last of her ten books, *From a New Garden,* to the memory of her mother-in-law Mrs. Henry W. King, recalling her displays of tulips in Elmhurst that sparked Louisa's interest in flower arrangement as a work of art. Louisa King died in 1948. She received many honors and awards. A memorial planting in the National Arboretum, Washington, D.C., "invites the visitor to sit in peace and enjoy the quietness and tranquility she considered so essential a part of any garden."

"EMERSON'S SUBDIVISION"

As refugees from the fire began to make Elmhurst their permanent home, development of a new subdivision followed. Mr. Emerson, about 1874, bought up a tract of land in the northwest section and arranged for a railway

Characteristic home of Emerson subdivision using Italianate style popular in the 1870s and 1880s.

excursion to sell plots. He staked off Addison, Larch, Maple, Elm, Evergreen and Myrtle streets. The subdivision was opened as a gala event advertising free beer, picnics, band concerts, and other entertainment for the visitors coming by the excursion trains. As a sales promotion it was not entirely successful, and later Henry L. Glos bought many of the unsold lots. The subdivision was platted as "Town of Elmhurst" but always referred to locally as "Emerson's Subdivision."

KOCH

Another refugee from the Chicago fire was Dr. Friedrich Koch whose wife, Louise, was the daughter of Frederick Fischer of the pioneer Addison Township family. Friederich Koch was the son of a landowner in Germany. He was a brilliant lad who read Latin at the age of 12, played piano like a master, and spoke French, Italian, and English as well as German, fluently. In the 1860s, at 17, he came to the United States for extensive travel; however, he returned to Germany to complete his medical education. After graduation, he returned to the United States and served in the Medical Department in the Union Army. For some unknown reason, Koch never had a private practice, but later his medical background had a great influence on his son who inherited a love for scientific investigation. Louise and Friedrich Koch were parents of seven daughters, including two who died in infancy, and one son, Fred Conrad Koch.

One of the daughters, Adheleid, related the family's taking up permanent residence in this manner:

> It was rumored Chicago was burning, and my mother was in Elmhurst helping her mother with sewing but feeling very worried about her Chicago house. It was October, 1871.
>
> When Grandfather Koch and my mother's father, Grandfather Fischer, went to Chicago in order to reassure my mother of the safety of our house, they found it in the direct path of the fire, with much of the furniture missing. Friends, as the fire approached, loaded their own furniture in coal carts with the intent of taking it to the Koch home which they believed would be safe from the fire. They found, however, that the fire was close on their heels and the Koch's were away (in Elmhurst). They added the Koch piano, finest china, and much of the furniture to their own and moved on again.
>
> After the Chicago Fire, we lived in our Grandfather Fischer's house on the farm for a while. Father had a house built at 175 Maple Avenue (in the Emerson Subdivision) in 1872 and the family has lived there ever since.

The only son, Fred Conrad, was born in Chicago May 16, 1876. He attended the German Lutheran School in Elmhurst and Elmhurst High School, not yet accredited. As a result, he finished at Oak Park High School. Fred Conrad Koch entered the University of Illinois in 1885 on a scholarship and with financial aid from his Grandfather Fischer, needed because of the early death of his father. He was graduated in chemistry in 1899 and remained for two years as an instructor. In 1902 he became a research chemist for Armour Co., Chicago. In 1909 he was awarded a graduate fellowship in chemistry

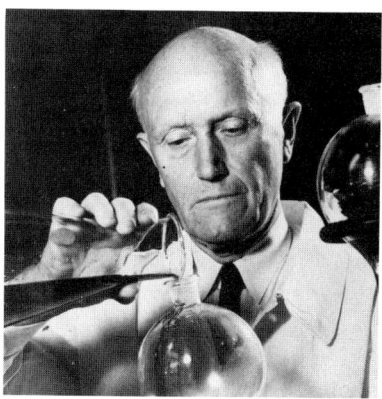

Dr. Fred Conrad Koch (1876-1948).

at the University of Chicago and remained there until 1941, being named distinguished service professor of biochemistry in 1926 and department chairman in 1929. He became internationally known for his studies of enzymes of the digestive tract, the gastric hormone, secretin, and the thyroid hormone. He was first to show that ultraviolet light converted cholesterol into Vitamin D. He was president of the Association for the Study of Internal Secretion, delegate to the League of Nations Conference on Standardization of Sex Hormones, and representative to the Pan American Conference on Endocronology. He was editor of the *Archives of Biochemistry* and received many awards and honors. After retirement from the university, he rejoined Armour Co., and continued research there until 1946.

This was a notable career for an Elmhurst boy of German descent. That he came of a family of inquiring and scientific minds is illustrated by a story told about his mother. During Elmhurst's first century there was considerable development in methods of home heating. Fireplaces gave way to wood-burning stoves, succeeded by coal stoves, culminating in the base burner which heated the living room and adjacent area when fed with anthracite coal from a scuttle. After the turn of the century most homes adopted central heating, consisting of a coal-fed furnace in the basement with asbestos-wrapped pipes sending heat to every room in the house.

When Mrs. Koch was 70, many of her neighbors were converting to automatic oil heating furnaces. She wondered if it would be economical. She calculated that every time she went to the furnace to put on coal, she turned on three lights and walked 100 steps. Counting the times she fired the furnace on a cold winter day, she discovered that she used three kilowatts of electricity and walked ten blocks. She installed the oil burner.

HIGGINSON

Also refugees from the Chicago fire were the George M. Higginsons. Their home on north Dearborn Street near Chicago Avenue was destroyed and their flight brought them to the Bryans' Byrd's Nest home where they were "most kindly cared for," wrote Mrs. Higginson in a letter to a friend. "The outpoured sympathy & kindness of the world is ours, & we need it." Anna Higginson mourned "our ruined homes, with all their years of accumulated treasures & associations of every kind. It is for those I Grieve, not over the loss of money - my Mother's Bible, the clothing & toys of my dead children, all the keepsakes & mementoes of a lifetime. People sometimes check me for being too despondent when I say I shall never have a home again; a house somewhere, undoubtedly I shall have....but a house which simply bears the mark of the builder & upholsterer could never be home to me if it were ever so elegant." Mr. Higginson, a real estate broker and president of the Illinois State Microscopic Society, bought land from Mr. Bryan and built a house on Virginia Street. Perhaps in time Anna E. Higginson accepted it as a home.

ELMHURST COLLEGE BEGINNINGS

In the same year that so many fugitives from the Chicago fire took up residence in Elmhurst, fourteen students and a professor arrived to start the Proseminary that was to become Elmhurst College. This was the result of a rather complicated series of efforts in religious education. The German Evangelical Synod of the West, organized in the St. Louis area in 1840, represented the Evangelical branch of the German Reformation, a Union Church, combining the Lutheran and Reformed branches. It established a theological seminary in Marthasville, Missouri, still existing as Eden Seminary, but plans for a college of general education, preparatory for the seminary, were abandoned during the Civil War. In 1871 it was decided to open

Kranz Hall, Elmhurst College, erected 1873.

"Old Main," Elmhurst College, dedicated 1878, declared a National Landmark 1976.

such a school in Evansville, Indiana.

Meanwhile, the German Evangelical Synod of the Northwest, centering about Chicago, planned similar schools. A seminary was established in Waukegan and later moved to Lake Zurich. Pastor Joseph Hartmann of St. Paul's Evangelical Church, Chicago, had become acquainted with Thomas B. Bryan and explained the synod's problems to him. Bryan offered twenty acres fronting on Prospect Avenue, Elmhurst, at a cost of $10,000, with an additional ten acres as outright gift. This offer was accepted and a two-story house on the property became Melanchton Seminary in 1869. In the fall of 1871, the synods of the West and of the Northwest, with great good sense decided to merge. They combined their educational program by moving all theological students to the seminary in Missouri, and transferring the Proseminary established that year in Evansville to the larger campus available in Elmhurst.

Carl F. Kranz, president and the only teacher of the Proseminary, arrived in Elmhurst with his fourteen students December 6, 1871. A freight car with their furniture and possessions had gone astray, the only house on the campus was bare, and the nearest Evangelical Church was three miles away. But farmers and church members took them in; the freight car arrived before the end of the month; and classes began January 4, 1872. Ten more students enrolled, bringing the student body to 24. It grew to 35 for the next term, 66 in 1873, 70 in 1874, and 97 by 1878. Students built a one-room addition to the first building. (Two sections of the house were later moved to Alexander Boulevard, where they became professors' houses.) In 1873 the building known as Kranz Hall was erected at a cost of $12,000. "Old Main," costing $25,000, was dedicated in 1878. It had a tower, classrooms, laboratory, reading room, chapel with a pipe organ, dormitories, washrooms, and the president's apartment.

Kranz resigned as Inspektor, his real title, in 1874, and was succeeded by the Rev. Philip F. Muench, a graduate of the seminary at Marthasville. Muench was responsible for the Proseminary's first catalog in 1878, which offered a four-year course covering Latin, Greek, German, English, religion, history, geography, mathematics, science, and music. There were 36 forty-five-minute class periods a week, "but the students are given time for exercise out of doors and for the preparation of lessons." However, "association with persons of feminine gender is strictly forbidden." A fee of $150 a year included tuition, board, room, and laundry - and this was continued without change until 1913. The curriculum was patterned on the German Gymnasium, which was also the model for much American education at that period, and the Proseminary was the equivalent of numerous academies that preceded the later-

Elmhurst College Faculty about 1900. Standing - left to right: C. Weisse, George Sorrick, C.G. Stanger, H. Brodt, Carl Bauer. Seated - Emil Otto, Daniel Irion, president; John Lueder.

day high school. The main purpose of the Proseminary was preparatory schooling for students who would enter the theological seminary and become pastors, and to train teachers for German Evangelical schools. However, from the beginning some 10 to 20 per cent enrolled as "college students" seeking a general classical education. What they got was more nearly equivalent to a present-day high school course except for greater emphasis on Latin, Greek, and classical literature. A proposal to add more "college students" was voted down in 1885.

President Muench died in 1880 at the age of 44 and was succeeded by the Rev. Peter Goebel. In 1885 the course was extended to five years, and the faculty, which had grown slowly, was enlarged. Included were such long-tenure teachers as John Lueder in history, Herman Brodt in pedagogy and German, and C.J. Albert in English. The Muench Literary Society started a library, and there were Saturday night entertainments by the Concordia, the Demosthenes Club, the Owl, and the Schiller Club in debate or oratory, or singing by the Orpheus Men's Chorus, started in 1884. An annual festival, the Seminar-fest, in June brought crowds from all over the Chicago area. With only three buildings erected, much of the campus was devoted to farming; cows roamed its pastures, corn, oats, and hay were grown, and a garden produced vegetables, all contributed to keeping the annual fee at $150 as well as assuring exercise out of doors for some students.

President Goebel resigned in 1887 and was succeeded by Daniel Irion, an alumnus of the school and pastor of St. Peter's Church. He was

Dr. Daniel Irion, President of the Proseminary (1887-1919).

to serve 32 years as president, until 1919, and then continue on the faculty until 1928. He died in 1935. Dr. Irion surrounded himself with an able faculty, including Emil Otto, Carl Bauer, George A. Sorrick, Christian G. Stanger, H. Arlt, Henry L. Breitenbach, Emil Hansen, and in the later years, Paul N. Crusius. In 1896 the Dining Hall, later called The Commons, replaced the original seminary building, but was razed in 1964 to make room for the College Union. A new dormitory, Irion Hall, was built in 1912 and incorporated a chapel, gymnasium, library, and assembly hall. However, the school had not kept up with the times of fading prestige for academy and preparatory school. Although calling itself Elmhurst College in a 1901 catalog, the five-year course prescribed was accredited only as four years of high school and a college year deficient in laboratory sciences.

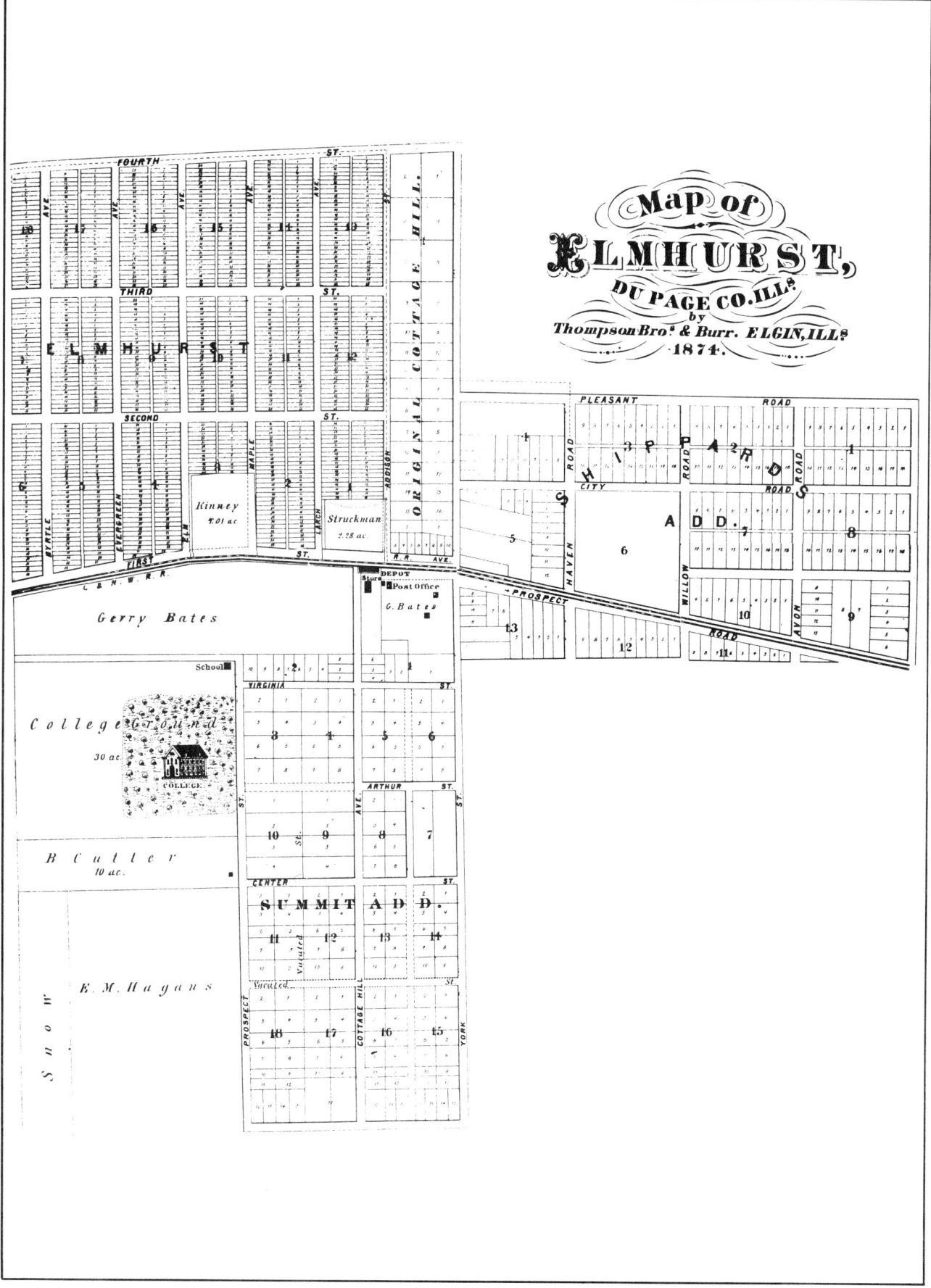

INCORPORATION AS A VILLAGE

During the period when fugitives from the Chicago Fire were finding Elmhurst attractive and staying on, there was a gradual growth in the community's facilities. Louis Balgemann started a blacksmith shop at 127 South York in 1870. Adam S. Glos opened a hardware store at 113 North York in 1872. Each of these businesses was to last fifty years. Henry L. Glos opened a general store in 1874. Dr. Frederick Fischer became Elmhurst's second physician in 1879. Albert S. Brownell, who had come as station agent in 1869, formed a partnership with Dederich Struckmann and they built a large warehouse for the sale of grain and feed. They also dealt in lumber and coal. Rudolph Kramer opened a butcher shop, and Charles Most had a general store at Addison Avenue and North Railroad Street, later First Street.

Elmhurst, however, was a community without boundaries and without a center; its only local government was that of county and townships. Dr. Frederick H. Bates stated that the primary reason a responsible local government was needed was the arrogance of four saloon keepers, who ignored laws against selling to minors and for Sunday closing, and sometimes refused to pay the $50 county license fee.

During the winter of 1880-1881, Henry L. Glos, began working to move sentiment toward incorporation. At first, the suggestion was met with indignation from many residents who protested incorporation as unnecessary and costly in tax money. However, the continued brash attitudes of the saloon keepers coupled with a state law "providing for an annual license of $250 for the sale of malt beverages and $500 for both malt and alcoholic drinks with local option" changed attitudes. The residents began to feel that saloon keepers had too much influence on the atmosphere of the town and the saloon keepers saw that with enforcement of license fees their free-wheeling business conduct was soon to be largely curtailed.

Mr. Glos went to the local leaders and persuaded them to agree to incorporation the following spring. "They (the leading saloon keepers) were pictured as public benefactors insomuch as the money they paid (for licenses) to sell liquor, after incorporation, would go into the village treasury." Feeling panicky and somewhat unpopular, the saloon keepers met with an argument they couldn't resist. Henry L. Glos was a man of determination and sagacity.

Henry L. Glos was responsible for a petition dated May 15, 1882, seeking to incorporate the east one-half of Section 2 and the west one-fourth of Section 1 of York Township as a village. This meant that the village of Elmhurst would extend from St. Charles Road to North Avenue and to one half mile west of York Street and to one-fourth mile east of York Street. When enough signatures were obtained, an election was held June 5, 1882, at the public school house. Of 88 votes cast, 60 favored village government, 28 opposed. An election of six village trustees followed July 1, 1882. Those chosen were Henry L. Glos, Peter A. Wolf, George Sawin, Christian Blievernicht, Ernst Balgemann, and Charles Wade. The Village Board of Trustees met eight days later and unanimously elected Glos as President, an office he was to hold for twenty years with one two-year interruption, 1886-1888 when Peter Wolf, harness maker and original trustee, served as president. Wolf was known as one of four Democrats voting in Elmhurst; his election came during the presidency of Grover Cleveland, first Democrat elected after the Civil War.

HENRY L. GLOS

Henry Glos is often called the founder of Elmhurst. Although Thomas B. Bryan gave the village its name. Henry L. Glos guided the growing settlement into a governed community.

Henry L. Glos was born on the Glos farm December 31, 1862, and spent all of his years

Henry L. Glos (1862-1905), village president, 1882-1887; 1888-1902.

within present Elmhurst bounds. He attended Cottage Hill public schools and the Bryant and Stratton Business College. He taught school until 1874 when he opened his brick store where he advertised that he was a "Dealer in Dry Goods, Groceries, Crockery, Hats and Caps, Boots and Shoes, Readymade Clothing, Notions, and all articles usually kept in a first-class country store." In 1876 Henry married Lucy Schween of Elgin. They lived above the store until 1892 when they built the Glos mansion, 104 South Kenilworth Avenue. (The Glos

Glos Mansion, built in 1892. The building is remarkable for its white oak woodwork, the solid brass doorknobs and hinges, the copper gutters and downspouts, and the outer walls of Bedford limestone.

home now houses the Elmhurst Historical Museum.) Eventually he gave up the store and gave his full attention to a real estate business. He founded the Henry L. Glos private bank in

The Henry L. Glos Private Bank at the southeast corner of York Street and Park Avenue, was also the third location for the Elmhurst Post Office. The library was housed from 1916-1922 in the small building at the rear.

The Glos Block Building, adjacent to the Glos Bank, was built in two different decades. The cast-iron store front, typical of the 1870s-1880s was a forerunner of the steel curtain wall. The use of pre-cast metal indicates the growth of industrial development and the fading of handicraft methods of building.

1894. This building also housed the post office for many years. For 25 years Henry Glos was York Township representative on the DuPage County Republican Central Committee. He also served a term as postmaster.

Newspaper articles about Henry Glos, and the obituaries following his death in 1905, are universally laudatory. It is repeatedly stated that "he was always ready to help those who came to him," and his banking business is said to have grown out of his frequent and generous loans to German farmers, many of whom bought farm machinery and implements from the hardware store of Adam S. Glos, Henry's brother.

Six years before his death, a special ordinance permitted him to erect the mausoleum in which he is buried in Glos Memorial Park across Kenilworth Avenue from the mansion. While Mrs. Glos survived, a rocking chair was kept within the mausoleum for her frequent visits. She deeded the house to the city in 1939 but continued residence there until her death June 29, 1941. The mansion's first civic use was by the wartime ration board in 1942. It was used as a city hall until 1970 when city offices were moved to Schiller Street. As an indication of inflation, it may be noted that in 1890 the estimated cost of building the mansion was $20,000. When the property was transferred, the estate's estimated worth was $75,000 including the park land.

VILLAGE ORDINANCES

The first action of the Village Board of Trustees after electing Glos as president was to name a special committee on ordinances. Important to this committee was a trustee who was a lawyer, George Sawin. A native of Boston, he had been active in organizing the town of DeSoto, Wisconsin; he had read law with G.S. Hilliard and was admitted to the bar before the Civil War in which he served as first lieutenant in the 58th Illinois Infantry. He was married to Carrie Rust and they had three children, George, Jr., Robert, and Gertrude when they moved to Elmhurst in 1870. He had been elected a justice of the peace before being chosen village trustee. He legally formulated the ordinances adopted during the early years of Elmhurst history as a village. His home and law offices were at 119 Virginia Street.

One of the first problems was to provide sidewalks in a less haphazard manner than the volunteer labor enlisted by Dr. Heidemann. H.C. Hohman was appointed constable and street commissioner, and an ordinance required him "to take charge of Village owned lumber for delivery and sale to property owners for sidewalk construction." A subsequent ordinance entitled "Labor on the Streets," subtitled "Poll Tax" was passed "to secure not less than two days' labor (or cash equivalent) from every able-bodied male between twenty-

Courtesy of Chicago Historical Society
Children walking on wooden sidewalks in the 1890s. Plank sidewalks were common in Elmhurst until the turn of the century.

one and fifty years of age for work on Village streets."

Air pollution, was one of the earliest concerns. Ordinance No. 8, on nuisances was passed July 22, 1882. Section No. 1 banned the keeping of more than ten cattle or swine in any yard, pen, place, or premises under penalty of a fine of not less than $5 and not exceeding $50, and to a like fine for every

Dick Schmidt, first Elmhurst Police Marshal, 1882.

day the offender neglected or refused to abate such nuisances. Another section provided that no privy should be "within forty feet from the street, or the dwelling house, shop, or well of any other person, unless the same be furnished with a substantial vault, six feet deep and made tight." Prohibited was "distilling and rendering of lard or tallow, or glue making from dead animals within the limits of one mile of the village boundaries." Chicken coops or stables could not be "nauseous, foul, offensive, or injurious to the public health."

An ordinance of July 29, 1882, listed punishable misdemeanors as assault and battery, disorderly conduct, concealed weapons, intoxication, vagrancy, and gambling. Disorderly conduct was a catchall for undesirable behavior.

September 15, 1883, Elmhurst authorized its first drainage sewer, "an eight-inch sewer tile sunk not less than one foot below grades, from Arthur Street north along the west side of York Street to an open ditch or into a sewer running along the south side of the Chicago & North Western right-of-way," and then into Salt Creek.

GROWTH AS A VILLAGE

In 1884, two years after incorporation, the village began to take more permanent form. Streets were named and platted. A road grader was purchased as was crushed stone to pave streets. A site was chosen for a new town hall on City Road (now Schiller Street, the site was that of the present fire station) and construction was ordered. The building was to be "a frame town

Elmhurst City Hall, 1886.

hall, 22 by 36 feet in size, and 18 feet high, joined by a 14 by 14 foot stone calaboose 9 feet high." A shed for housing the grader and other equipment was also provided. A second floor was added to the town hall in 1886.

Contracts were let in 1885 for twenty-five kerosene street lamps and Fred Schroerine was hired as lamplighter. He agreed to light, clean, and fill the lamps for $85 for one year. The village minutes of May 1, 1886, record the hiring of the first permanent village employee in this manner: the village published an "advertisement" for "services of able-bodied man to be furnished to the village for one year." Mr. John Ohlschefski was among three men who bid for the position. Mr. Ohlschefski's bid was to serve as general help, lamplighter, and calaboose keeper. (He rounded up vagrants, put them into jail, and also released them.) All these services were bid for $250 a year and living quarters in the upper floor of the town hall. The same year Mr. Ohlschefski was hired, more street lamps were installed. In 1888, the village purchased a cart for use in filling and lighting street lamps.

Henry Glos resumed the village presidency in 1888 after Peter Wolf's two-year term. An

Peter A. Wolf, village president (1886-1888).

ordinance was passed February 4, 1888, forbidding the village's three saloons to sell or give away intoxicating liquor to a "black list" of habitual drunkards under threat of losing their licenses. Names were added to the list from time to time. The "black list" was officially rescinded July 7, 1900, but the procedure seems to have continued for seven more years.

A resolution was approved August 3, 1889, "requesting the Chicago and North Western Railway Company to erect a gate and station a flagman at York Street crossing within thirty days."

This continuing civic activity would seem to indicate a growing village. By 1885, with a population of 300, there were some forty businesses. Adolph Hammerschmidt and Henry Assman in 1883 organized a company for the quarrying of cut stone and the making of clay brick and tile. During 1883-1885, they rented a small quarry and clay pit on part of Ludwig Graue's farm about one mile west of the village center, now West Avenue and West First Street. In 1885 they purchased eleven acres of the Graue farm for $3,300 and built kilns for the manufacture of clay products. In 1893, Adolph Hammerschmidt

Adolph Hammerschmidt, founder of the Elmhurst-Chicago Stone Company.

bought out Assman's interest and incorporated the business as Elmhurst-Chicago Stone Company. His son "Max" Hammerschmidt came from Naperville to help manage the business.

Many buildings in Chicago stand on "dimension" stone cut from the Elmhurst quarry.

Through the years growth was matched by an increasingly complex plant and equipment. In 1915 screening and crushing equipment were installed; 1920 marked the initial manufacture of cement blocks. By 1929, crushed stone products were the quarry's major output. In 1940, the Hammerschmidts entered the redi-mix concrete business. More modernization came in 1950.

By the 1970s members of the fourth generation of the Hammerschmidt family were operating the stone quarry and several generations of some Elmhurst families had worked at Elmhurst-Chicago Stone Company. It is one of the oldest and has remained one of the most constant business factors in the Elmhurst community.

The Robbins Cheese Factory was at the northeast corner of Larch Avenue and West First Street, near the turntable of the Chicago and North Western Railroad. East of the cheese factory was the Brownell and Stange Lumber Yard, offering lumber, grain, feed, flour, and coal. Next to the east, at Addison Avenue, was the Hohmann Saloon and Dance Hall.

In 1885, August Graue's general store advertised groceries, dry goods, notions, paint and shoes. Three horses and wagons were kept in barns at the rear of the store for prompt free delivery service. The brick building store at Park Avenue near Cottage Hill

Elmhurst Stone Quarry, 1894

Avenue was later operated by August's sons, William and Julius. When August was propriretor with his son William helping, and later when Julius and William ran Graue's together, the store stayed open late Saturday evenings and was opened early Sunday mornings. The store became a social center. Julius and William operated the store until 1921. Since then the building has been remodeled and has been occupied for many years by Better Radio and TV. The building used by Gerry Bates as post office and general store, discontinued in deference to the Graue store, was rented in 1879 by Henry Tedrahn for a general store which he had moved by 1886 to North York Street where he paid $5 a month rent. Mr. Tedrahn constructed a large frame building at Schiller Street and Haven Road. His son, Fred H. Tedrahn, a Spanish-Americn war veteran, took over the store in 1926.

At the northeast corner of First Street and Addison Avenue, William Most offered "stoves, stove repairs, tin and copper ware, etc." Later he moved to the west side of Addison Avenue. Charles Most had a general store on First Street. The official village scale was on First, west of York.

Elmhurst's first shoemaker probably was Nicolaus Peter whose shop was on South York Street, north of Marion. His land extended east to Kenilworth. D. Benjamin Miche had his shoemaker shop on the west side of South York Street. Rudolph Kramer's meat market was south of the Balgemann home and blacksmith shop. Another blacksmith and wagon maker was Louis Rakow, who lived at York and Marion Street. North of Balgemann's was William Ulrich's saloon. Next to the north was a brick building that was a general store until 1885; then it was used by Henry Glos as a real estate and insurance office, and after 1894 as his bank. The building was razed in 1927 and replaced by the building which in 1976 housed the Elmhurst National Bank.

Continuing north on York Street, the first building across the tracks was the saloon of Frank Baeder; and north of it was the Cottage Hill House, the public house of Christian Blievernicht, who later converted it into a general store. At 113 North York Street was the hardware store of Adam S. Glos, born in 1846, grandson of pioneer John Glos and brother of Henry L. Glos. Besides hardware, Adam S. Glos sold farm machinery and implements, and stoves, and was agent for Singer and Wilson sewing machines. He became president of the Elmhurst State Bank and president of the Addison Farmers Mutual Insurance Company but continued

Adam Glos Store, business founded 1872 at 111 North York Street, now the location of York Furrier.

operating his hardware store until his death in 1927. The Gloses generally resisted electric lighting. Old timers recalled his store, dimly lit with kerosene lamps, with Adam seated in a chair in its middle aisle. If anything was wanted, he would direct his customer where to find it, then accept the pay for it without getting up. Perhaps he was the inventor of the self-service of the supermarkets. He lived upstairs, over the store and his widow, Emily, resided there for a time after his death.

The next building, a frame structure with porch, was Carl Bauer's Tin and Stove Store, also dealing in hardware and copperware. Between the Bauer store and the Giese blacksmith shop at the Schiller Street corner was the harness shop of Peter A. Wolf, who was also a saddler. Henry Moeller was a wagon maker in the area. On Schiller Street, adjoining the Village Hall, was the home of Julius Heegard, housepainter and interior decorator. He painted the murals inside the original St. Peter's Church. Other painters and paperhangers were Jacob Wittenburg and

Frank Blau. North of Schiller at 144 North York Street was the home of John Hahn.

Hahn residence, 144 North York Street

Born in Germany in 1819, Hahn was the community's first carpenter, and the only one until 1860. He built St. Peter's Church. He also built coffins, and Mrs. Hahn lined them and made the mourning crepes hung on doors. Their son-in-law John Keiler, was the village's first undertaker. Hahn Street marks the area where John Hahn used to graze his cow.

Other carpenters and joiners were William Hanebuth of Marion Street, William Schaper of Schiller Street, Henry Battermann and Ernest Balgemann, both of Addison Avenue; Arthur Sievers, Hermann Warnecke, and Hermann Conrad. Balgemann charged 30 cents an hour in 1902 for repairs to the post office in the Glos Building. Inflation had started. Carpenter bills show 40 cents an hour in 1907, 50 cents in 1910, 60 cents in 1912, and 70 cents in 1917.

Masons of 1882 were Henry Boettcher, Henry Morwitzer, and Henry Wiegrefe. Henry R. Uhlhorn was a teamster and did odd jobs of excavating, hauling, and road grading. Edward Dolberg had a butcher shop at the southwest corner of York Street and North Avenue. Tailors included John Barge, Henry Gekrke, and Albert T. Schultz. In those days a man needing a suit of clothes went to a tailor. There were no "hand-me-downs" as tailors scornfully called ready-made suits which were handed down from a shelf and in their opinion, ill-fitting.

Many early merchants and artisans were men of many talents. John Keiler, son-in-law of John Hahn, has been mentioned as Elmhurst's first undertaker. Keiler came to Elmhurst about 1882. When he married to Johanna Hahn, he was working as a house

John Keiler (1859-1905).

painter. Then he opened a store on York Street, the site of the present Elks Club Building, advertising as a "dealer in all kinds of Furniture, Picture Frames, Mouldings, Mirrors, Stoves, Heaters and Ranges, Hardware, Paints, Oils, Glass. Undertaking and Embalming a Specialty. Furniture Repaired." The combination of furniture store and undertaking was common in small towns when coffins were made by hand, using the skills that could be employed in furniture making

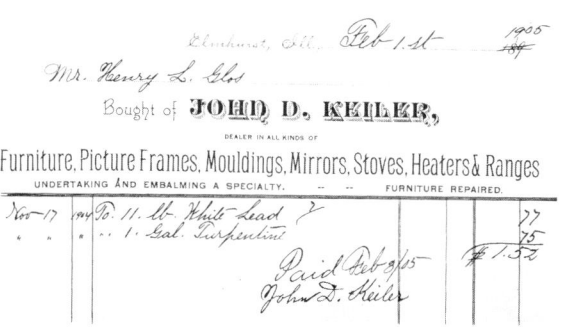
Invoice from Keiler store.

and repairing or picture framing. In this case father-in-law Hahn built the coffins. A complete funeral service included the hiring of two women at two dollars each to make house-to-house calls (one on each side of the railroad tracks) to announce the deaths and the day the wake would be held, probably in the home of the deceased, although occasionally in the paint shop.

Dr. Frederick H. Bates, born in Cottage Hill in 1857, the son of pioneer settlers Gerry and Georgia Bates, built a home and office at the southwest corner of York Street and Park

Avenue in 1884. He had attended the Brown School in Chicago and Rush Medical College, graduated in 1878, and had practiced medicine in Elgin and Bensenville before returning to his home town. As was not un-

Dr. Frederick Bates (1857-1920).

common among doctors of that time, he also operated a drug store, the first in Elmhurst, and he succeeded his father as postmaster. Dr. Bates was married in 1885 to Nellie Porter Emery. He maintained a home and office in the same location until 1913, when he sold the property, and moved the house to Cottage Hill Avenue. There, Dr. Lester H. Hills took over the practice. Dr. Bates died in 1920. He had been village trustee, member of the school board, president of the Building and Loan Association, and treasurer of the Electric Light Company. He organized Elmhurst's first library in Hawthorne School, and often served as volunteer librarian. That library was destroyed in the Hawthorne School Fire in 1917. Dr. Bates was also Elmhurst's first historian. A series of his articles in the Elmhurst Press was published in 1920 as *"Old Elmhurst" Being the Personal Recollections of a Native.*

The decade of the 1880s was a quiet one in American history. The long hot summer when President Garfield lay dying of an assassin's bullet was remembered; the Statue of Liberty was erected and dedicated. The Haymarket Riot in Chicago and the Johnstown flood were events that might have been less noticed in times of wars, want, and worries. It must have been quiet in Elmhurst for those who walked its wooden sidewalks bordering its newly macadamized streets, lit dimly at night by kerosene lamps. During the day except when a train came through or school or church bells clanged, the only noise to be heard might be that of the blacksmith's hammer.

Louis Balgemann started a blacksmith shop at 127 South York Street in 1870, with his home next door to the south. His son, Louis A. Balgemann, eventually took over and continued the business into the 1940s. Theodore Kross, who was himself a student at the time, wrote his reminiscences of the younger Balgemann's shop as an attraction for Hawthorne School students in the 1920s:

> The big doors to the shop opened onto the sidewalk and always attracted an attentive gathering at lunch time and after school. Sometimes the show involved the making or repair of a farm tool. A black piece of cold iron was put into a hearth of black, cold-looking coals. Then Louis would turn the switch and the electric bellows would start rumbling. (Louis the elder would have operated the bellows by hand, pulling on a rope.) In a few minutes the hearth came alive with a cherry glow, sending up a shower of golden sparks whenever the iron was turned over for more heating. The subsequent clanging of the smithy's hammer was loud enough to attract a few more spectators. Of course the hammer had to hit the glowing iron from time to time to flatten or shape it, but that sound was dull. I am sure the frequent bounce strokes on the anvil were made just because they made such a fine sound.
>
> The best show was when one or two horses were waiting for new shoes. The horses always had a wild, apprehensive look in their eyes, although their owners, or young helpers, tried to keep them calm. We did not blame them a bit when they snorted, reared up, and stamped the floor as the smithy started cutting and filing their hooves, then pressed on a red-hot shoe for size. When the shaping was completed, the shoe, held with long-handled tongs, was still red

Interior of Balgemann blacksmith shop about 1910. (R to L) William Harger, Sr., George Balgemann, (at anvil), Louis A. Balgemann, and helper, repairing wagon box.

hot, and was then plunged into a trough of cold water. The resulting "swishhh" and a cloud of steam marked the climax of the show. The steam helped intensify the friendly aroma of horses and the acrid odor of scorched hooves. The cold shoe was then nailed into the bottom of the hoof, another stage in the procedure not always appreciated by the horse.

Louie was not markedly friendly to children, but occasionally he would hand out new horseshoe nails to his audience. If you were alone late in the afternoon, he might make a horseshoe nail ring for you, but always with the admonition, "Don't show it to anyone and don't tell anyone where you got it."

A frame blacksmith shop was built about 1885 at the southeast corner of York and Schiller streets. It was operated for many years by the William Giese family who lived next door. In later years, Charles Johnson was the smith. With fewer horses to shoe, he sharpened lawn mowers and did odd jobs of repairing and welding. The building was demolished in 1953 to make way for the Elm Square Building and the Walgreen Drug Store.

The other Elmhurst blacksmith at the turn of the century was Frederick H. Goltermann, "practical horse shoer and general blacksmith," at 149 North York Street. Invoices from 1902 through 1909 show that his prices remained constant, $2 for four new horseshoes; 50 cents for a bottle of linament. He retired in 1923.

Giese's Blacksmith Shop, later Johnson's welding shop. At one time Francis Neumann had a wagon shop at the rear of the building.

Growth As A Village

By that time horse-and-buggy days were nearly over. The buggy was never the vehicle common to everyone that the motor car has become. Keeping a horse required a barn to store hay and feed. The horse required constant care; it had to be fed, watered, and curried. Harnessing horse to buggy took much

Dr. Frederick Bates and Charles Michaels in a single buggy about 1890.

more time than stepping on the starter. A busy man usually had to hire a hostler or coachman, unless he had a small boy at home, capable and dependable. Keeping a horse and buggy was mainly for the rich, or well-to-do, and in the early days of the automobile it was supposed that the wealthy would continue to have their fine horses and carriages - a prediction partly realized in the continuing popularity of saddle horses.

However, the horse and cart performed many services now forgotten. Before the days of telephones, the grocer would take his cart to his customers, take orders, return to the store, make up his orders, and deliver the day's needs. The milkman made daily deliveries, and notoriously the milkman's horse knew the route so well that he would move the wagon along from stop to stop without direction. The baker delivered bread (unwrapped), pies, cakes, and cookies. The iceman made his daily rounds, cutting the huge cakes in accordance with the sign in the window that could be turned to show at top 25, 50, 75, or 100 pounds. He would then lift the ice with a pair of tongs (such tongs now mystify antique collectors), sling it over his padded shoulder, and put it in the top of the ice box. Some oldsters still call a refrigerator an ice box. On hot summer days, children hopped on the rear end of the wagon to fill their mouths with ice chips.

Louis Balgemann and Cramer Heineman in front of Heineman's Market about 1890.

One could have stayed home throughout those far-off days without starving. Perhaps the last to offer such service in Elmhurst was Martin F. Krage and his wife Mathilda who for a decade or so, before and after 1938, operated Store-at-your-Door, abbreviated "Storchy" by a generation of youngsters who stormed about his truck for penny candy and bubble gum. Krage had been a carpenter. When building halted during the Depression, he fitted out a truck as a miniature grocery and notions store

Ed Baethke in Grampa Baethke's delivery wagon. Note the fly net on the horse.

and drove it on a route from his home at 262 Third Street.

If one could not stay home in horse-and-buggy days, he called for an express wagon to take his trunk, suitcase, "telescope" (an expandable canvas-covered box with handle on top), and bandbox (for hats) to the North Western station, where the baggage could be checked to any depot in the United States and where through trains going west might stop; Elmhurst was a flag-stop, meaning a stop would be made when the station agent put out a red flag or a lantern at night. The express wagon was not exclusively for railroad use; it could be hired for any minor hauling. For major hauling there were large wagons drawn by huge horses - Belgians, Clydesdales, Percherone, Westphalians. The beer wagons used these horses; Anheuser Busch has maintained a team for show purposes. It must have taken a considerable number of wagons to move John R. Case's annual crop of 2,000 bushels of cherries and 3,000 barrels of apples from his orchard at York Street and St. Charles Road. James Wakeman, nurseryman on East Lake Street, was also a large shipper.

EMERY

Another prominent Elmhurst family arrived in 1889. William Harrison Emery came to Chicago in 1869 to establish a business as a hide broker. Born in Fairfield Center, Maine, in 1840, his first business experience was in Waterville, Maine, where his father had moved

William Harrison Emery (1840-1903)

to establish a sheepskin tanning and dying shop. William shared this experience with his brothers, James and Alben. Before his arrival in Chicago, William and James had established Indian trading posts in many locations, including one in Montana. William Emery took goods to the trading posts in the spring when the Missouri River was high and steamboats could go far up the river. His brother James was Indian agent and trader at the posts.

William opposed the use of alcohol in trading with the Indians, but he found another article of barter which seemed to be acceptable. When the Indians came to trade, they would sit, forming a large circle. After speeches and before trading began, a barrel of brown sugar would be rolled into the center of the circle; one by one the Indians would come to the barrel and their extended bandana handkerchiefs would be filled with sugar. Each one would go back to his place, eat the sugar, and the trading would start.

Eventually all three Emery brothers had interests in and lived in Elmhurst, but it was William who came to Elmhurst from Oak Park in 1889. While continuing his trading and hide broking interests, he began to take a major part

Emery House, 284 Kenilworth, built in the late 1880s, residence of the William Emerys.

in Elmhurst social activity and land development. Mr. Emery built his home, now an Illinois landmark home, on the northwest corner of Kenilworth and Adelia avenues. He then developed the seventy acres, the old Wadhams farm, which he had purchased with the house, making $100,000 worth of improvements including streets, trees and shrubs, and houses. This investment made the Emery land, or Emery Subdivision as it became known, one of the most attractive areas of Elmhurst. Emery Subdivision includes the area from Kenilworth Avenue east to Poplar Avenue, and from north of Church Street to just north of St. Charles Road.

In the interest of his land development, Emery encouraged the establishment of utility services in Elmhurst. He was an organizer of both the Elmhurst Spring Water Company and the Elmhurst Power and Light Company. William Emery also served on the Board of Education. William died in 1903. He was survived by his wife, Mary Adelia Toby Emery, and his four children, John, William H. Jr., Ida (Mrs. Albert Ullman), and Grace (Mrs. Berkeley Brandt).

Of William's brothers, James Emery made his major contribution in the development of one of the churches of the community, Alben Emery was a stock holder in the Spring Water Company. Alben lived in Elmhurst while operating a large teaming business in Chicago. Alben Emery's daughter, Nellie, married Dr. Frederick Bates, hence the given name of their son Alben Bates.

GROWTH OF SCHOOLS

In 1887 a Board of Education, consisting of a president and six members, replaced the three member board established in 1850 and it appealed for help from the civic minded citizens in building the two-story brick school at Cottage Hill Avenue and Arthur Street which opened in 1888. The site was purchased from Thomas

Old Hawthorne School

Bryan for $3,300 and the Bryan family donated $300 toward the purchase. A two year high school course was started in the same building in 1893. Taught by Principal Stoop, the course proved adequate for the three students in the first graduating class.

However, by 1904 the school was overcrowded, so that in 1905, during A.A. Kester's principalship, a four room addition was built. The high school curriculum was expanded to four years and offered the standard courses. To better facilitate the teaching of the expanded high school curriculum, a fully-equipped physics laboratory, a manual training shop, and a domestic science area with cooking equipment were added in 1906. At the time of the building addition, the school which had been called Elmhurst School was renamed Hawthorne for author Nathaniel Hawthorne.

NEW CHURCHES

First Congregational Church

The First Congregational Church had its beginning in 1887-1888 in a movement for a union church, led by George F. Rosche, Harry G. Brownell, and C.J. Albert. In 1889, seven families were charter members at the organizing conference on June 12, 1889. Meetings were held at Byrd's Nest Chapel with the Rev. James Wykoff of the Congregational Board preaching

Old Christ Church, built 1890.

occasionally. Most meetings were held in homes and a Sunday School was organized with John R. Case as superintendent. The Rev. F.W. Cooley was invited to preach, succeeded by the Rev. M.L. Williston. Permanent organization as the Union Congregational Church was effected September 14, 1890. William H. Emery donated land on the southeast corner of Kenilworth Avenue and Church Street and a building on that site was completed for services December 14, 1890. The Rev. T.E. Barr became pastor in 1896 and in 1897 the church was reorganized as an interdenominational church with no affiliation with any sect, and was renamed Christ Church. William G. Danforth, who was also religion editor of *Chicago Inter-Ocean*, served as pastor from 1900 to 1916. Under his leadership, the Community House was built in 1914.

Immanuel Lutheran Church

Another church which influenced community development in early days was Immanuel Evangelical Lutheran Church. Although the original church, Zion Lutheran, was established in 1859 in an area now known as Churchville, a large portion of the attending membership came from Cottage Hill. Among these members were Ernst and Louis Balgemann who interested others of the group in purchasing land for a parochial school in Cottage Hill. With this purchase and the building of a school on the land, the history of Immanuel Lutheran Church began in Cottage Hill; however, church membership remained for a time with the mother church. Bi-monthly services were held in the school until a church was built in 1892. In the same year, the Rev. Hild was installed as pastor. With continued growth of the school, the Rev. A. Baumann was installed as a full-time teacher in 1894. The same year saw the purchase of lots at York and Lake streets for use as a cemetery. The Elmhurst congregation, firmly established with not only school but a permanent church, felt the need of a second pastor. Mr. Baumann was hired to fill the post and to serve as a second teacher in 1905.

Immanuel Lutheran Church, built 1892.

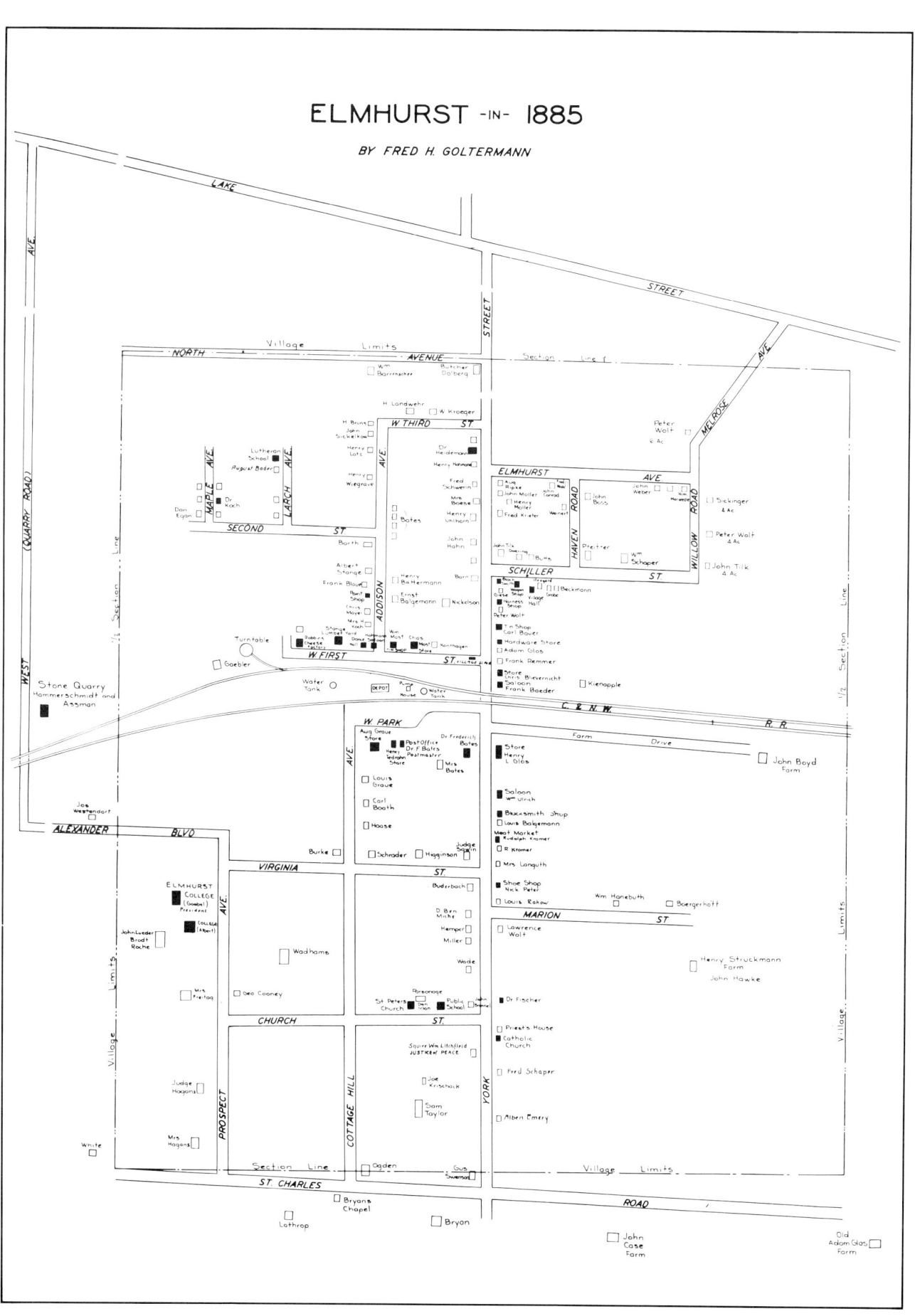

ELMHURST IN THE 1890s

The census of 1890, the first for Elmhurst as a village with legal boundaries, showed a population of 1,050, a considerable increase over the 300 estimated at the time of incorporation, or even the 750 estimated in 1882 which possibly included areas considered a part of Elmhurst although not within the corporate limits.

The decade of the 1890s, sometimes called the Gay Nineties, was perhaps a time when Americans began to enjoy themselves, taking life less seriously than their parents who had been influenced by puritan tradition. It was a time of dancing and picnics, of croquet and church socials, of buggy rides, sleigh rides, and skating, of lawn swings and parasols, of folding fans and flowers, of growing interest in sports, especially baseball and football, and of the invention of basketball. It was truly a period of transition, when many conveniences now regarded as essentials of modern life, made their first appearances. During that decade Elmhurst acquired running water, electricity, and telephones. The automobile had been invented, and was on its way to revolutionize life in America.

Water was a primary necessity for the growing village, dependent upon wells and what use could be made of Salt Creek and other small streams. One night in 1861, a great explosion

Mammoth Spring on Talmadge Farm about 1890.

rocked the farm of George Talmadge, three and one-half miles south of Cottage Hill. Next morning the Talmadge family found that a clear, sparkling spring had burst from the earth. (This spring still exists on the site of the Hyatt House in Oak Brook.) Talmadge banked up the spring and dug a ditch to Salt Creek for the overflow. He used some of the water for irrigation. Mammoth Spring, as it was called, remained mainly a picnic spot.

Exactly when Lucian Hagans and Thomas Bryan purchased the land and spring from the Talmadge family is not clear, but the property was in their possession when, along with Bryan's son Charles, they incorporated the Elm-

Water tower of Elmhurst Spring Water Company.

hurst Spring Water Company on October 7, 1890. The village board passed an ordinance December 6, 1890, giving the company a thirty year franchise for the establishment of a waterworks to supply residents with running water. Private residences paid $7 yearly for the first faucet and $3 for each additional faucet. George C. Morgan, Chicago hydraulic engineer, was employed to install the plant. Wooden mains, six inches in diameter, were laid and the water from Mammoth Spring was pumped to the water tower on the east side of South York Street.

The Rev. M.L. Williston, who was living in the first house north of St. Charles Road on the east side of Kenilworth Avenue was the first resident to be supplied with running water.

At that time water at the turn of the tap was such a luxury that some users did not realize the water supply had a limit. Wilbur Hagans told of some hoses being left running over night. Morning found lakes around newly planted trees and no water in the 1,000 barrel water tower. Needless to say, the result was that meters were installed. Water was metered beginning in 1902. The Elmhurst Spring Water Company was dissolved in 1923.

FIRST FIRE DEPARTMENT

There had been volunteer firemen since 1883, but the Volunteer Fire Department was organized by an ordinance of July 15, 1893, to consist of a marshal, assistant marshal, hook and ladder men, hose men, saw men, and bucket men. Herman Overkamp was the first fire chief. Equipment included a wheeled horse reel, horse-drawn hand pumper, and horse

Fire Station and equipment about 1898.

drawn ladder and paid wagon. The ladder truck was purchased at the Columbian Exposition. Until 1895 the village had depended entirely on barrels for the storage of water for fire protection. Barrels had been purchased from the Chicago Hose and Reel Company. However in 1895 the Elmhurst Spring Water Company installed five fire plugs on trial and as a result in 1896 installed 26 more.

The fire department was reorganized in 1896 to consist of two companies, each of eleven men, headed by a captain and a lieutenant. Assigned to the hose company were four pipemen, five couplers, and a plug man. The hook-and-ladder company included two ladder men, two pole men, two axe men, and four unassigned firemen. Officers, including a secretary, were elected for one year by vote of the members. Registered firemen were exempt from paying village taxes. A code relating to uniforms provided for a $3 fine for anyone wearing a fire hat who was not a member of the fire company.

As reported in the *Elmhurst Enterprise*, August 31, 1894, the work of the volunteer fire department was harried and sometimes unsuccessful:

> Situated on the Chicago Great Western Railroad in south Elmhurst, a mile and a quarter from the village proper, a week ago there stood a large cleaning elevator belonging to W.R. Luce of Minneapolis, Minnesota. It was the largest of 60 such buildings owned by Mr. Luce. It was 36 x 100 feet in size and 76 feet or five stories high. It had a capacity of 250,000 bushels and cost $250,000. The machinery was complicated and expensive, $50,000 and a capacity of 1,500 bushels an hour.
>
> Today nothing marks the spot where the busy din of industry was heard, but the blackened ruins and a lot of twisted, warped, and spoiled machinery....the most plausible story for cause of the blaze is that a spark from a passing train engine must have blown into the fourth story which had been accidently left open when the men cleaned the machinery on Saturday. As the manager reached the hotel where he stayed, he heard the cry of fire and saw the black bellowing clouds coming from the elevator....when he reached the site the top story was ablaze and fire was spreading fast.
>
> Citizens promptly responded to the call, the fire company quickly turned out, even the Bensenville boys, seeing the fire, came over with their rigs but nothing could be done to save it.

The Grain Elevator fire loss was $50,000.

ELMHURST ELECTRIC LIGHT AND POWER COMPANY

Electricity came to Elmhurst following adoption of an ordinance of October 7, 1891, offering a 25-year contract for lighting streets and public places. The Elmhurst Electric Light and Power Company was incorporated under Illinois law

Elmhurst Electric Light and Power Company, 1900.

November 19, 1891, with a capital of $15,000. Incorporators were William H. Emery, president; Warren Buckner, Wilbur E. Hagans, and Dr. Frederick H. Bates. Dr. Bates headed the board of directors which included vice president H.F. Meyer; secretary and superintendent Fred H. Rohmeyer; and treasurer Max Hammerschmidt. For convenience in receiving coal, the plant was erected on the Illinois Central Railroad at its St. Charles Road crossing. The company owned a large brick powerhouse with a boiler house attached, two large dynamos, two boilers, two high-speed New York safety engines, and nine miles of poles to carry the wiring. Electric lights soon illuminated public buildings, churches, the college, most businesses, and a large number of private residences. The Elmhurst Electric Light and Power Company is said to have been the only civic project in Elmhurst to pay dividends. It was later sold to Public Service of Northern Illinois, which dismantled the plant and supplied current through its Maywood plant.

RAILROADS

The Illinois Central line running diagonally through Elmhurst was a branch, completed in 1888 as the Chicago, Madison, and Northern Railroad to connect the Chicago branch with the main stem at Freeport. There was a spur to Addison and for many years a diminutive locomotive named *Addison* with its tender, an integral part of the engine, took commuters daily, with a stop at Elmhurst, to the Chicago terminal at Michigan Avenue and Twelfth Street (Roosevelt Road). As late as 1934, the Illinois Central scheduled three trains daily each way with stops at Elmhurst.

The Chicago Great Western was completed through Elmhurst in 1887. In early days its local trains took a few passengers from Elmhurst to Chicago, but by 1934 this had been reduced to one scheduled flag stop although two trains going west would stop for paying passengers.

Children of the day liked to go into the Great Western Railroad Station to watch George Meister, green visor pulled low over his eyes, sending telegraph messages. The click of the keys always drew the children as did George Meister's friendliness. There was always a welcome even when he was busy as station master.

Elmhurst's first drainage district was created by an ordinance of May 7, 1892, which resulted in construction of a large brick sewer, five feet in diameter, paid for by assessments. It relieved spring flooding of some areas, notably between Prospect Street and Myrtle Avenue, which had frequently been under two to five feet of water. It had not been uncommon to see wooden sidewalks floating away. That sight was eliminated with the building of the first concrete sidewalk in 1897, the year that saw established the first Board of Local Improvements.

WORLDS FAIR OF 1893

The World's Columbian Exposition of 1893 held special interest for Elmhurst. The oratory of Thomas Barbour Bryan before the United States Senate in 1890 is credited with obtaining the World's Fair for Chicago. President Benjamin Harrison appointed Bryan special commissioner-at-large for the exposition and he traveled to many countries accompanied by his son, Charles Page Bryan, to urge them to send exhibits to Chicago. He was highly successful. During the Fair, visitors from many nations were entertained in Elmhurst. An article in the *Chicago Graphic* reported: "The recent reception of the foreign commissioners of the World's

Fair at 'Byrd's Nest' was an enjoyable affair. The house was handsomely decorated with flags of the various nations represented by the visitors, and a brass band concealed in the shrubbery discoursed the various national airs....Art treasures were inspected and admired by the guests who did ample justice to the generous hospitality for which Mr. and Mrs. Bryan are noted. A large number of prominent society ladies....were present and assisted the hostess and her daughter, Miss Bryan, in the entertainment."

A less distinguished, but certainly colorful World's Fair visitor was the Turkish guide and linguist dubbed Far-Away Moses by Mark Twain in *Innocents Abroad*. Wilbur Hagans had met Far-Away Moses in Constantinople (now Istanbul) and in Cairo, Egypt. Hagans wrote: "We made various short trips in the vicinity together....He had a bazaar at the World's Fair in 1893 and remembering me, came out to Hawthorne to visit me three or four times."

It was during the decade of the 1890s that sons of several prominent early Cottage Hill families began active participation in the community. Charles Page Bryan returned from travels to aid his father in work for the Chicago

John R. Case, Jr. (1860-1947).

World's Fair. At the same time, John Case, Jr. took a more active part in management of the Case lands and, despite having built a large addition to Bingham Tavern in which he had lived as a child, he offered to buy *Hill Cottage* from Frank Sturges in 1891. Sturges wanted it removed from his property so he could build another house. John Jr. had the Hill Cottage Tavern moved to the Case property on South York Street and changed the name *Hill Cottage* to *Orchard House*.

In 1907 John Case, Jr. subdivided the land which had been the Case Cherry Orchards and family farm. The resulting Cherry Farm subdivision to the east of York Street and south of St. Charles Road, is marked by names such as Orchard Street, Hill Avenue, and South Street, which Mr. Case thought would remain the southern boundary of Elmhurst.

HAGANS

Wilbur Eggleston Hagans, son of Lucian and Lovela Hagans, was born July 23, 1852, in Kingwood, Virginia. He was brought to Cottage Hill in 1857, and attended the original Cottage Hill School on Church Street in 1861 and 1862, although the family home was in Wheel-

Wilbur Hagans (1855-1942).

ing, Virginia (West Virginia) during most of the period, 1861-73. Wilbur attended Highland Military Academy, Worcester, Massachusetts; Northwestern University, and Dickinson College, Carlisle, Pennsylvania.

At Dickinson he was a member of Sigma Chi Fraternity, and in 1941 was honored as one of its oldest members. Wilbur worked two years for the Baltimore and Ohio Railroad, then became a superintendent for Rand, McNally & Company, Chicago publishers, in which his father was a large stock holder. Wilbur was employed there until 1886 except for a year's absence for travel in Europe.

Despite his many and extended travels abroad, Wilbur Hagans found time to do much for Elmhurst, including work for the water company, the electric light company and the Chicago, Aurora & Elgin.

Just before a four-year stay abroad, he contracted for construction of his home, *Villa Virginia*, at St. Charles Road and Hagans Avenue, west of *Hawthorne*, the estate of his parents.

Villa Virginia, Wilbur Hagans residence built between 1886-90 at the north-east corner of Hagans Avenue and St. Charles Road.

Villa Virginia as remodeled by Winfield Day about 1916.

When he returned to Elmhurst in 1890, the house was completed and he set about landscaping the grounds. He built a racetrack and kennels across St. Charles Road from his home, between Argyle and Mitchell avenues. He brought Great Danes from Germany - one of them wore a diamond-studded collar - and imported English setters. Children of that era aspired to drive a pony-cart and Hagans became interested in the popular Shetland ponies. He visited the Shetland Islands and bought seven ponies at Leith, Scotland, bringing them back to *Hawthorne*. There were also race horses and an annual horse and dog show. The *Hawthorne* track was abandoned in 1896 but the name lives on; two grooms, Ed Corrigan and John Condon, having taken the name and the horses, "without warrant from me," Wilbur Hagans wrote, to a new site, and established Hawthorne Track at 3501 South Laramie Avenue, Cicero.

In the late 1880s, Wilbur Hagans developed the Elm Park subdivision, naming many of its streets for relatives and friends. Among them are Hagans, Argyle for his great grandmother's family name; Eggleston, his middle name; Grace for Grace Hagans; Mitchell for Arthur Mitchell, a boyhood friend; Fairfield for a family in Connecticut; Alexander for Alexander McDonald, who had owned part of the land; and Utley for Edward Utley who bought the first lot. Wilbur Hagans retired to Florida and *Villa Virginia* was sold to Winfield Day about 1915. Hagans returned to Chicago and was living in the home of his stepdaughter, Dr. Grace Jerger, when he died in 1942 at the age of ninety. *Villa Virginia* later became the home of Dr. Richard M. Cronin.

It was likely Hagans and others like him, with an interest in horses, especially saddle horses, who inspired N.W. Murphy to found the Elmhurst Saddle Club. Equestrian activities were prominent in the social life of Elmhurst in the late 1890s. While Mr. Murphy served as first president of the saddle club, he planned many activities for club members.

Every Saturday afternoon, some twenty or more members gathered at an appointed spot. Giving two or three of their number a five minute start to lay a trail of bits of paper, they followed over fields and roads until the fastest horse or the keenest-eyed rider arrived at the rendezvous. A supper dance would round out the evening.

COMING OF THE TELEPHONE

The telephone came to Elmhurst in 1897. An ordinance of March 18 granted a franchise to the Chicago Telephone Company, permitting the company to erect and maintain poles and wires, provided that the poles be located under the supervision of the Commissioner of Streets and Alleys, and placed and maintained so as not to interfere with ordinary travel, or with any water or sewer pipe. The company agreed to furnish one telephone with local exchange service, free of charge, for each fire house. The first telephone was in the Henry L. Glos building at York Street and Park Avenue. The second was in the Denig Drug Store at 128 West Park, across from the railway station. The Denig store served for a time as telephone exchange. (The drug store of Dr. Bates was destroyed by fire in 1891, and Louis A. Denig established a pharmacy at the same site about a year later.)

The second telephone exchange was located above the Heinemann Grocery Store, 1904.

Employees at the telephone office, 124 South York, about 1910 were (L to R) Anna Heinemann, Manager; Lydia Heinemann (Anna's daughter); Julia Malone; Clara Schoenbeider (Miller); Hattie Cordt; Mamie Reusch (Specht); Florence Nordmeyer.

The telephone exchange was moved in 1902 when a switchboard was installed in Edwin Heinemann's grocery at 124 South York Street. Mrs. Heinemann was the first telephone operator, assisted by her daughters Amanda and Lydia. Amanda Dammier was the first "central" outside the family. Calls to Chicago were routed to Bensenville and then either by way of Elgin, or Oak Park. When a second switchboard was needed the two were moved upstairs to the Heinemann living room, and later to an adjacent building to the south. In 1922 the telephone office was moved to 111-113 South York Street. In 1952 a telephone building was erected at York and Virginia streets, and a second building was later added at 162 South York Street.

In 1898 the Spanish-American War interrupted the decades of peace that had marked the close of the 19th century. It was a short war, with naval victories at Manila and Santiago and army campaigns in Cuba, Puerto Rico, and the Philippines, but the little remembered Philippine Insurrection dragged on through 1902, with sporadic fighting after that. Illinois sent volunteers, notably the "Dandy First" Infantry, and many Elmhurst men served. Henry Tedrahn has been mentioned. Carl Sandburg was a Spanish War veteran, as was Harry Grass, Sr. After the war there was organized a DuPage Camp of Spanish-American War Veterans and an Auxiliary. In the southeast corner of Elmhurst's Arlington Cemetery, near Lake Street, 297 veterans are buried, said to be the largest number of Spanish-American War Veterans buried in any one place. The memorial plot was sponsored by William McKinley Camp No. 6, Chicago.

NEWSPAPERS

The *Elmhurst Press* has been published for 66 years and traces its continuity one or two decades before that. No early files are known to exist, hence it is not certain when it assumed its present name. Copies dated 1911 are designated Volume 20, indicating that it was the successor of the *Elmhurst News*. The earliest Elmhurst newspaper was the *Eagle*, which was an Elmhurst edition of the newspaper published in Wheaton by H.C. Paddock, who later headed Paddock Publications, centered in Arlington Heights. The *Eagle*, with Elmhurst section, was published from January 2, 1885, to November 15, 1889, perhaps longer. Next came the *Elmhurst Enterprise*, published by John Neltor from 1894 to 1899. A rival weekly was the *Elmhurst News*, started as early as January

Elmhurst Eagle, May 30, 1884 - Elmhurst News, June 13, 1896.

6, 1894, by Cushing & Company. Louis A. Denig, who opened the Denig Drug Store in 1891, apparently took over the *Elmhurst News* in 1900 and continued publishing it until his death in 1906. Both businesses were carried on by his son A.M. Denig. In 1908 Alben F. Bates took over the *Elmhurst News* to finance his legal education. A 1909 listing shows the publishing company's officers to be F.W.M. Hammerschmidt, president; Alben F. Bates, vice president; and Herbert Johnson, manager. Bates was also secretary of the Board of Review in Wheaton. After his marriage in 1911 to Clara Glos, his professional interests increased and he gave less time to the newspaper. In 1911 Hammerschmidt became mayor, so Johnson was left in active control of the newspaper. His tenure was brief, as he died in a drowning accident. His interest was taken over by James S. Buley. At about this time, the newspaper's name was changed from *News* to *Press*. Buley's interest was sold to Alonzo Fischer. From 1918 to 1922 the *Elmhurst Press* was published by Mr. and Mrs. H. Beetlestone, aided by their son Robert. During this period the *Press* was published in a building owned by Fischer at 105 West First Street.

In 1922 the Cruger family began its long interest in the newspaper when John Wesley Cruger, of Watertown, Wisconsin, bought the *Elmhurst Press*. He began expansion by buying the *Villa Park Argus*, founded in 1923, and starting the *DuPage Press* in 1924, published under a Bensenville dateline. He also acquired the *Lombard Press* and later its rival, the *Lombard Spectator*, started in 1926. The several newspapers were organized as Press Publications, eventually including also the *Addison Press*, *West Cook County Press*, and *Oak Brook Press*.

A competitor, the *Elmhurst Leader* was started in 1926 in the York Theatre Building by William S. Gillespie, publisher, Camilla Thomason, editor, and C. Edward Riener, advertising manager. It was published weekly until 1929, when it was sold to Mr. Cruger. J.W. Cruger died in 1932 and was succeeded by his son Harold J. Cruger. In 1933 Press Publications was moved to a former motion picture theatre at 112 South York Street and after acquiring a garage to the north, the buildings were remodeled with Bedford stone front. Harold J. Cruger died in 1962 and was succeeded by his son Melvin J. Cruger. A disastrous fire November 26, 1966, destroyed much equipment and all early files of the newspaper. Damage was repaired and the newspaper continued publication in the same building. The *Elmhurst Press* is published twice weekly, once during some holiday weeks.

Elmhurst In The 1890s

Courtesy of Chicago Historical Society

First Street in the 1890s. These buildings were situated on the north side of the Northwestern Railroad track. The buildings included a carriage repository, the Pusatere store, and the Most Building. The buildings were moved to the alley behind Soukup's when modern buildings were constructed on First Street. The buildings were demolished to make room for a parking lot.

First Street in the early 1900s showing the new structures tenanted by Balgemann and Rathje's Hardware, the Palace Meats, and Howard Cafe, and First National Bank - York and First.

TURN OF THE CENTURY

Elmhurst entered the twentieth century with a population of 1,728, a modest increase of 678. This census included an area running west between the C. & N.W. tracks and St. Charles Road annexed in 1892. There was no more optimistic period in America than those opening years of the new century. Progress seemed unlimited, until the disillusionment of World War I. "Twentieth Century" was the trademark of the new, the modern, the unprecedented, a predecessor of the TV commercial's "Introducing...." An example of this optimism was the Twentieth Century Limited, the fastest and most luxurious of all railway passenger trains. It barely survived to mid-century.

Elmhurst had acquired running water, electricity, and the telephone in the 1890s and the first concrete sidewalk in 1897. In 1903 Harry W. Darling was granted a franchise, permitting him to maintain and operate a system of gas pipes in the village. The first gas mains were laid on Addison, Third and York streets, north of First. In 1904, the franchise was sold to the LaGrange Gas Company which was ultimately absorbed by Northern Illinois Gas.

1907 Reo, the second Elmhurst automobile owned by Dr. H.F. Langhorst. Mrs. Langhorst stands at the rear of the car. The other couple is Dr. Langhorst's parents.

The automobile, which was to have so profound an effect on twentieth century living, was still regarded as a rich man's toy. An ordinance of 1903 set a speed limit of eight miles an hour and demanded that each "automobile, auto-car, or other similar vehicle....be equipped with an alarm bell or gong of not more than 4" in diameter, and the same shall be sounded at all street crossings and whenever else deemed advisable by the operator." Adam Glos bought an early Ford, drove it to Lombard, ran out of gasoline, and was ignominiously hauled home by horse. He put the car in a shed and never drove it again. A large tree had grown up outside the shed door when the car was recovered as an antique many years after its owner's death.

ELECTRIC RAILWAY

One of the early applications of electricity was to transportation. Trolley cars were replacing horse cars and cable cars on Chicago streets in the 1890s. Elevated lines were built for faster service at long distances. A network of electric railways blanketed the country in the first quarter of the twentieth century, particularly in Illinois, Indiana, and Ohio. They were commonly called interurban lines because of their frequent service, often hourly, between cities. One such line was incorporated in 1899 as the Aurora, Wheaton, & Chicago Railroad. It became the Aurora, Elgin & Chicago in 1901 and ran its first trains in 1902. In 1906 it absorbed the Cook County & Southern, and the Aurora & Southern, and was renamed Chicago, Aurora & Elgin.

Wilbur Hagans was employed by the promoters to buy the right of way and found much opposition both from residents fearing it would hamper C. & N.W. service and from merchants thinking it would draw away business. Those objections may have induced Hagans to locate the right of way through Elmhurst fully a mile from the line of the North Western. (In suburbs

Turn Of The Century

Spring Road station of the Chicago Aurora, and Elgin Railroad, 1940. Used as a station until 1957.

farther west the two lines ran side by side). The result was a considerable expansion of Elmhurst south of St. Charles Road and the growth of business sections around the York Street and Spring Road stations. Development of the area served by the Poplar Street station was much slower. As late as the 1920s, Mrs. C.S. Hotchkiss told of living in the only house in the Stratford Hills section, when it was easier to shop in Oak Park than to get over to the Elmhurst business district. "The motorman on the 2 p.m. freight on the Aurora Elgin would toot if there was a shipment for the family and unload furniture or food on the station platform. A whole winter's supply of food was purchased at one time, with the accommodating C.A. & E. delivering cartons of canned goods, bushel baskets of apples, and sacks of potatoes. It was easier to travel by train than to shop in Elmhurst, and an unlimited monthly ticket amounted to less than $7 or about 7 cents a ride."

The C.A. & E. was a third rail system, the electric power obtained from a third rail instead of overhead wire connected by trolley. The third rail could be highly dangerous to trespassers, but it enabled the C.A. & E. to use Chicago's elevated tracks. The C.A. & E. carried hordes of commuters, with the frequent rush-hour trains often of seven or eight cars. There was also hourly all night service, reduced to one car in the late hours. As the third rail was not laid through crossings, the lights blinked on and off with annoying frequency. It was a great convenience for night workers, and for those who wanted to attend the theatre or other late entertainment in Chicago. After midnight, the North Western offered only the "scoot" which left from the Kedzie Avenue Station at 2 and 4 a.m.. A strike halted the Aurora for two weeks in 1946, but disaster came with the building of the Eisenhower Expressway. A track down the middle, now used by elevated trains, was planned for use by the Aurora. But during construc-

Typical Chicago, Aurora, and Elgin commuter train using the third rail power.

tion, a temporary track was laid alongside on the surface; the resulting traffic congestion slowed the time from less than one hour to more than two hours. After one day of this C.A. & E. commuters stormed the C. & N.W. trains to standing-room only capacity. The Chicago, Aurora & Elgin suspended service April 26, 1957. The roadbed was dismantled in 1962 and much of it became the Illinois Prairie Path.

Frank Koval, an Elmhurst resident and executive of the North Western Railroad, who established its public relations division, was then the director of commuter services. He helped the North Western meet the unexpected crisis by borrowing coaches from all over the country, and the commuter might find himself in a red Pennsylvania car that had taken his grandfather to the Centennial Exposition. This was no great hardship, however, as commuter trains in those days were made up of discards from the sleek passenger trains such as the Columbine, painted purple, and the Portland Rose that sped through Elmhurst. Many of these obsolete coaches were lit by gas lights. Few windows could be opened. Air conditioning was unheard of. The windows that did open allowed cinders from the locomotive to shower in on passengers. Although the transportation was sometimes less than desirable, a well remembered ticket agent provided some relief.

For two generations of Elmhurst residents, the Winchesters were an integral part of the old North Western station. William Winchester, with his visored eye-shade, was the telegrapher and station and express master, for nearly fifty years. His wife, Wilhelmina, was the ticket agent for forty years. Both made the station a friendly small-town travel center.

Through the efforts of men like Frank Koval, the grimy commuter at last got a break. The North Western, realizing that it was stuck with providing commuter services, decided about 1959 to see if it could be made to pay. A fleet of double-decked, streamlined, air-conditioned cars began to appear, powered by push-pull diesel locomotives. Switching of locomotives was eliminated; all were headed out from Chicago and returned by pushing the trains from the rear. In 1961 service was made hourly during off-peak times instead of at odd hours dictated by Proviso yard convenience. For the first time, suburban service was in the black. There were boasts of no fare increases in four years. Unhappily, that did not last; inflation set a faster schedule.

The Elmhurst Model Railroad Club and the Salt Creek Society of Model Engineers indicate a widespread hobby interest in all that concerns railroads. There are histories of all lines from the Baltimore & Ohio to the Virginia & Truckee, including logging roads and narrow-gauge mine roads. Collectors can give the dimensions and performance of every steam locomotive that ever rolled. Others specialize in the electric or "juice" railways, but almost nothing has been written about commuting, which has been a fact of life for several generations of suburban dwellers.

WAYS OF COMMUTERS

Helmut Berens tells of the one-room, stove-heated station of the North Western before the turn of the century: "Each morning the commuters arrived to take the 7:30 train into Chicago. Here in carriages, driven by coachmen and drawn by fine horses, came Thomas B. Bryan and his neighbors - Jedediah Lathrop and Lucian Hagans, Seth Wadhams, William Rand, Andrew McNally, the Rockwood brothers, and Francis Taylor. On the platform and in the train, they were joined by others who lived nearer the station and walked: George F.

Courtesy of Chicago North Western Railway Public Relations Department
Built in 1862, the Chicago North Western Railway Station, pictured in 1904, was housed in this building until 1964.

Rosche, C.J. Albert, George Marks, and George Higginson. On board the train, friendships were extended and business talks begun. New acquaintances were made with residents from towns farther west. For example, Mr. Bryan and Benjamin Franklin Taylor, the poet and newspaper man from Wheaton, became great friends. Taylor was reporter and literary editor on the staff of the *Chicago Evening Journal*. He was also a war correspondent; the book of his collected Civil War sketches, *In Camp and Field*, was dedicated to Bryan.

Taylor also wrote a book about railroading, *The World on Wheels*, published in 1874. It includes one paragraph on commuting:

"There was a time when people put on their slippers, took a night-lamp, bade each other good night, and went upstairs to bed. Those people now go to bed by railway. They think nothing of fifty miles between counting-room and bed-room. They die out of the city every evening, and are born into it with newness of life every morning. It is a good thing. They live more, and they live longer, if the engine behaves itself; but when it gets a notion to pass a sister engine on a single track, or to try the bare ground, like a horse with his shoes off that kicks up its heels in the pasture, or to climb aboard the train and be a passenger itself, perhaps the bedroom may be a few miles too far away, and the old geography be best." Perhaps Taylor was first to call a suburb a bedroom town.

Similar to the train's conversational society led by Bryan was one of a later day that may be said to have centered on J. Christian Bay, librarian of the John Crerar Library who took up residence in Elmhurst in 1929. He was author of many small books and numerous articles, many of which were assembled in 1941 in a large book, *The Fortune of Books*. His professional work was with a scientific library, but his personal collection ranged from Charles Dickens, James Whitcomb Riley and Roswell Field, brother of Eugene Field, to that represented by his *A Handful of Western Books*, a listing of rarities that itself became a high-priced rarity. A bibliography compiled when he was 70, in 1941, shows 160 items. One of them was *100 Years of Elmhurst News*, 1936, to which he made an important contribution. He received many honorary degrees but would not allow anyone to address him as "Dr. Bay." That title, he insisted, belonged to the medical profession. He had strong opinions, but they could be altered. He was incensed at the appointment of Archibald MacLeish, a poet, as librarian of the Library of Congress. But after Bay attended a library meeting in Washington, he asserted that MacLeish "addresses himself to our responsible intelligence" and from then on he supported MacLeish whole-heartedly. One morning at the train, Mr. Bay denounced a copy reader from the *Chicago Daily News* because that newspaper had published the story of Vidkun Quisling aiding the German Nazis in their invasion of Norway. Bay, a native of Denmark, could not believe that any Scandinavian could be guilty of treason. Yet that outburst affected not a bit the friendship of Bay and the newspaperman. Bay was always ready to share his interests with a PTA meeting, the Friends of the Elmhurst Public Library, or his companions on the 8:11 a.m. train.

One of these companions was Miles Sater, artist in oils and stone lithography, then living on Kenilworth Avenue. Sater had a unique ability to translate a builder's blueprint into a colorful picture showing how the building would look when completed. For many years he did his work for the Subway Commission of Chicago. Others in the group were Guy Housley, who wrote hunting and fishing articles for the *Chicago Daily News* when he was not, as a reporter, helping the police solve murder mysteries; John P. Hinkley, proofreader for the *Daily News;* Abram L. Schafer, printer for the *Journal*, later *Times,* who remembered the Chicago Fire; and Arthur Valair Fraser who devised window displays "to make people think" and originated the famed Christmas window displays for Marshall Field & Company. They gathered five days a week in the forward two seats facing each other on the right side of the first car, a smoker, with hangers-on, literally, on the next seat back, and commonly an overflow on the facing forward seats across the aisle.

It is a peculiarity of commuter transit that despite the rush and push to get into cars, the same patrons are commonly to be found in the same seats each morning. In time, the commuter acquires vested rights to his customary seat. This of course is taken for granted by the bridge players, whose games go on year after year, with some kibitzers waiting patiently for years for a seat to become vacant. Such rights were claimed by Miss Caroline Wade, one of Elmhurst's most distinguished citizens. She cared naught for fashion's changes, dressed as she always had, and always carried an umbrella. She was usually waiting when an early afternoon train backed into the North Western Station and took her place at the right of the first

Caroline Wade (1857-1947). Shown with faculty members at the Chicago Art Institute about 1890.

forward facing seat on the right side of the last car. If by chance anyone got to it first, she politely but firmly asserted her claim, and always won her point.

Miss Wade was born in Chicago in 1857. She studied at the Art Institute and in Paris and won the anatomy prize in drawing at the Institute in 1881. Just before she sailed for Europe, she started what is known as the "Saturday Class" at the Art Institute. These classes especially for children continue today and are still called "Saturday Class." She began with two pupils; when she left her class numbered 150.

When Miss Wade returned from Europe, she became an instructor in oil and water colors, and instructor of water colors for architecture. She was at one time president of the Art Students League of Chicago and a charter member of the Palette Club.

She exhibited at the Interstate Exposition, and the St. Louis, Jacksonville, and Minneapolis expositions. She was one of only three women who exhibited at the Chicago World's Fair in 1893, showing "Lady in Grey."

Caroline Wade - Self Portrait, donated to the Elmhurst Public Library, 1941.

Caroline Wade's self-portrait hangs in the King Room of the Elmhurst Public Library.

LAST YEARS AS A VILLAGE

Elmhurst's progress was further marked in 1900 by adoption of an ordinance providing a street numbering plan, accompanied by the renaming of major streets. Railroad Street became First Street; City Road was changed to Schiller Street. In 1902 Henry Glos announced his retirement as village president in leaflets separately printed in English and German. He died three years later. Succeeding as village president was Edwin Heidemann, son of Dr. George Heidemann, Elmhurst's first doctor.

Dr. Heidemann was born in Hanover, Germany, February 10, 1839, came to Illinois at 15, and served in the Civil War. He then opened practice in Elmhurst. Dr. Heidemann served as village treasurer and was county coroner for eight years. With this background, Edwin Heidemann, born in 1877, was ably fitted to

Edwin Heidemann, village president (1902-1905).

direct village affairs from 1902 to 1905. He had attended Northwestern University, was admitted to the bar in 1899, and was married to Martha Ostrum of Hinsdale in 1902, the year he became village president.

Henry Schumacher was village president from 1905 to 1908. Two years later in 1910, he was elected Elmhurst's first mayor. He was

Henry C. Schumacher, village president (1905-1909), first mayor (1910-1911).

born in Chicago, August 8, 1870, attended schools in Oak Park and the Chicago School of Telegraphy. Mr. Schumacher came to Elmhurst in 1888 as telegrapher for the North Western Railroad. After three years as bookkeeper for the Chicago Stone Company, he became the first cashier in the Henry Glos bank in 1893. He continued as cashier when the Elmhurst State Bank was organized in 1903 and served as its president from 1926 to 1935. He married Mary Hohmann in 1891. He was long active in civic affairs, serving as village clerk, 1894-1904; village collector, 1897-1903; York Township school trustee, 1905-1908; and school treasurer, 1908-1940.

During Schumacher's term as village president, Elmhurst established May 20, 1905, a datum base, used thereafter as the reference point for all measurements of elevation for public works and improvements. It was especially useful in sewer installations. Concrete sidewalks were built over much of the village in this period, and by 1910 almost all wooden walks had been replaced.

The last village president was Christopher J. Albert, elected in 1908. A native of Preble

C.J. Albert, village president, (1909-1910).

County, Ohio, he received his B.S. and M.A. degrees from Baldwin University and taught school in Dayton. In 1884 he married Lillie Pauley. They had one son, Eugene Pauley Albert. In 1884, C.J. Albert accepted a position teaching English at Elmhurst College, but resigned in 1892 to establish Albert's Teachers Agency, with offices in the Studebaker Building, Chicago. His home was at York and Church, Elmhurst. He served five years as a member of the Elmhurst School Board. Part of his term, he served as board president. Mr. Albert was active in the Masonic Order and in organizing the Union Congregational Church and the Elmhurst Golf Club. In 1920, the Albert family moved to Kenilworth, Illinois, but the Paul Albert family remained in Elmhurst until 1960. Paul was married to Mildred Pentecost, daughter of an old Elmhurst family, and both were active in social and civic affairs.

WILDER

In 1905 the T. E. Wilders who had been living in Elmhurst in the Challacombe House for 10 or 12 years, purchased the Wadhams-King estate. Wilder, who was born in Lancaster, Mas-

T.E. Wilder (1855-1919).

sachusetts in 1855, received his formal education at Lancaster Academy and Worcester Polytechnical Institute. Wilder arrived in Chicago in 1878 and established a leather commission business. He became a magnate in the leather industry, and his company eventually became the Chicago Rawhide Company. Considering his Massachusetts background, the source for Mr. Wilder's new name for the White Birch estate is clear; after the purchase, the estate house was renamed *Lancaster Lodge*.

The Wilders held many social events in *Lancaster Lodge*, including musicales in the north east wing. This big drawing room later housed the Arts Division of the Elmhurst Public Library.

T. E. Wilder served as president of the Elmhurst School Board, president of the Elmhurst Golf Club, was a member of Christ Church, and served as president of the New England Society of Chicago. In 1908 he was general secretary of the Chicago Association of Commerce which he aided in organizing. Wilder also served as Director of the Great Lakes District of the National Rivers and Harbors Congress.

Although Mr. Wilder had commissioned Walter Burley Griffin to design a subdivision for the Wilder estate, he stipulated in his will that the estate should first be offered to the City with the provision that a library be built on a portion of the property. (The Griffin design for a subdivision of the Wilder property is on exhibit at the Chicago Art Institute.)

ELMHURST BECOMES A CITY

The census of 1910 showed a population of 2,360 for Elmhurst, almost double that of 1900. Village government, depending largely on voluntary services, was proving inadequate. Incorporation as a city was proposed in a petition signed by 107 voters and a special election was called for March 29, 1909. The result was 156 votes for incorporation, 155 against, and two unintelligible ballots. The immediate ruling was that the proposition had failed to get a majority of the votes cast, but a canvassing board found that incorporation had been approved. The village trustees called a special election for May 10, 1910, and at their final session May 14 announced the results: Henry C. Schumacher, mayor; Julius J. Braun, clerk; Richard Hammerschmidt, treasurer; F.C. Harbour, city attorney, and six aldermen, William Meyer, G. Weber, George F. Rosche, John Mueller, C.J. Albert, and C.J. Marhoefer. The aldermen represented three wards, two north of the North Western tracks, divided by York Street; the other, south of the tracks.

The city government approved the following officers: marshal, Herman Trenn at $65 a month; special policeman, William Baethke at $15 a month; Saturday and Sunday evening policeman, Fritz Ernst at $8 a month; street commissioner and day policeman, Fritz Ernst at $150 a month, and city collector, G.S. Burmeister, who was paid 1.5 per cent of collections on posting a $10,000 bond. The village government had employed a police marshal, that office having been held successively by Dick Schmidt, Otto Remmer, August Wirkus, Herman Schmidt, Ed Benson, and Henry Uhlhorn.

Robertson and Young, land developers, opened a subdivision in 1910 west of Spring Road and south of the Aurora Elgin Railroad. Its streets included Berkley, Fairview, and Sunnyside avenues.

F.W.M. Hammerschmidt was elected second mayor of Elmhurst in 1911 and served until 1919. In 1890 as a young man Frederick William Maximillian Hammerschmidt, known as "Max," came to Elmhurst from Naperville to

F.W.M. Hammerschmidt, mayor (1911-1919).

manage his father's stone quarry. In 1902 he decided to purchase with Gustav Franzen a coal, lumber, and ice company from E.W. Fischer and together the two men formed the Hammerschmidt and Franzen Grain, Feed, Coal, Ice, and Lumber Company.

Records of the city during Mayor Hammerschmidt's term show many changes: 1911 saw the issuing of a license to a movie theater, consideration of the establishment of a Carnegie Library in Elmhurst, and the annexation of both the Oaklawn and East End Park subdivisions; 1912 brought the public library ordinance; and 1913 saw the extension of sewers, and the franchisement of the Western Gas and Electric Company. In 1916, the year after a $35,000 bond issue had been passed, the municipal water plant, including reservoir and water house, was constructed. It was a period of growth in Elmhurst's municipal development.

EXPANDING SCHOOLS

School District 1 was reorganized as School District 46 in 1901 and soon was faced with the problems of a growing city and expanding school enrollment, crowding Hawthorne School to capacity. In 1911 Eugene Field School was built at York and Third streets. This

York Street entrance of old Field School about 1940.

Emroy Street facade of new Field School, 1966.

was the first school to be named for anyone of local interest, for Field had conducted the "Sharps and Flats" column in the *Chicago Daily News* for many years and his major work was done while a resident of Chicago. To preserve the name, when a new building was erected in 1930 it became the "New" Eugene Field School while classes continued for some time in the "old" Eugene Field School. The "old" Field School still exists, now occupied by the Providence Washington Insurance Company. Lincoln School, Hillside Avenue, was built in 1916.

The school district faced disaster when Hawthorne School was destroyed by fire December 12, 1917. Nearby residents carried out a few books and desks, but the building was a total loss. The school board met the crisis by rapid improvisation. By Monday following the fire, classes resumed: high school students at Christ Church Community House; sixth grade girls at the Chinese Laundry on Addison Avenue; seventh and eighth grade boys in the basement of Old Main, Elmhurst College; seventh and eighth grade girls in the school of St. Peter's Church; others found desks at Eugene Field School and some classes were taught in private homes.

NEW CHURCHES
Episcopal Church of Our Saviour

The increased population also brought a demand for more churches.

In 1914 the Byrd's Nest congregation was recognized as an organized mission of the Episcopal Church and received the name Church of Our Saviour. In the same year property at Church Street and Kenilworth Avenue was donated by J.L. Greaves and Mrs. A.I. Ullman. Stone from the court house destroyed by the Chicago Fire of 1871 was used in construction of the church, opened for services April 18, 1915, with the Rev. John Arthur as priest in charge. He served for nine years and was succeeded by the Rev. Thomas B. Foster. Next came the Rev. W. Ridley Parson, who served fifteen years; then the Rev. Chandler Sterling, 1945-1951, notable for his interest in youth groups in Elmhurst; and the Rev. James Plankey. An addition to the church was completed in 1960. The Rev. Paul Stewart began his pastorate in 1971.

First Methodist Church of Elmhurst

The First Methodist Church of Elmhurst was first organized in 1911 at Glos Hall and soon moved to Elmhurst's first motion picture theater (site of *Elmhurst Press* offices). A building was started in 1913 at York and Arthur streets and was dedicated as the Methodist Church by the Rev. John I. McVey on Easter, April 12, 1914. During World War I, the congregation disbanded, the church closed its doors, and the mortgage was foreclosed. The building became the Masonic Temple. In 1924 a group of seven, including members of the former church, received a new charter and reorganized as the Elmhurst Methodist Church April 27, 1924 in a Roosevelt School classroom. Services were held in the old Elm Theater on First Street and the Rev. Charles Ray Goff became the first pastor in October with a fifty-member congregation. Beginning in 1935, services were held at the York Theater and in 1929 a lot was purchased at York and Church streets just before the beginning of the Great Depression. It was pay-as-you-go this time, with the Rev. Joseph Burrows arriving in 1935 to push it along. Young people of the church remodeled a frame stable on the parsonage grounds, dubbed it "The Shack," and held MYF activities there, led by Rosemary Musil. A small unit, unfinished but usable, was dedicated Palm Sunday, 1935, by 451 members. Methodist discipline had disparaged theater-going, but this Methodist Church had held services in three theaters! The church sanctuary was consecrated October 27, 1950, by the Rev. Frank Countryman and 1,027 members. A balcony and educational unit were added in 1955; the adjoining former American Legion building was purchased for $75,000, and an addition to the sanctuary was dedicated in 1961. The Rev. Howard Benson assumed the pastorate in 1975.

Faith United Methodist

Faith United Methodist Church was originally Faith Evangelical United Brethren Church, founded April 26, 1911, as a mission by 27 charter members. Services were held in Mahler Hall, Park Avenue, until 1914 when the church erected at a cost of $12,500 at North Avenue and York Street was opened by the Rev. J.W. Davis. This was the first English-speaking congregation on the north side of Elmhurst. A frame educational building was erected in 1927; it was replaced by a new educational unit in 1951 when the Rev. G.D. Nielson was pastor. In 1968 the Evangelical United Brethren and the Methodist denominations merged and the church was renamed Faith United Methodist Church. The Rev. Edward Stach assumed the pastorate in 1972.

First Baptist Church of Elmhurst

The First Baptist Church of Elmhurst started as a Sunday School sponsored by the First Baptist Church of Wheaton in the fall of 1911 at Crescent Street and Sunnyside Avenue. Dr. R.R. Kennan was pastor. A church was dedicated April 11, 1915, at Berkley and Eggleston but it was destroyed by fire in 1921. A new church was built at Berkley and Eggleston avenues (site of Grace Bible Church) and served until October 12, 1941, when the building at the northeast corner of St. Charles and York was dedicated during the pastorate of the Rev. W.S. Sommerschield. The Rev. Donald Bjork was serving as pastor in 1976.

First Church of Christ Scientist

The First Church of Christ Scientist was founded in 1918 and held its first service January 5, 1919, in Mahler Hall. Services were held in the Masonic Temple from 1920 to 1941. The cornerstone for the building at Prospect Avenue and Claremont Avenue was laid April 26, 1941, and the first service was held in the completed building July 11, 1948. In 1952 dedication services were held for a completely mortgage free church.

First Congregational Church

From 1900 to 1915, Rev. W.C. Danforth had been serving as the pastor of Christ Church. He was also religious editor of *Interocean*. During his pastorate, the Community House was built at a cost of $13,000. The building architect was Charles Bohassek. In 1926 Christ Church became the First Congregational Church of Elmhurst and in 1927 the congregation saw the dedication of a new church under the pastorate of the Rev. Fred Harrison, who was a continual participant in Masquers, a forerunner of the Elmhurst Community Theater, a lecturer and book reviewer, and a friend of Elmhurst youth. In 1956 a new church addition was dedicated. 1957 saw the church renamed the First Congregational United Church of Christ. In 1967 the Rev. Ernest Huntzinger, Jr. began serving First Church as their tenth minister.

DOWNTOWN ELMHURST IN 1910

Elmhurst was bounded in 1910 on the north by North Avenue, on the south by St. Charles Road, on the east by Poplar Avenue and Avon Road and on the west by Myrtle and Villa avenues. The business district had grown with increased population. William Baethke offered baggage transfer service at 101, later 103, North York Street, in addition to general merchandise, dry goods, groceries, fruits, and vegeta-

Exterior of William Baethke store about 1910; A creamery was located at the rear of the building.

William Baethke store at 101-103 North York Street. Clerks are Dorothy Baethke Krause and Hannah Baethke.

bles. He had previously operated the Elmhurst Creamery at First Street and Larch Avenue.

M. Stuenkel, Edwin Heinemann's brother-in-law, managed the family grocery and dry goods store at 124 South York. In earlier days before Edwin Heinemann's death, so much German was spoken in the store that old timers remember Edwin telling his son, "Willie, hal de buttle..."- meaning, Willie get the bottle for flavoring. (The south wall of the store had an ice cream counter.) Henry A. Fiene purchased the Keiler paint store and added dry goods and groceries in 1910. Other grocers were Henry Asing, 116 North York Street; Henry Laatz, 226 Addison Avenue; and W.P. Trenkler, 120 West Park Avenue.

The butcher shop of L.H. Heinemann was at 135 South York Street and that of Henry G. Fritz at 132 West Park Avenue. Bessie Hilliard recalled that her mother would order a nice sirloin steak from Fritz's butcher shop for 35 cents. That included delivery. Wendland Brothers at 113 West First Street were among the first to deal in meat products exclusively. Their shop had butcher blocks, "honest weight" scales, and sawdust on the floor. Youngsters got a free cold, uncooked weiner, often to the consternation of their mothers. The bakery of G. Weber at 112 North York Street

Weber's Bakery, 112 North York Street about 1910.

was operated by John and Emma Bartman from 1912 to 1955. Mrs. J.L. Howard had an ice cream parlor and restaurant at 110 Addison Avenue. The business was later moved to First Street. The Elmhurst Ice Cream Parlor of Christ Poulos at 111 West First Street, featured home-made ice cream and candy, and sold fruit and cigars. With his brother James he later operated a tavern at 104 South York Street. The Poulos brothers were in business in Elmhurst for 33 years.

The Ward H. Wilcox drug store was at 124 West Park Avenue in a building erected in 1895 by Fred H. Mahler, who conducted his business as merchant tailor in the building. His son William H. Mahler studied pharmacy and took over the Wilcox drug store in 1919, continuing that business until his retirement in 1953. The store then became Karstens Pharmacy.

An Elmhurst resident recalls accompanying his father to Mahler's in the 1930s to have a prescription filled. He remembers the pleasant medicinal odor that permeated drug stores when they were primarily drug stores, but finding most important and attractive, in an unlighted part of the store, the white marble soda fountain with mirrored back bar and Coca Cola art calendars. Two or three marble topped tables with wire backed chairs were in front of the fountain.

> On top of the fountain was a glass dispenser for soda straws. Pull up on a silver ring and you had a choice of straws, but only one to a customer. Next to it was a dispenser which offered an endless supply of ice cream cones. On the back bar were Coca Cola glasses stacked in layers with cardboard dividers, the malted milk mixer, and the large container of Horlick's malted milk powder. A nearby canister had packages of two cookies, served with the malteds. Waiting for the prescription seemed endless, but at last Mr. Mahler turned on the lights and awaited the order: Should it be a Hires root beer, directly from the tap; a double-dip strawberry ice cream cone; a chocolate soda; a sundae with a cherry on top? The cone was the choice, and happily Mr. Mahler never bothered to trim off the excess ice cream the scoop would pick up. A quart of ice cream, hand packed in a wire-handled paper container, might be taken home.

Before Frieda Mahler, William's sister, opened her shop at 126 West Park Avenue the space had been occupied by Gustav L. "Shorty" Burmeister with his barber shop, billiard and pool parlor, and laundry agency. Later he cut hair with Edward Mueller at 142 South York Street. Frieda's shop, known as the Park Avenue Variety Store, was in front of her father's tailor shop and was connected by an open door to her brother's drug store, so that all members of the family could help out when one or another was busy. Frieda Mahler stocked all kinds of utensils for the kitchen, the office, the workshop, drawing materials, paper goods, school supplies, gifts, post cards that had survived from an earlier day in Elmhurst, and much miscellany. If an item was not on display, Frieda would go to the basement and hunt for twenty minutes although the result might be only a five cent sale.

Mahler's Hall was overhead on the second floor, a social center for lodge ceremonies, club

Mahler Building, 124 West Park Avenue. The second floor was used for dances receptions, and recitals for many years.

meetings, receptions, dances and dancing classes, recitals and elocution lessons.

Dorothy Hobein Wetzel recalls two candy stores of the era- Mrs. Blau's Candy Store and the old "Dew Drop Inn". Mrs. Blau's store was on the east corner of York and First streets and children could choose "tiny wax bottles that held fruit juice, marshmallow ice cream cones, strips of paper with colored dots of sugar, licorice tails, and even candies that looked like fried eggs in a tin pan."

The old fashioned Ice Cream Parlor owned by Miss Clara Olson was on South York Street. "Here were twisted metal framed tables and chairs. 'Sundae Delights' were served and chocolate creams and home made candies came from her own kitchen."

Dr. T.B. Galbraith, DVM, of Park Avenue was a veterinary surgeon and dentist. Physicians in 1910 were Dr. Frederick H. Bates, 104 West Park; Dr. Henry F. Langhorst, 175 South them in both programs. The lady's escort claimed the first and last dances from his companion, and a number in between depending upon the degree of attachment he wished made known, but for the rest she was on her own. These were family affairs, and polite young men were careful to seek dances from their hostess, their boss's wife, relatives and friends of the family. Their mothers frequently commanded them to ask some of the less popular and less pretty girls who had long blank spaces in their programs and sat the dances out in the chairs against the wall; thus the derivation of the term "wallflower."

The Elmhurst Dancing Society was organized in 1893, and held its first reception in School Hall. However, it does not appear to be a forerunner of the more formal Elmhurst Dance Club which was organized December 31, 1918, at a New Year's party in the home of G.F. Kennedy. The party included the Bosworths, Cadwells, Hultquists, Rueblings, and Shipeks. The first officers of the club were E.W. Bosworth, president and Sue Kennedy, secretary-treasurer. A paragraph from a pamphlet, "History of the Elmhurst Dance Club," states:

> The first dance was a great success and enough members were obtained to start it (the club) off with a bang. The meeting place was the old Glos Hall, which had a good dance floor on the third story. This was reached by three flights of iron steps hanging on the outside of the building.

In 1922 the dances were moved to the Masonic Temple. Dances were held there for many years with a club membership varying from 18 to 48. The Elmhurst Dance Club disbanded in the early 1970s.

The ballrooms also housed receptions and card parties, evenings for husbands and wives, afternoons for ladies only, developing into ladies card clubs. The women played euchre and five hundred. Mrs. Henry Glos was a member of a 500 club and many early citizens recall playing 500 in the bay window of the Glos mansion. Men played pinochle, poker, or rum, later corrupted to rummy.

In the first decade of the twentieth century the ancient game of whist, played in Queen Anne's day, was modified into bridge whist and became widely popular, especially in its later manifestations of auction bridge and contract bridge. Those with religious scruples against playing cards, banned by some denominations, played invented card games such as Flinch, Rook, or Authors.

In time dancing and card playing were taken over by organizations on a more public basis. Among the earliest in the village were German organizations: Sangvereine, Kirchenchore, Unterstutzungsvereine, Frauenvereine, Jugendvereine, and Plattdeutsche Gilde, and the Elmhurst Mannachor. The Grand Army of the Republic, veterans of the Civil War, took charge of Memorial Day, set for May 30 by their commander-in-chief, General John A. Logan, later senator from Illinois. They were joined in Elmhurst parades by the Kriegerverein, veterans of the Franco-Prussian War of 1871, and after 1898 by the United Spanish War Veterans. The Spanish-American War stimulated interest in things military and many lodges uniformed and drilled members to march in the parades of Memorial Day and the Fourth of July. The

Mrs. Otto Stange driving south on Addison Avenue in a Fourth of July parade in the early 1900s. George Balgemann's house in the background.

bright and shining nickel plated axes of Elmhurst Camp No. 4126, Modern Woodmen of America, were especially spectacular.

The marching tradition has been continued by Elmhurst Council No. 1911, Knights of Columbus, chartered in 1918 under leadership of the Rev. David L. McDonald, and renamed Father McDonald Council in 1938. Fourth Degree members organized the Christopher Club in 1946 while S.K. John Frendrels was grand knight. The Ladies Auxiliary was formed in 1959 under the guidance of G.K. Joseph Gallagher. The Council led the state in 1965 in adding new members, its additional 120 members meriting "Century Club" designation. It was named Number One Council in the state in 1972, 1973, 1974, and 1975, and took first place in family activity in 1970. The Council has published the *Knightly News* since 1963. Its retarded children program is outstanding in the state. It assists the Catholic School System, the EYO and Newman Club, and sponsors a Columbus Day radio program.

Masonry came to Elmhurst in 1911 with the chartering of Elmhurst Lodge No. 941, Ancient Free and Accepted Masons, followed by Cottage Hill Lodge No. 1120. Elmhurst Chapter No. 699, Order of the Eastern Star also dates from 1911. It assists in supporting a home for the aged at Rockford and a home for the ill and handicapped at Macon, and has a scholarship program. Elmhurst Chapter, Royal Arch Masons was organized in 1921, about the time the Masonic Temple at 103 Arthur Street was acquired from the Methodist Church. DuPage Commandery No. 88, Knights Templar was chartered in 1945 and consolidated with Maywood Commandery No. 87 in 1969. Since 1968 meetings have been at Lombard Masonic Temple.

Elmhurst Lodge No. 1531, Benevolent and Protective Order of Elks was chartered in 1925 with 89 members, and occupies its own building at 136 North York Street. Its 400 members support programs for crippled children, veterans and the Little League, as well as Americanism and scholarship projects. The Elks donated a room at Elmhurst Memorial Hospital and all patients there are visited during the yearly Easter Bunny Program. The Ladies of the Elks was organized in 1937 in the home of Mrs. George Bright; the 32 charter members elected Mrs. J. Oleschlaeger president. Among charities its members support are the Elmhurst Welfare Association, United Charities, National Foundation for Infantile Paralysis, the Hospital Guild, Bensenville Home's Foster Children's Fund, the Lutheran Home in Addison, and the Clothes Closet in Elmhurst.

Elmhurst Lodge No. 420, Independant Order of Odd Fellows represents one of the oldest of fraternal orders. Its auxiliary, Rebekah Lodge No. 122, I.O.O.F. was organized in 1927 at Laundry Hall, First Street. It helps support the Old Folks Home, Mattoon; the Children's Home, Lincoln, and an education fund. Each year the lodge sends a boy or girl on the United Nations Pilgrimage.

Other fraternal orders that have flourished in Elmhurst include Elmhurst Lodge No. 1553, Loyal Order of Moose and Women of the Moose; Elmhurst Lodge No. 6900, Royal Neighbors; St. John's Court No. 1591, Catholic Order of Foresters; and Elmhurst Lodge No. 1173, Woman's Catholic Order of Foresters.

Lodges having no home of their own met at Mahler's Hall, which was also the scene of their dances and other entertainments.

THE AUTO REVOLUTION

Dances, card parties, picnics, and lodge meetings did not add up to continuous entertainment. At times one was left to his own resources. Then he could always go on a buggy ride, perhaps in the family surrey with the fringe on top, but the young man of the family, taking out his best girl, would prefer the single seat buggy. Either could be purchased from Otto Strauschild's Harness and Horse Clothing

Strauschild Harness Horse Clothing Shop, 140 South York Street, 1912.

Store at 133, later 140, South York Street. Strauschild, agent for the Banner Buggy Company, also sold shoes and rubbers and did shoe repairing. If one owned neither horse nor buggy, he could rent either in 1903 from D.W. Thoma at 136 Addison Avenue. This business was taken over by E.A. Langkafel and moved to 127-129 East First Street as Elmhurst Livery, offering stables for livery, boarding, and sale of horses. Langkafel then converted the building into a garage for the Packard agency, continuing it for as long as that luxury car was made. The building was last occupied by West Suburban Saab and was demolished in 1976 to make way for the North Western underpass.

One of the earliest automobile sales agencies was the Elmhurst Garage at York Street and Elmhurst Avenue, operated by C. Beringer and Theodore H. Wolf. They sold Overland and Ford cars, offered a taxicab service, had a machine shop for repairs, and recharged the batteries used in electric cars. George Bright, Sr. founded Bright Auto and Repair Company in 1912 at 131 Schiller Street. It was operated for many years by George Bright, Jr. and Ralph H. Mears. The Bright Agency was a dealership for Plymouth, Studebaker, and Lincoln-Mercury. In 1969, the agency was moved to West Grand Avenue. Elmhurst Motor Sales Company, 108-110 South York, offered Fords and Hudsons, and rented, stored, and repaired automobiles. Walter B. Kidder was president of the company and Frederick H. Bates vice-president.

When Ed Schram moved his Buick agency from Addison in 1924, he settled at a previous site of the Hammerschmidt Lumber Company. The Schram location is now a parking lot for Elmhurst Federal Savings and Loan.

If an auto dealer could not repair a car because of limited experience, one might try William A. Robbins at the Homer E. Egolf draying and storage quarters at 137-141 South York Street. Robbins was also a plumber, steam and hot water heating contractor, electrical contractor, and gas fitter. William J. Hilliard operated the heating, plumbing, and electrical business at 134 North York Street from 1885 until 1928. He was also an expert on sewerage and sold, rented, and repaired bicycles, as well as being the agent for Thor motorcycles.

YOUTH ORGANIZATIONS

New recognition of a community problem-too many boys and young men with undirected time-came in the early 1900s, perhaps sparked by the stories of Horatio Alger, Jr., about homeless boys and by boys with homes, having fewer chores in a changing economy, which often lead to trouble. In 1908 Lieutenant General, R.S.S. Baden-Powell wrote *Scouting for Boys;* his ideas quickly spread from England to America. W.D. Boyce, Chicago publisher, led in incorporating the Boy Scouts of America in 1910.

Boyce had the cooperation of two writers and illustrators who had formed similar organizations, Dan Beard and Ernest Thompson Seton. Seton became Chief Scout; he wrote the first *Handbook for Boys;* and he had much to do with the success of the movement.

Elmhurst had a front row view of these developments because of visits here by Ernest Thompson Seton, whose niece was Mrs. Helmut Berens and whose brother George Seton-Thompson, lived in Chicago and later stayed for a time at the Berens residence. Seton was born in England in 1860 and came to Canada with his family when he was six. He studied two years at the Royal Academy in London and illustrated many of his 42 books, most of them written while he lived in the United States, in later years at Seton Village near Santa Fe. Seton died October 17, 1935.

It was Seton who inspired Helmut Berens, historian of Elmhurst and DuPage County to join in application for two troops of Boy Scouts of America in 1914. He became scoutmaster of Troop No. 2. Members of Troop No. 2 included James Burns, Harrison, Jack, and Munson Emery; Joseph Gray, Jr., Norman Hanson, Arthur Heine, Brad Hilliard, Willard Mowers, William Pearn, Byron Stevens, Stuart Ullman, and Walter Weiser.

The designation of "Troop 1" was applied for in 1914 for a group at the Baptist Church on Spring Road; however, the troop was not actually organized until 1917 when Ira Stone became scoutmaster. Members of this troop included Walter Bartusch, Wray Finnemore, Alfred Hanscom, Waldo Hansen, Roger Olson, Earl Strand and Gerald Stringer. (These troops still exist as renumbered No. 71 and 72.) The first campout was held in June, 1919, at Pick's farm on Salt Creek.

Another Elmhurst resident who contributed greatly to the early Boy Scout movement was A. Neely Hall, author of *The Boy Craftsman* and numerous other how-to books for young people. He opened his studio to boys and taught them skills such as type-setting, photography and carpentry. These skills could be used in fund-raising projects or in earning merit badges. His studio grew into Craft Patterns at North Avenue and Route 83. Another project of Boy Scouts was operating the only movie theatre in Elmhurst during May, 1923. A series of three films shown in the basement of Hawthorne

School netted $223.05.

Cub Scouts was founded nationally in 1933 and came to Elmhurst the same year with the forming of Cub Pack No. 21 in Roosevelt School; Pack 23 in Lincoln School and Pack 26 in Eugene Field School. Six Explorer Posts appeal to students of high school age. Most of Elmhurst's 32 packs and troops are sponsored by P.T.A. groups and meet in the schools. There are about 800 cubs and 400 scouts.

Camp Fire Girls, founded nationally in 1910, came to Elmhurst in 1917 with formation of a group by Mrs. Bert A. Davis, Sr. However, during World War I, it was absorbed by a Girl Scout group led by Miss Mabelle Glos. Camp Fire Girls was revived in 1929 by Miss Betty Reinhardt, a teacher at Washington School. She also formed a Blue Bird group. The first executive committee included Mrs. G. Harding, Mrs. Charles Gallup, and Mrs. John Golden. Among early volunteer leaders were Mrs. Guy Housley, Mrs. Herbert Morrison, Mrs. Lester LeVesconte, Mrs. E.C. Sullivan, Mrs. Norman Keller, and Mrs. William Brice.

Mrs. Harlan Tarbell organized the first high school Camp Fire group in 1931, and started a Horizon Club chapter at Immaculate Conception High School in 1941. At the same time, Mrs. Philip T. Ewan organized a Horizon Club from a group of York High School girls who had been together since they started as Blue Birds in Roosevelt School in 1933. These two clubs were among the first Horizon Club chapters in the nation. A cabin was built in 1950 at North Avenue and Route 83, and the first summer day camp was conducted in 1947 in Wilder Park by Mrs. Norman Keller, Mrs. M.M. Moen, Mrs. Elton Discher, and Mrs. George Thorpe.

When membership reached 1,100 girls and 250 adult leaders in 1956, the Elmhurst Area Council of Camp Fire Girls was formed with Mrs. C.A. Linder, president, and Mrs. Howard Larson, executive director. Mrs. Larson served through 1975 and was succeeded by Mrs. Lee Wachenheim. In 1972 boys became eligible as members and leaders in the Horizon Club. Total membership is about 2,800.

The Girl Scout movement started nationally in 1912 and the first Elmhurst troop was organized in 1918 at Spring Road Community Church, Eggleston and Berkeley avenues, by Mrs. Ira Stone, assisted by Mrs. Montgomery Harris, Mildred Schulke, and Blanche Randolph. Girl Scouts names early roster: Beda Carlson, Margaret and Miriam Carlson; Evelyn and Margaret Hansen; Gladys Johnstone, Ann Keller, Myrtle Olson, Vera Schulke, Bernadine and Geraldine Stone; Lucile and Ruth Strand.

An early activity was tacking a comforter to be raffled for money to buy uniform cloth. Cooking, sewing, signalling with flags, and hikes to Graue Mill or to Glen Ellyn were scheduled. More troops were added, usually meeting in churches. The troops adopted names, such as Cardinals, Sunflowers and Pine Cones. They joined the Chicago Council in 1920, and in 1928 the Elmhurst Girl Scout Council was organized with some 20 troops. Summer camps were in Saginaw, Michigan, in 1929, and Wilmington, Illinois, in 1930, called the "year of the tornado" by Mrs. David Kinnett, director, because high winds destroyed many tents. In 1933 the only Golden Eaglet ceremony held in Elmhurst gave this award to Frances Kinnett and Ruth Patton. During World War II, a cabin was built in Salt Creek forest preserve on plans drawn by V. Viscariello with fireplace donated by Mr. and Mrs. R.A. Raab. It served as a camp into the 1960s. Later camps were at Chippewa Bay, New Auburn, Wisconsin, and Camp Greenwood, Woodridge. In 1948 the Elmhurst Council was merged into the DuPage Area Council, with Mrs. Louis Garbi, president, and Mrs. Ben O. Anderson, executive director. In 1970 Project Amigo was adopted as a Senior Service, centering on a three-week summer program at Cornille School for Spanish-speaking children. Elmhurst Girl Scouts enroll 1,400 girls and 400 adult leaders.

LINDLAHR SANITARIUM

One institution in Elmhurst that was without a like or an equal during the years 1914 to 1929 was The Lindlahr Sanitarium on West St. Charles Road. Henry Lindlahr, its founder, was born in Germany, March 1, 1862, and came to the United States when he was 20, and ten years later was prospering in business in Kalispell, Montana. Then he was stricken with a kidney ailment, and his wife Anna with Bright's disease, and as he put it, "At the age of 35 years I found myself a physical and mental wreck, without faith in God, in nature, or myself." Then a book on German nature cure "came as a great revelation." They found relief. In 1899

Lindlahr Health Resort, former Lathrop home on St. Charles Road at Prospect Avenue.

Lindlahr gave up his business and with his wife went to Europe to study nature cures in Germany, Austria-Hungary, and Switzerland. He returned to the United States in 1900, studied osteopathy, homeopathy, allopathy, and eclectic medicine; passed the examination of the Illinois State Board of Health, and was licensed to practice as physician and surgeon. He opened offices at 232 Michigan Avenue, Chicago, and in 1906 established Lindlahr College and Lindlahr School of Nursing at 525 South Ashland Avenue, Chicago. Neither school was accredited.

Patients at the Lindlahr Sanitarium, exercising as part of the "Rational Therapeutics" system.

In 1914 Dr. Lindlahr bought eight acres of the Lathrop property on West St. Charles Road, Elmhurst. The Lathrop home became the Manor House, with offices for doctors and secretaries, dining room, reception room, and parlors with billiard table, piano, phonograph, and lecture facilities. A three story annex had bedrooms, baths, parlors and treatment rooms. There were also one and two room bungalows. In summer a "Tent City" was set up, screened and electric lighted.

Dr. Lindlahr's system of "Rational Therapeutics" included natural diet, strictly vegetarian; sun baths, air baths, hydrotherapy, electrotherapy, and manipulation. While most of this was rejected by the medical profession of the time, later discoveries in vitamins, mineral salts, and the importance of diet came close to Dr. Lindlahr's ideas. He also lectured, wrote five volumes on his medical theories, and collaborated with his wife in a *Nature Cure Cookbook*. In his Elmhurst sanitarium, and another in Chicago, he is estimated to have treated 80,000 patients. Among patients in the Elmhurst Sanitarium were Sinclair Lewis, author of *Main Street;* Clarence Darrow, famed defense attorney; Kathleen McBain, author of *The Queen's Rings* and mother of Hughston McBain of Marshall Field & Company; Mary King Estill of the King Ranch of Texas; Gretchen Esterbrook, wife of Howard Esterbrook, movie producer; Paul Swan, actor and dancer; George E.Q. Johnson, district attorney who prosecuted Al Capone, and perhaps most notably, Eugene V. Debs, five times Presidential candidate on the Socialist Party ticket.

Dr. Henry Lindlahr died March 26, 1924. His son Victor took over the Sanitarium while also broadcasting a daily health program by radio and editing *Journal for Living*. His father had banned the sale of any kind of drugs, even including German herb teas, at the sanitarium, but Victor Lindlahr made a fortune in the development of patent medicines. They included Geritol, Serutan, Sominex, and Zuramen.

CRANE SANITARIUM

According to his son Riley, Dr. Milo A. Crane was a disciple of Bernarr Macfadden, physical culturist and publicist. Born in

The Crane Sanitarium, former home of Dr. Frederick J.T. Fischer, built in 1891 at 203 South York Street.

Saginaw, Michigan in 1874, Dr. Crane was educated at the Wayne Medical School of Detroit. As a practicing physician he came to Elmhurst in 1914 as a specialist in stomach disorders. He took over the building which had been Dr. Frederick J.T. Fischer's offices and home at 203 South York Street.

The philosophy of the Crane Sanitarium (Dr. Crane called it the Natural Therapeutic Institute) is stated in a brochure published in 1922: "Nature's methods have been reduced to a science and the application of these laws has been a constant study for many years. We are pioneers in the modern treatment of chronic diseases by the great curative sources of nature, and we are devoting our life to the alleviation of suffering humanity." Dr. Crane was a member of Elmhurst Elk Lodge 1531 and Elmhurst Lodge 941 of Masons. He died in 1944. His son Dr. Riley Crane, DDS. continued to occupy the Crane building for many years.

SPORTS IN ELMHURST

The preoccupation of most Americans with spectator sports would probably have amazed their pioneer ancestors. In earlier days there were many games, some of them practical like corn-shucking, but in most of them everyone took part, with few left to look-on. If anyone was regarded as a professional, it probably would be the owner of a fast horse, and he was looked on askance. Games such as town ball, tap ball, sock ball, and rounders developed into baseball.

BASEBALL

As early as 1900 an independent team was organized as the Elmhurst White Sox, adopting the name of the Chicago team as later Little Leaguers assumed the trappings of big time contenders. The Elmhurst White Sox played until 1915 on a diamond at the southeast corner of Third and Illinois streets, against teams from DuPage and Cook county towns and Chicago. "Shorty" Burmeister, barber and postmaster, was team manager, and the players included Al Struckman, Frank Hestermann, Art Boeger, Herman Jaeger, Tenny Woodruff, Paul Hild, C. Heidemann, Lem Brodt, Ted Bright, Dick Most, and Emil Kruckow.

The Elmhurst Tigers was organized in 1915, succeeding the White Sox, and played at the southeast corner of York Street and North Avenue until it disbanded in 1919. Manager was Art Schumacher, Jr., son of the banker, and players included "Skim" Moeller, Adolph Hintz, Richard Haak, Alvin Hintz, August Kraus, Walter Hild, Vern Conrad, John Hintz, Zan Hintz, George Steinhebel, Walter Treptow, Herman Hertzfeld, Art Stegen, and John Lawson.

The first Elmhurst Boosters baseball team played from 1918 to 1922, at first at Park and Chandler avenues; later at Myrtle Avenue and Walter Street, against teams from nearby towns

ELMHURST WHITE SOX BASEBALL TEAM
1908 CHAMPIONS OF DUPAGE COUNTY
BACK ROW: Ted Bright, Emil Kruckow, Ewald Balgemann, George Struckman, Otto Nemitz, Hugo Brodt, William Dammeier.
FRONT ROW: Emil Dumke, Tenny Woodruff, Mgr. "Shorty" Burmeister, Frank Hesterman, Herman Weinert, Paul Hild.
The Dog Mascot — Kum—Fuz—Lum.
(Given to Shorty by City Attorney Fred C. Harbour)

and from Chicago. Raymond Allen was manager and players included: Al Watts, Robert Crumpton, Owen Phillips, Harvey Froeming, John Ronske, William Rosenfeldt, Henry Kiting, Melvin Alexander, Frank (Cy) Ronske, Red Hagermann, and A. Dixon.

The Elmhurst Flashes played during the seasons of 1926, 1927, and 1928 in the DuPage County League and twice were league champions. Players included J. Seeck, R. Hesterman, H. Seeck, H. Reuter, S. Ochefski, H. Hintz, R. Krisch, A. Rudolph, L. Froeming, W. Burke, E. Ronske, T. Woeller, A. Stegen, and W. Davis. Managers were George Rudolph and H. Gauger.

The Elmhurst Travelers baseball team was an outgrowth of the Travelers football team, and played from 1928 to 1931. Having no home diamond, they played all games on the road, mostly against teams in the Fox River valley, including Aurora, Batavia, Dundee, and St. Charles. George Kulton was manager and players included Lawton Davis, Shorty Pillatt, Bob Crumpton, Mickey Hild, Ed Farrell, Ed Schweppe, Adam Hohman, Lefty Ewald, Paul Brettman, and Augie Hawkins.

The Elmhurst Aces, organized in 1930, won the city championship in 1931 and played in the Midwest League. The team was sponsored by Alonzo Fischer, president of the First National Bank of Elmhurst, who furnished equipment and built bleacher stands for the field at Lake Street and Milton Avenue (now Armitage). The players included R. May, E. Heinke, L. Ball, W. Smotherman, A. Benson, B. Burke, E. Beckman, E. Pearson, R. Bigalke, F. Sieloff, A. Rudolph, W. Burke, and W. Rieger.

ELMHURST INDIANS BASEBALL TEAM
1946
BACK ROW: Irv Niemeyer-Mgr., Bob Pierce, Vince Bennett, Wally Newlander.
FRONT ROW: Bud Keir, Harold Pierce, Snipe Hanson, Art Niemeyer, Wally Rude, Marty Schwarz, Bill Kruse.

The Elmhurst Indians started as the Elmhurst Comets in 1934, organized by Irv Niemeyer, Charley "Snipe" Hanson, Bud Keir and Joe Hesterman. They played at Lake Street and Milton Avenue, got uniforms in 1935 and in 1936 changed their name to York Indians. Harold Lind was manager. They lost their playing field to the reorganized Elmhurst Arrows, but regained it, 1937-39. In 1940 Irv Niemeyer, manager, moved the team to East End Park, where they built stands, dugout, and score board and leveled the diamond. Among the players were Bud Metz, Bill Kruse, Frank O'Regan, Ed Fiene, Bob Phillips, George Criswell, Lee Pfund, and Norm Asche. They disbanded in wartime-1943, but were reorganized by Niemeyer in 1946. The Indians joined the Midwest "B" League in 1947. They won 12 and lost 3, finishing second to the Chicago Bisons in a league that included four Chicago teams, one from Berwyn, and the Elmhurst Boosters. In 1948 the Indians joined the DuPage County League in which they finished second for the four years 1948-51. The team disbanded in 1952, some players going to the Boosters. Among players not previously mentioned were Vince Bennett, Bill Balgemann, Art Niemeyer, Hutch Niemeyer, Jack Freimuth, Art Commare, Luke Leyden, Marty Schwarz, Lyle Pladna, Jim Stopka, Bob Pierce, Harold Pierce, Wally Newlander, John Dickson, Tex Simon, Ralph Mottashed, W. Runge, Ray Mensching, Wally Rude, and Russ Boeger. Irv Niemeyer, Hanson, and Keir played from the start in 1934 to the finish.

The second Elmhurst Boosters was organized in 1946 by Bob Backhaus, and in 1947, with Frank Peters as manager, joined the Midwest "B" League. Players included Harold Pierce, Warren Melgard, Gunther Ahlf, Hub Griffith, Bob Thollander, Marty Schwarz, Bill Van Mater, Ed Kabat, Harold Bates, Jack Brumm, Louis Oehlerking, and Jack Gaare. The Boosters played in the DuPage County League in 1948 and 1949, winning the championship both years. Additional players included Lyle McIntyre, Howie Goetschell, Wally Newlander, and Hub Stolper. Marty Schwarz was manager. The Boosters played in the West Suburban League in 1950 and 1951, and returned to the DuPage League in 1952, winning a third championship and also the Lockport District Baseball Tournament, going on to the state finals. Among players were W. Sellergren, Jack Freimuth, Bill Balgemann, Vince Bennett, Del Mittelhauser, Harry Fawell, Hal Luhring and R. Sellergren. In 1953 the Boosters finished second in the league and second in the state district tourney. Howie Goetschell, manager, was succeeded by Charley Hanson, who had pitched 19 years for the Elmhurst Indians. Other players were Art Benedetto, E. McPartland, O. McPartland, Dale Shynikevich, and Luke Leyden. This was the last season for the Boosters. Among its players, Lee Pfund and Hub Stolper were in the Brooklyn Dodger farm system for several years and tryouts were offered Ed Fiene, St. Louis Cardinals; Bill Balgemann, Chicago White Sox; and Norm Asche, Chicago Cubs. Bud Henning of the first Boosters played several years in minor leagues.

SOFTBALL

The Elmhurst Men's Softball League was organized in 1932 by George Kulton with eight teams sponsored by merchants, and varied from five to twelve teams until disbanded after the 1951 season. Kulton's teams, at various times called Travelers, Elks, and Stone Crushers, won 14 championships. Games were played at East End Park, and in 1937 at Poplar Avenue and South Street. The 16-inch ball was used except in 1935 when the 12-inch ball was accepted. Players included Don Olson, Carl Vertovec, Al Kentgen, Clyde Metz, Jack Dagley, Bill Schwerin, Wally Klasen, Bill Raese, Irv Kirch, Warren Cooney, Bob Webster, Tom Oliva, Joe Mann, and Al Bayer.

Elmhurst Orioles

No Elmhurst team ever received wider acclaim and publicity than the first and only girls softball team, the Elmhurst Orioles, organized in 1936 by Fred Nieman because a teacher at Hawthorne School had urged that teenage girls could and should participate in organized sports. Merchants backed the team by providing uniforms, bats, balls, and other equipment. Early games were played on the property of Gustav Schmitz at Maple and Milton avenues, but as a lighted field for night games became desirable Otto Balgemann, realtor, and Albert Glos, owner of the property, offered a field in East First Street near Haven Road, which became known as Rabe's Field because it adjoined Rabe's Dairy. A backstop, screens, and bleachers were built, and all seats were filled, with spectators lining the foul lines for games with teams from Lombard, Maywood, Westmont, Brookfield, Arlington Heights, and Blue Island. Lights were sufficient to illuminate home plate and some of the infield, but a ball hit to the outfield might disappear in the dark, along with the fielder chasing it. But these were Depression days, and spectators were uncritical. Members of the original team were Mickie McDaniels, Viola Kolvitz, Kay Ehlers, Olive Rhode, Bernice Baethke, Vivian Hargreaves, Fran Kulton, Blanche Nieman, Marion Krause, Ruth Ferguson, Dorothy Heinberg, Grace Heinke, June Carney, Polly Rebek, and Jo Dezutel, with bat boy Johnny Weber and coach Art Heinke. The team became known as the Elmhurst V-8's after Cooper-Pollack Ford took over as sole sponsor, and continued playing through 1941, but was then disbanded because of the war. Fred Nieman, 183 Hampshire Avenue, has become an Elmhurst legend as organizer of one of the most famous of girls softball teams.

ELMHURST ORIOLES GIRLS SOFTBALL TEAM 1936-42
TOP ROW: Mickie McDanials, Kay Ehlers, Vida Kolvitz, Mr. Fred Nieman, Olive Rhode, Bernice Baethke, Vivian Hargraves.
MIDDLE ROW: Fran Kulton, Blanche Nieman, Marion Krause, Ruth Ferguson, Dorthy Heinberg, Grace Heinke, June Carney.
BOTTOM ROW: Polly Rebek, Johnny Weber-bat boy, Jo Dezutel.

LITTLE AND PONY LEAGUES

The Elmhurst Baseball League, Inc.

The Elmhurst Baseball League, Inc. had its beginning in the East DuPage Little League, established in 1952 and affiliated with the National Little League. Two teams from Elmhurst, one from Villa Park and one from Bensenville formed a National league and the same number formed an American league, eight teams in all. Each team had 18 players and played 18 games within its own league. The four teams in Elmhurst were managed by Emil Golub, Bob Boke, Art Niemeyer, and Don Cooper. Games were played at I.C. Field (now Plunkett Field) and Elmhurst Junior High School (now Sandburg).

The first officers were: president, E.E. Mundt; vice president W.A. Eggert; secretary, A.L. Tennyson; and treasurer, V.O. Schradel. Others who helped organize and were active in the beginning were Bill Newell, Don English, Charley Adams, Charley Johnson, Henry Banser, Elmer Malecha and Bob Stumpf. Each team included six boys, 9 and 10 years old, six boys 11 years old, and six boys 12 years old.

In 1953 the Pony League was established for boys 13 and 14 years old. It was affiliated with the East DuPage Little League. There were four teams: the Broncos, Colts, Mustangs, and Pintos. There were fifteen boys on each team, and a fifteen game schedule was played with an all star team playing in the National Pony League tournament at the end of the season. The first managers included Nick Ermisch, John Spratt, Bert Hough and Ray Berg. Don Cooper served as Commissioner. Games were played at East End Park.

To give the graduates of the Little League and Pony League programs an opportunity to continue playing in organized baseball, the West Suburban Colt League was formed in 1956. This consisted of eight teams: Elmhurst, Glen Ellyn, Villa Park, and Itasca in a Northern Division and Naperville, Downers Grove, Hinsdale and LaGrange in a Southern Division. Each team played 16 games and at the end of the season the champions of each division met in a play-off. The Colt League was for 15 and 16 year old boys. The Elmhurst team had 20 players. The organizer and manager of the Elmhurst team was John Spratt, with the help of Coaches Jack Wilkins, Earl Grimshaw, Joe Mahoney, Bill Krueger, and Don Cooper, business manager. The Elmhurst team finished second the first year with a 12-4 won-lost record. In 1957 the team won the championship with a 12-2 record.

The Little, Pony, and Colt Leagues, continued to grow with many added teams. Elmhurst withdrew from the National Little League and formed an independent organization, the Elmhurst Little League, Inc., which later became the Elmhurst Baseball League, Inc. In 1976 the organization entered its twenty-fifth year with an expanded program, reaching 1100 boys and girls.

There are sixteen teams each in the Farm, Minor and Major leagues for boys ages 9 through 12; fifteen teams in the Pony League, ages 13 and 14; six teams in the Colt League, ages 15 and 16; three teams in the Babe Ruth League, ages 17 and 18. There are eight teams in the Pee-Wee League, age 8. There are six teams for girls, ages 8 through 16. In all there are 86 teams involving 275 adults as coaches and managers! A "no-cut rule" insures an opportunity for everyone to play. Each member must play at least three consecutive innings each game.

The budget for 1976 was $50,000.00. The money was raised by player fees, business sponsorships and benefits. The whole program is one of the most comprehensive of any in the State of Illinois. The 1976 officers were president, Jim LaSpisa; Ex Vice President - Joseph Marrs; first vice president, Ray Ranger; secretary, Dick Stanton; treasurer, Ron Hain. Others active in management are Joe Tiberi, Ernie Weber, Ralph Cohrs, and Frank Maggio. A major contribution to youth baseball was made by Art Niemeyer who managed teams in the Little League for fifteen years, the Pony League for two years, and the American Legion for two years. Mr. Niemeyer had been a participant on the Elmhurst semi-pro teams, the Indians and the Boosters.

An additional outlet for youth interested in sports was provided by an independent organization. In 1967 the Churchville Boys Baseball Association was organized with six Little League teams of boys 8 to 12 years old, representing north Elmhurst, east Addison, and south Bensenville. The next year a Pony League team, boys 13 and 14 years old, was added. By 1968 there were eleven Little League teams, one Pony League team, and one Colt League team, boys 15 and 16 years old, a total of 178 boys. In 1970 when the Association adopted the present name of Elmhurst North Baseball Association, men's and girl's softball were added, with over-all participation of Little League Minors, ages 8 and 9; five of Majors, ages 10 to 12; three Pony League teams; five softball teams, ages 15 and up; five girl softball juniors, ages 9 to 14, and four seniors, ages 15 and up. The association is a community project, not affiliated with national youth baseball organizations. The first president was James Pickell, succeeded by Frank France, James Gabelman, Jay Ricki, and Tom Kulik. Long serving as managers and coaches are Ed Osmanski, Tom Enlow, John Hermansen, and William Fiedler.

FOOTBALL

Football is a game of ancient origin, developed mainly in England where it took two forms, Rugby, from which the United States game derived, and the game of the London Football Association, which got its designation

Sports In Elmhurst

when "association" was corrupted to soccer. In the United States the first intercollegiate football game was played in 1869 when Rutgers defeated Princeton, 6 to 4. It was mainly a college game, of primary interest to alumni, until 1924 when Notre Dame's "Four Horsemen" attracted national interest. There were professional teams as early as 1895, but they got little notice until 1925 when Red Grange (of Wheaton), all-American at the University of Illinois, joined the Chicago Bears. Broadcasts by radio, and later by television, vastly increased the national following.

The Elmhurst Teddy Bears, an independent football team, played from 1910 to 1917, mostly

ELMHURST TEDDY BEARS YEAR 1910
Picture taken at corner of Addison and 2nd. SEATED L TO R: Ray Ruffan, Alvin Maloit, Harry Bleich, Stanley Krisch, Arthur Hintz, Michael Krause, Bruno Hintz, Walter Hild, and Adolph Hintz. BACK ROW: Arthur Schumacher - Mgr., Otto Haack, Richard Hintz (killed in World War I), George Krischak, Anton Hintz, Coach Paul Hild (Son of Lutheran Minister).

at home in its field at Elmhurst Avenue and Haven Road, against teams that could use C. & N.W. trains. An exception was an annual Thanksgiving Day game at Palatine. The team rode a horse drawn hayrack, leaving Wednesday, playing on the holiday, and returning Friday after spending two nights in a Palatine hotel. Among the players were Ray Ruffan, Alvin Maloit, Harry Bleich, Stanley Krisch, Arthur Hintz, Michael Krause, Bruno Hintz, Walter Hild, Adolph Hintz, Otto Haack, Richard Hintz, George Krischak, Anton Hintz, Ed Anderson, Frank Maloit, Albert Keller, Frank (Cy) Ronske, George Kruskow, Arthur Schumacher, manager, and Paul Hild, coach.

For nearly fifty years George Kulton was active in athletics in Elmhurst as a player, organizer of teams, manager and coach. His record with the Elmhurst Travelers, an independent football team that won 292, lost 80 and tied 30 games over thirty-eight playing seasons from 1927 to 1967 is outstanding. Kulton also organized and played with a number of basketball and baseball teams in Elmhurst.

In 1927 Kulton, Mickey Hild, and Lawton Davis organized the Elmhurst Travelers football team, recruiting ten former York High School players and nine others. The team was called the Travelers because it had no home field. In 1928 the Travelers played back of the Mill on Walter Street, with barely room for a regulation field; then moved to Maple Avenue and Lake Street from 1929 to 1932; back to the Mill field, 1933 to 1938; and then to East End

THE FIRST ELMHURST TRAVELERS
FOOTBALL TEAM - 1927
TOP ROW: Mielke, Stellman, Bucholz, Black, Hohman, Pillatte, Robbins, Miller, E. Ronske.
BOTTOM ROW: Hawk, Leeseberg, F. Ronske, Berlien, Davis, Kulton, Weller, Hild, Jepsen, Stott.

Park with occasional big games at Elmhurst College Field. The 1927 squad of 19 included the three organizers and H. Mielke, M. Stellman, Fred Bucholz, Phil Black, Eddie Hohman, H. Pillatt, G. Robbins, H. Miller, E. Ronske, R. Hawk, Ray Leeseberg, F. Ronske, Herb Berlien, Stan Weller, Bill Jepson, and Dan Stott. Only two games were lost during the first three seasons, and as the team's reputation grew, players were recruited from far distances and games were played with teams from Chicago and distant suburbs. From 1927 through 1951, excluding the war years 1943-45 when the team was disbanded, the Travelers were consistently champions of DuPage County and had a record of 182 won, 23 lost, and 22 tied.

One of the most thrilling plays occurred in the 1937 undefeated season when the Travelers were 7 to 6 behind the Melrose Park Rams with a little more than one minute to play. Four out-of-bounds passes took the ball from deep in Travelers territory to the Rams 43 yard line. With time for one play, quarterback Bud Voelz called on Shine Robbins to try for a field goal. Bud teed the ball on the mid-field line and Shine booted it 60 yards into a cross wind, clearing the bar by inches as the game ended.

The Travelers played in the Bi-State League, 1952 through 1956, winning the league championship in 1955 and the southern division championship in 1956. They played in the Tri-State League, 1957 through 1959, winning the championship each year. In the Central States Football League, 1960 through 1967, they won three southern division championships and one league championship. During 38 seasons the Travelers won 292, lost 80, and tied 30. In 1941 they won 11 with no losses or ties and had only 6 points scored against them. In 1949 they won 11, with one tie and no losses, scoring 311 against 31 for all opponents. In 1968, because of increasing costs and decreasing attendance, the Travelers franchise was sold to Rockford, Illinois, and the team ceased to exist.

George Kulton, one of the originators, played and then coached throughout the 38 seasons. Among players after the original roster were Marvin and Ed Voelz, Carl and Frank Vertovec, James Smotherman, Wallace Baucke, Al Klaeren, Frank Grady, Frank Morris, Norman Nissen, Fuzz Adams, Pat Albanese, Don Busch, Tom Nagle, Don Olson, George Johnson, PeeWee Anderman, Jack Schumacher, Bugs Newlander, Al Dobbeck, Monte Brethauer, Joe Turyna, Henry Tiedemann, Leon McCrae, Fred Fiorelli, Red Harbour, and Bill Smotherman.

Boy's Football

Elmhurst Boys Football is the outgrowth of the Pop Warner League system, sponsored by Elmhurst YMCA and started there in 1962 by Bob Myers. A league was formed including two Elmhurst teams and YMCA teams from Thornton-Harvey, Downers Grove, Montclair, and Hi-Ridge. Forty to fifty boys, ages 10-13, participated. Weight limit was 130 pounds. After two years Elmhurst withdrew from the YMCA program and Elmhurst Boys Football was organized with Jerry Spaeth as president. Two Elmhurst teams entered the Fox Valley League, which included two Naperville teams, two from Glen Ellyn, and one each from LaGrange, Lombard, Elk Grove Village, Geneva, and Wheaton. In addition to the two traveling teams, Elmhurst had four city teams. There were two weight divisions, 135 pounds for ages 13 to 14, and 105 for ages 11 to 12. Beginning in 1970 Elmhurst had only one traveling team, ages 13 to 14, with no weight restriction, and 16 teams; four for age 9; six for ages 10 to 11; six for ages 12 to 13, totaling 280 boys, with 75 girl cheerleaders. Rules require each qualified boy to play two minutes of each game. Games are played at Plunkett Field and Butterfield Park, with some championships at Clarence East Field and Elmhurst College Field. Ted Zajac has been head coach for 11 years; others of dedicated service are Ray Jordan and Jerry Wiemanski.

BASKETBALL

Basketball was invented by James Naismith in 1891 at the YMCA in Springfield, Massachusetts. It was designed as a game to be played in gymnasiums, although it could be played outdoors, by men or women, although somewhat neglected by women after its early years, until rediscovered by woman's lib. Within a decade or two basketball became popular in small country high schools where a team of five players could more easily be put together than a baseball nine or a football eleven. Early development of regional and state tournaments made basketball a leading high school sport, especially in Illinois. Interest in collegiate and professional teams is more recent.

The Elmhurst Travelers Basketball Team was organized in 1926 by George Kulton as an independent team, and continued playing until 1940. For part of the time it was sponsored by the Elks. Home games were played at York High School against Hinsdale, Glen Ellyn, Wheaton, Villa Park, and other DuPage County teams. The Travelers won a CYO tournament held in Elmhurst. The 1930 team included Harold Miller, Fred Bucholz, John Weiser, Pat Hansen, Myron Krom, and Kulton. Among later players were Irwin Krieter, Ted Lesney, Frank Vertovec, Jim Smotherman, Red Burke, Jack Kennedy, Chester Baucke, and Ed Nowak.

The Elmhurst Rockets were organized in 1943 by Jack Van Voorst. The Rockets played

Sports In Elmhurst

ELMHURST ROCKETS - 1946
FRONT ROW: Don Olson, Byron Dixon, Jack Van Voorst, Bob Thompson, Ed Fiene.
BACK ROW: Buzz Rosback, Norm Frega, Norm Steingraber, Marv Fleege, Fred Moeller.

some of the strongest teams in the Chicago area, including the Wabash YMCA, Chicago Shamrocks, Glenview Nas, Naperville Moose and Brookfield Pandas, as well as nationally known teams such as the Harlem Globetrotters, the House of David, and the Detroit Rams. The Rockets won the Press Publications Invitational Tournament and the Warrenville Park District championship in 1948. Home games were played at Hawthorne Junior High School with some major games at York High School. The team dispanded in 1952 after nine years of competition, the last game being played against the House of David at Elmhurst Junior High School (Sandburg). Van Voorst was manager and coach. Among players were Bob Thompson, Ray Sieloff, Ed Fiene, Marv Fleege, Fred Woeller, Norm Steingraber, Norm Frega, Byron Dixon, Doug Cunningham, Buzz Rosback, Ed Voelz, John McArthur, Gunner Ahlf, Ken Johnson, Harry Kindl, Don Olson, Ed Vertovec, and Joe Remec.

The Red Devils Basketball Team was a woman's team organized and coached by Russ Perry in 1928. Players included Fran Davis, Marge Eastham, Katherine Wright, Marge Colby, Pat Burke, Mildred Burke, Anne Keller, Josephine Hobein, and Marge Harbour. In 1931 the team became the Elmhurst Travelerettes. Coached by George Kulton, they played through 1933 and then disbanded. Home games were played in York High School and opponents were other Girls' teams, mostly in DuPage County.

YORK COMMUNITY HIGH SCHOOL

The first football teams at York High School were coached in 1918 and 1919 by its principal J.H. Crann. The practice field was the King nursery on Arlington Avenue. In 1920 a new high school was erected in the prairie west of town and designated York Community High School. With the new school came a new coach, Clarence East, who was to remain as a coach and teacher and athletic director for thirty-six years. In 1921 York had teams in football, basketball, baseball and swimming. There was also a girls' basketball team. York competed in 1922 in the County League made up of Hinsdale, Downers Grove, West Chicago, Glenbard and York. That first year York won the football, basketball and baseball championships. The West Suburban Conference consisting of Glenbard, Downers Grove, Hinsdale, Maine, Riverside and York was formed in 1923. That year York repeated its championships in football and baseball. In 1924 track was added. In the following years cross country, tennis, golf, wrestling and gymnastics were added and swimming was discontinued.

IMMACULATE CONCEPTION HIGH SCHOOL

Immaculate Conception High School has been a member of the West Suburban Catholic Conference, formerly the North-East Catholic Conference, for a quarter century. The 1971 football team was conference champion and first to complete a season without a defeat. The record was 9-0-1. The football teams won conference titles in 1971, 1973, 1974, and 1976. The 1974 team was Illinois state semi-finalist. The 1966-67 basketball team was conference champion with a 23-3 record. The 1973-74 basketball team won conference and regional titles. The 1972 baseball team won the conference and regional championships. The track teams have consistently sent competitors to the state track meet.

WORLD WAR I CHANGES

World War I marked the end of an era for Elmhurst as for the rest of the world. For almost a century wars had been localized and there was hope of ending war altogether. There was a belief in something called civilization that was enlightening the dark places on the map. Peace, progress, and prosperity seemed no empty promise. Mankind was never more idealistic or optimistic than in the early years of the twentieth century. The war brought disillusionment and skepticism from which we have not recovered. To the people of Elmhurst the war in 1914 was more than a history lesson that had strayed from textbook to newspaper front pages. Because Elmhurst was a community of two major national backgrounds, it was bound to feel the impact of the English - German discord firsthand.

Germans had come to America to escape military conscription, cited as one of the causes of the war, but they retained an understandable loyalty to the fatherland. There seemed no reason they should not express it in those early days when the war was remote and the United States was neutral. But this expression was devisive. Not all English-speaking residents supported England; some were anti-English, but many saw American interests threatened by the German war machine. There was much hot argument, resulting in bitterness and misunderstanding that continued after the United States entered the war. Dr. Stanger recalls the absurdity of someone asking him if Elmhurst College students were required to salute the Kaiser! There are stories of a store front daubed with yellow paint. Pro-German talk was based more on sentiment than on principle. When the United States declared war there was no opposition. Young men who were second-generation Germans had become Americans. They volunteered, or were drafted, with as much enthusiasm as those of other national origins. At the time the war was considered as necessary; it was not unpopular.

On the home front, there was no rationing, but proclaimed meatless days and wheatless days were accepted with patriotic fervor. There were shortages of sugar and razor blades. There was much knitting of socks and sweaters for soldiers and rolling of newspapers into wax soaked trench candles. Collecting balls of tinfoil made more sense, as tin had been recklessly used to wrap candy. There were service flags in businesses, churches, schools, and in the windows of many homes, a red-bordered white flag with a blue star for each serviceman, a gold star for each youth killed. It was a time for everyone's doing one's bit, but it was soon over, for participation of the United States lasted only one year and nine months. It spawned a "lost generation" that was lost mainly in not knowing what to do next. After a world war the world would never be the same.

REMEMBERING THE WARS

American Legion T.H.B. Post 187 was chartered September 26, 1919, the year the national organization was founded. The initials T.H.B. memorialize three Elmhurst men killed in World War I: Ernest Timrott, Richard Hintz, and Kingsley Buck. A plaque on a granite stone in Wilder Park was dedicated May 30, 1927. Three trees were planted and a flagpole erected as a tribute to them and others who served. Here every Memorial Day three volleys are fired and taps is sounded. The American Legion Home, Butterfield and Spring roads, was completed in 1958. The Legion sponsors Boy Scout Troop 187, a baseball program, high school oratorical contests, Boys' and Girls' State; a children's Christmas party, and Vaqueros Drum and Bugle Corps. T.H.B. Unit 187, American Legion Auxiliary, was organized in 1922 and has as a major project aiding in rehabilitating disabled veterans of all wars in hospitals and in a program for the education and welfare of their children.

Walter A. Glos Post 2048, Veterans of Foreign Wars was chartered April 21, 1931. It sponsors youth and civic projects, but its most spectacular contributions to civic ceremony are

Harold Wilder, son of T.E. Wilder, in World War I uniform.

the Highlander Pipe Band and the Highlander Color Guard that wear Gordon kilts from Scotland. The Color Guard has won three national and seven department competitions. The Ladies Auxiliary to Walter A. Glos Post 2048 was chartered March 24, 1932, and assists the post in community service, with special attention to the National VFW Home for Widows and Orphans, Eaton Rapids, Michigan, and the Illinois Soldiers and Sailors Home, Normal. The Military Order of Cooties, Pup Tent Box Car 66, chartered in 1949, and its Women's Auxiliary, chartered in 1975, give attention to work in veterans' hospitals. Junior Girls Unit, VFW, instituted in 1962, maintains a drill team and joins with the Sons of the VFW in collecting gifts for needy families.

The Martha Ibbetson Chapter, Daughters of the American Revolution, was organized January 26, 1933, by twelve descendants of those who helped win the War for Independence. Martha Ibbetson was notable in caring for prisoners of war and her home, Whitby Hall, is preserved in Philadelphia. Historic preservation is a D.A.R. objective. In 1936 the Elmhurst chapter erected a bronze tablet marking the location of Hill Cottage Tavern and the first post office. In 1940 the chapter sponsored Mrs. William H. Wood in organizing the Elmhurst Production Unit of the Chicago Chapter of the American Red Cross, which has given a total of 14,501 hours of service, Mrs. Wood alone giving 5,500 hours of service. D.A.R. members collect and copy geneological records of churches, cemeteries, counties, and families for deposit in the Newberry Library, the Illinois Geneological Library, and the D.A.R. library in Washington, D.C. The society sponsors American history essay contests in Elmhurst and Bensenville schools. Good Citizenship awards and scholarships are other school projects.

BUSINESS MENS ORGANIZATIONS

Another area of civic responsibility was represented by the organization in 1918 of the Elmhurst Boosters Club by 60 business and professional men. The first meeting was held in the home of Francis O. Stevens, 440 South Kenilworth Avenue. H.H. Robillard was elected president. Boosters' clubs were popular across the country in those years, but they succumbed to a national organization with what some considered a more dignified name. In 1926 the Boosters became the Elmhurst Chamber of Commerce with Robillard as president. In 1937, when Matt Lockwood, manager of a furniture store, was elected president, the organization became the Elmhurst Trade & Civic Association, but in 1940 resumed the name Elmhurst Chamber of Commerce. Harold Cruger of the Elmhurst Press was elected president and Irving W. Giese was part-time executive secretary.

ELMHURST COLLEGE

World War I shook the old foundations of the Proseminary that had become known semi-officially as Elmhurst College. Wartime prejudice against all things German included elements of German culture that previously had been admired and imitated. Teaching in Elmhurst College was still largely in German. Student enrollment increased from 103 in 1887 to 133 in 1892, and reached a peak of 170 during the presidency of Dr. Daniel Irion, but then declined. A demand for change and for the establishment of a full-scale college was voiced in the denominational journal *Messenger of Peace,* and in the student magazine *The Keryx.* Dr. Irion, recognizing the need for younger leadership, resigned as president, an office he had held for 32 years. He continued as teacher until 1928. He died October 25, 1935.

The new president was the Rev. Herman J. Schick of Evansville, Indiana, an alumnus of the Proseminary with master of arts degree from the University of Chicago. The school was reorganized in 1919 as an Academy and Junior College, President Schick serving also as dean of the Junior College. Paul N. Crusius, professor of history, was also principal of the Academy. Additions to the faculty included Karl Henning Carlson in English, Homer Helmick in chemistry, and Theophil W. Mueller in sociology. The Rev. Robert Leonhardt was registrar, physical education director, and football coach, the college's first official recognition of athletics. The Memorial Library was built in 1921. Miss Grace Barbee was first fulltime librarian. In 1923 South Hall (now Schick Hall) replaced the barn and vegetable garden.

The first fulltime football coach was Robert Hale, who came from Miami University in 1922. In 1923 Elmhurst College joined the North Illinois Junior College Athletic Conference, including Crane, Elgin, St. Procopius, North Park, and Chicago Normal.

The official name of the school became Elmhurst College in 1923. It had been so called popularly and unofficially since the first decade of the century. Dr. Schick resigned as president in 1924 and returned to parish ministry in Chicago.

The new president was H. Richard Niebuhr, who as a member of the Class of 1914 had clamored for relevancy (well before the time for demands and protest marches.) He had gone on to Eden Seminary, Washington University, and Yale University. He was Elmhurst's first president trained in the American university system. A School of Music was established. A long-range plan of campus development was laid out by Benjamin Franklin Olson, Chicago architect. Academic ranks were established and faculty members became specialists. In 1927 before much of his program could be carried out, Dr. Niebuhr was forced to resign because of ill health. For the next year the college was administered by Dean Mueller, Principal Crusius, and Dr. Helmick. During this time, it was decided to close the Academy.

The Rev. Timothy Lehman of Columbus, Ohio, an alumnus, assumed the presidency in 1928 and held the position through twenty years of financial difficulties including the Depression and a pressing need for accreditation as a four-year college. A new President's House and a new Gymnasium were built in 1928 as a result of a $25,000 gift from William A. Wieboldt of the Chicago department store. This was the last construction for two decades.

Dr. Lehman interested himself in civic affairs, serving on the city's welfare board and the county's Selective Service Board, and joining the Kiwanis Club. Elmhurst College joined the Intercollegiate Conference and Oliver ("Pete") Langhorst began his 36 years as coach and athletic director. A marching band turned out for football games. Coeducation was authorized in 1919 and forty-six women enrolled in the fall of 1930. Mrs. Lehman served as dean of women the first year; Miss Grace Falck, history teacher, the second. Then Miss Genevieve Staudt began thirty years of service as dean of women and teacher of education.

After a number of rejections, the North Central Association of Colleges fully accredited Elmhurst as a four year liberal arts college, April 24, 1934. It was a day of parade and jubilation for the student body. In the same year the Evangelical Synod united with the Reformed Church in the United States to form the Evangelical and Reformed Church. This altered the status of Elmhurst College, as the Reformed Church brought seven colleges into the denomination, all of them financially more secure and with larger endowments than Elmhurst. In 1942 Elmhurst received a charter with a board only half of whose members represented the denomination. The further merger of the Evangelical and Reformed with Congregational Christian churches to form the United Church of Christ brought more changes as the numerous Congregational colleges had a tradition of independence and limited denominational support.

In 1939 the Challacombe property at Prospect Street and Elm Park Avenue was added to the campus. (In the late 1800's The Challacombe House had been the Cutter School for Girls). World War II brought declining enrollment and financial stringency. After the war, government scholarship assistance for veterans

World War I Changes

Originally the home of the Cutter School for Girls about 1870, later the George Challacombe residence and a college residence. The site at Elm Park Avenue and Prospect Street is now occupied by the Elmhurst College Science Building.

sharply increased enrollment from 300 to 500 and then to 650. The neglected facilities were suddenly overcrowded. Temporary barracks were set up and a dormitory improvised. President Lehman resigned in 1947. Theophil W. Mueller resigned as dean, but continued as professor and head of the sociology department until 1962. Professor Mueller had given 41 years of service to the college.

The new president was the Rev. Henry W. Dinkmeyer of Chicago, another Elmhurst College alumnus, and for years a member of the board of directors. Alfred Friedli of St. Louis became dean of the college. In 1949 Dr. Clarence E. Josephson became assistant to the president with duties as business manager. Financial conditions improved, but there remained great need for new buildings. Of top priority was a new dormitory. President Dinkmeyer picked a site, hired a bulldozer to dig an excavation, and put up a sign, "A Hole to Be Filled With Faith.". This publicity was successful; gifts poured in and the idea was continued. Lehman Hall and Dinkmeyer Hall were built; then a $300,000 gift from Louis M. Hammerschmidt, lawyer of South Bend, Indiana, sparked a campaign for a chapel and classrooms. Two weeks after announcing his retirement in 1957, President Dinkmeyer died of a heart attack.

The Rev. Robert C. Stanger was the first president of Elmhurst College to have been born on the campus. His father was Professor Christian G. Stanger who had served on the faculty for fifty years. Dr. Stanger, a graduate of one of the last Proseminary classes in 1918, had gone on to Eden Seminary, Yale University, and the University of Chicago. He had been an instructor and dean of men at Elmhurst, and had followed Dr. Dinkmeyer as pastor of a Chicago church. He came to the presidency at a time of population explosion, the Russian Sputnik, and the consequent boom in the sciences. A study of the college's needs was made and a "Decade of Development" program was adopted in 1961, updating the Niebuhr plan. Hammerschmidt Memorial Chapel was dedicated in 1959 and a Moeller pipe organ installed. Niebuhr Hall, completed in 1961, included a health facility. The College Union was added in 1964. Enrollment had reached 1,000 students by the time Dr. Stanger retired in 1965.

Dr. Stanger continued to have a close relationship with the college after his retirement and was a vital link between Elmhurst College and the community. He served on the boards of directors of the Elmhurst Y.M.C.A., Elmhurst Symphony Orchestra, the Lizzadro Museum, and Elmhurst Senior Citizens Commission. He was an active member of the Elmhurst Historical Commission and the Elmhurst Historical Society. He was instrumental in aiding in the establishment of the Elmhurst Historical Museum. He was co-chairman of the Elmhurst Bicentennial Commission and the main guide and force behind the writing of the Bicentennial history. Dr. Stanger died November 2, 1976.

Dr. Donald C. Kleckner was the first president of Elmhurst College not to have served a church pastorate, his background being entirely academic. He was educated at Heidelberg College and the University of Michigan. He had been at Elmhurst since 1962. His administration was marked by building of the Science Center, the A.C. Buehler Library, and Stanger Hall, named for the Stangers, father and son, and by the celebration of the 100th anniversary of the school.

In 1972 Dr. Kleckner was succeeded by Dr. Ivan Frick. The economic and the educational climate and needs of our time required Dr. Frick's concentrated attention and leadership. Under his guidance the academic program of the college has undergone many changes. While the traditional liberal arts patterns of education have been maintained, changes and expansions have taken place. Some of the changes are the establishment of the "Center for Business and Economics" and the "Center for Special Programs." These and other innovations enable Elmhurst College to address itself to the needs of today. Dr. Frick serves on the Board of Directors of the Y.M.C.A. and is a member of St. Peter's Church.

View of Elmhurst College Commons, 1960s.

YEARS OF SUBURBAN EXPANSION

Otto W. Balgemann was elected mayor in 1919 and remained in that office until 1931. During that time the population of Elmhurst more than tripled, from 4,594 in 1920 to 14,055 in 1930. Said the *Elmhurst Press*, "Those were the years when Elmhurst ceased to become a farmer's shopping center, and became instead a suburban community." Balgemann was born in

Otto Balgemann, city mayor (1919-1931).

1874 in a house on the east side of York Street, north of Marion Street, the son of Louis Balgemann, blacksmith. Otto worked for Henry L. Glos and learned the real estate business. He served as postmaster and as village treasurer, and became a member of the county Republican Central Committee. He was elected Mayor as candidate of the local People's Party.

When Balgemann became mayor there were no paved streets in Elmhurst. His campaign slogan had been: "Get Elmhurst out of the mud". Before paving could be laid, wooden water pipes had to be replaced by iron pipes and sewer mains put down. The first sewage disposal plant, Rex Boulevard and Crescent Avenue, was built in 1916, ending the dumping of sewage into Salt Creek. In 1919 the City Water Department was created; a second treatment plant and three new sewage districts were completed between 1919 and 1926. The Office of Superintendent of Streets was established in 1920. Immediately that office had problems. York Street was first to be paved; there was an argument whether it should be paved with brick or with blacktop and accusations that contractors were seeking to influence city officials. The improvements were backed by the Booster's Club and merchants but opposed by those who feared that taxes and special assessments would drive people out of town. Costs of home ownership did go up, but the census shows that there were many more home owners to share the burden.

Under Balgemann's administration in 1920 the Council minutes record the establishment of a Library Board and plans to build a library. That same year voters said "No" to a proposition to establish a city hospital. In 1923 the Elmhurst Zoning Ordinance was enacted, and in 1924 the Zoning Board was established. In 1927 the Board of Local Improvements installed a comprehensive lighting system for the City.

City Hall was still the wooden building that housed the fire station. How City business was conducted during these controversial years was related by Claude Van Auken, who was then Alderman: "We met in one corner of the fire station on Schiller Street, our seats being ordinary school desks, while Otto presided from his position at a small table. When hearings were held, the fire apparatus was moved out on the macadam paved street, and benches were placed in the vacated space." It was from this location that Otto Balgemann envisioned a greater Elmhurst.

In 1924 the first paid full-time fireman was employed. He and his family lived upstairs over the fire station that was also City Hall. He was assisted by 25 volunteer firemen. Harry Magers succeeded Henry Hohman as city marshal in 1919 and was shot to death October 30, 1920, by

Harry Magers, city Marshall, and his wife.

robbers who were preying on persons returning from the Masonic Temple dedication. Magers was followed in quick succession by Frank Lloyd, Ed Flynn and Henry Wolf.

In 1925 Wolf was named Chief of Police, assisted by William Trenn, motorcycle policeman. After Trenn was disabled in an accident, Charles Fuller assisted. Other policemen added that year were John Martens, who was Chief of Police from 1927 to 1931, Albert Nelson, and George Kummerow. For the first time policemen wore uniforms. The city marshals had worn badges as their only identification. A 50-trunk switchboard and 25 call boxes were installed. In 1926 a squad car and ambulance patrol wagon were added to police equipment, which had been limited to motorcycles. City offices were moved to 132 Addison Avenue in 1927, giving more room to the Police Department, which had occupied three rooms. By 1929 there were 10 policemen.

In 1930 a City plan commission was created, to consist of the Mayor, President of the Board of Local Improvements, and five citizens, paid $5 for one meeting weekly. The five were: Frank W. Newman, Chester A. Ragland, Emmett M. McQuillan, Grover C. Babcock, and William R. Cadwell. The privately owned water works was taken over by the city in 1931 as one of the last acts of Mayor Balgemann's administration. Otto Balgemann continued his real estate business, and at his last residence, 667 Hawthorne Avenue, celebrated his 80th and 85th birthdays. He had guided the city through the period of recovery from World War I and a rapidly expanding economy into the beginnings of the Great Depression.

Elmhurst grew physically in the first quarter of the twentieth century, but most annexations were in small bits and pieces. The Pick subdivision, opened in the 1920s, included 80 acres fronting St. Charles Road west of Salt Creek, plus 40 acres including the Cottage Hill Cemetery. Tuxedo Park subdivision was plotted in southeast Elmhurst. Expansion was limited on the east by the Cook County line, and on the west by Villa Park, subdivided in 1908 and incorporated as Ardmore in 1914. It became Villa Park in 1917.

In that period suburban growth followed the lines of commuting railroads, with large areas of farm land in between. In Elmhurst homes were sought within walking distance of the Chicago & North Western and the Chicago, Aurora & Elgin.

Elmhurst acquired an airport in 1929 at Lake Street and Church Road. It accommodated training classes, the Moody Bible Institute Flying School, and private planes. It supplied the Elmhurst Post Office with helicopter service from 1946 to 1949. The airport succumbed to urban sprawl and was closed in 1956.

SCHOOLS

The year 1920 was a banner year in school development in Elmhurst for three reasons. First, the board of District 46 had decided Hawthorne School should be rebuilt; it had burned in 1917. Second, because there had already been over-crowding and strain as a result of trying to take care of high school and grade school in one building (and for a period after the fire, the high school students (118) had to convene in the Congregational Church for school classes), a new organization was affected by which High School District No. 88 took over the building of York Community High School on a 23 acre plot that had been the Lathrop farm. When it opened in the Fall of 1920, it had 116 students. The third reason 1920 was an important year is that in that year two women were elected to the District No. 46 School Board; they were Mrs. George Griffin and Mr. Anton Nelson. It may be well stated that this was a singular event as women in office were still unusual in the western suburbs.

Years Of Suburban Expansion

First unit of York Community High School opened in 1920.

As Elmhurst extended into Addison Township, the high school was not entirely a York Township school, hence "community" in the name. But, after eleven major additions it was still crowded and Willowbrook High School was built in Villa Park in 1956. In 1972 the schools were separated and Elmhurst Community Unit District 205 took over direction of York High School and all Elmhurst grade and junior high schools, including Churchville Junior high school, opened in 1969. Yorkfield School, built in 1940, was annexed to the Elmhurst School System in 1959.

The rapid growth of Elmhurst from 4,294 population in 1920 to 50,547 in 1970 necessitated a corresponding increase in schools. Roosevelt School, named for President Theodore Roosevelt, was built in 1922; Washington School in 1928; the new Eugene Field School in 1930. Junior high school started at Hawthorne, enlarged in 1932. Elmhurst Junior High School was built on St. Charles Road, near Poplar, in

Helmut Berens and Carl Sandburg at the rededication of Sandburg Junior High School, May 4, 1960.

1949, later named for Carl Sandburg, poet and Lincoln biographer who lived in Elmhurst from 1919 to 1930. Bryan Junior High School, named for Elmhurst's famed early citizen Thomas Barbour Bryan, opened its doors in 1960.

Eventually there were 15 elementary schools with a student body of 6,400 pupils and 401

Washington School built in 1928

teachers. Jackson School was added in 1952; Jefferson School and Emerson School in 1954; Edison School in 1956; Madison School in 1958; Eldridge School in 1962, followed by Conrad Fischer School, Cornille School, and Crestview School. There has been little pattern in their naming. Presidents honored are Lincoln, Roosevelt, Washington, Jackson, Jefferson and

Eldridge School built in 1962.

Madison, with the naming of Madison influenced by the street on which it is located. Literary figures are Hawthorne, Field, Sandburg and Emerson, and just possibly it was remembered that Ralph Waldo Emerson lectured as far west as Chicago. Edison commemorates Thomas Alva Edison, inventor. Conrad Fischer School was named for a settler who came from Germany to Addison Township in 1834. Cornille School was named for Louis Cornille, school board member, and Crestview for the street on which it is located.

PARKS AND PLAYGROUNDS

The Elmhurst Park District was organized June 5, 1920, as a separate governing body with tax levying powers, and with its boundaries not always coinciding with that of the City. The headquarters for the newly organized Park District was in Wilder Park which remains Park District Headquarters today. Otto Heper was first President, and Commissioners included Thomas W. Claridge, Winfield S. Day, Gertrude A. Golden, and William J. Keimel. The first acquisition was Wilder Park. Louis G. Linnewah was employed as head gardener in 1930 and developed the flower shows in the Conservatory. Miss Caroline Hohmann who served the District as secretary for 30 years was responsible for the "Music under the Stars" program of summer concerts started in 1942.

In Wilder Park the conservatory was built in 1923, the greenhouse in 1926, the Park District Administration Building in 1923 and the recreation building in 1972. Also in the park are the World War I Memorial, the 1893 fire bell dedicated to the men of the Elmhurst Volunteer Fire Department, and the urn that was one of the capstones of the Cook County Court House before the Chicago fire of 1871 and brought to the estate by Seth Wadhams.

Salt Creek Park was acquired in 1927. Its ten acres are used for playgrounds and picnic areas. A camp of the Civilian Conservation Corps (CCC) helped to develop it during the Depression. East End Park, a tract of 18 acres that had been part of the Albert Bucholz farm, was purchased in 1929, and its swimming pool was opened in 1937. Butterfield Park, acquired in 1930, is the site of Memorial Field, a lighted athletic field, built with help from the Lions Club, Evening Women's Club, and the Jaycees. Eldridge Park, named for Edward Eldridge, a pioneer of 1835, was a swamp unsuitable for the construction of buildings when the Park District took it over in 1954. A program of sanitary land-fill received national recognition as a method of reclaiming submarginal land for recreational purposes.

The Elmhurst Recreational Council was organized in 1957 under the leadership of Norma Davenport to co-ordinate planning for the best use of parks and recreational facilities. After a successful campaign to increase the tax rate for the Park District, a full-time executive director was employed in 1960. Ronald Johnson held this post until 1971. He was succeeded after a two-year interim by Mick Pope.

The Board of Commissioners and the park district staff have developed an imaginative and creative program designed for young and old. The program includes sports, crafts, trips, and special interest clubs.

Ben Allison Playground was named for the mayor who served from 1957 to 1961; Berens Park for Helmut Berens, Elmhurst historian; Conrad Fischer Park for the German immigrant of 1836 who had settled in the vicinity of the park, and Plunkett Park for Rt. Rev. Msgr. William J. Plunkett, founder of Immaculate Conception High School. The Abbey, 407 West St. Charles Road, was formerly the Youth Center, dedicated in 1953 and taken over by the Park District in 1964. It is used largely by senior citizens.

A second swimming pool was built at York Commons, York Street and Cayuga Avenue, acquired in 1966, the property formerly being owned by Dramm Greenhouses. Jaycee Tot Lot was landscaped by a gift from the Jaycees in 1970. The Courts, 186 South West Avenue, has courts for indoor tennis, handball, and racketball. Other parks are Crestview Park, Golden Meadows, Jefferson Park, Maple Trail Woods, Pioneer Park, Sleepy Hollow Park, Wild Meadows, and its extension Wild Meadows Trace, following the abandoned Chicago Great Western Railway. The 1887 passenger depot was purchased by the Park District in 1972 and remodeled as a meeting place.

Prairie Path

The Prairie Path following the route of the abandoned Chicago, Aurora & Elgin Railroad is leased from a private corporation and DuPage County, which owns the right-of-way and is operated by a specially chartered corporation.

CHURCHES

The 1900s saw the expansion of the well-established churches and addition of several others.

Over the four year period from 1920-24, the original St. Peter's Church was torn down and a new structure erected on the same site. In the 1920s a number of distinct changes took place in this long-established congregation. The Repke pastorate from 1916-1922 had encouraged a

Years Of Suburban Expansion

larger use of the English language by enlisting new and younger lay leadership, by modernizing the Sunday School, and by promotion of the effort to build a new church. The next pastor of St. Peter's Church was Karl M. Chworowsky. He was a dynamic and modern pastor with strong ideas about church service structure, hymnal use, and Sunday School organization. In these areas he took positive steps to reorder the church. It was also his drive and enthusiasm which saw the actual dedication of the church building. The total cost was an astounding $120,000 as compared to $3,900 in 1877 for the first church building. Reverend Chworowsky was a liberal in social and political outlook and often lectured on these topics. In relation to his achievements within the church from 1922 to 1934, it is said Rev. Chworowsky brought St. Peter's into the American mainstream. It is a mark of St. Peter's recognition of its German heritage that some German services were held at late as 1956. That was during the ministry of the Rev. Edwin Koch. In 1959 St. Peter's remodeled its educational facilities and while our country celebrated its bi-centennial, St. Peter's Church (United Church of Christ) celebrated its centennial year. The Rev. Robert O. Laaser, pastor, shared with the congregation in the celebration.

Among the long established churches, St. Mary's, or Immaculate Conception as it is properly called, knew a renewed growth beginning in the 1920s. The Rev. David McDonald purchased additional property and in 1920 the Rev. P.H. Hennessy built a new school, which was soon overcrowded. In 1928 the Rev. John Foley completed a new church and elementary school. The Rev. William J. Plunkett began his long pastorate in 1932, and three years later opened Immaculate Conception High School. Its building was dedicated in 1950. An eight-room addition to the grammar school was dedicated in 1958 and the Sacred Heart Chapel and Parish Center was started in 1960. A special jubilee mass celebrated Monsignor Plunkett's 60th anniversary as priest June 17, 1976, during the pastorate of the Rev. Arthur J. Maher.

St. Lukes Evangelical Lutheran

St. Luke's Evangelical Lutheran Church had its first meeting in February 1923, at the old Elm Theatre, West First Street, with nine persons present contributing an offering of $1.85. The church was formally organized April 29, with seventeen charter members. The Rev. Carl H. Walter was the first pastor. In 1924 a bungalow chapel was built at North and Larch avenues. A new church was completed in 1961. The Rev. L. Yarger Seibert became pastor in 1931 and served for nearly forty years. He was succeeded by the Rev. Carl H. Obert in 1967.

Epiphany Evangelical Lutheran

Epiphany Evangelical Lutheran Church was organized February 22, 1925 with 17 charter members as the result of a meeting in 1924 with Dr. Thomas B. Hersch, Missionary Superintendent of the Illinois Synod. Services were held in Lincoln School until completion of a chapel at 590 Spring Road, corner of Vallette Street, April 19, 1926. The church on the same site was dedicated June 17, 1947. The first section of the present church was completed in 1955; the fully completed church was dedicated in 1970. During the church's growth, which began with the pastorate of the Rev. Eldon G. Ernst in 1927, the congregation received the Rev. Frobenius, Boldt, Irvin, and Addy as pastors in turn. The Rev. Robert L. Hooker became pastor in 1963.

Redeemer Evangelical Lutheran

Redeemer Evangelical Lutheran Church was founded in October, 1928, by about fifty persons, most of whom had been released by Immanuel Lutheran Church of Elmhurst, and Trinity of Villa Park to form an English Lutheran congregation, affiliated with the Missouri Synod. Services were held in Hawthorne School until the church was dedicated May 18, 1930 at Kenilworth Avenue and St. Charles Road. Educational annexes were completed in 1955 and in 1972. Only three ministers served during this period: Rev. W. H. Setzer, 1928 to 59; Rev. Geo. W. Bornemann, 1959 to 67; and Rev. Richard D. Drews, who has been pastor since 1967.

Grace Bible Church

Grace Bible Church was founded in 1930 by the Rev. Edward Theo. Holtdorf and two laymen. Early meetings were held in a store room on Spring Road. In 1941 Grace Bible Church bought the building at Berkley and Eggleston avenues formerly occupied by the First Baptist Church. An addition was dedicated in 1961. Pastors have included Edwin German, Harry Bryant, Wright Van Plew, Joseph Palmer, Jack McDonald, Elmer F. Fitch, and

Howard L. Brumme, and the Rev. Paul Hunter.

BUSINESS IN THE 1920s

The *Elmhurst, Lombard, and Villa Park City Directory,* dated 1928-29, gave a false impression with its long lists of real estate dealers, architects, 23 building contractors, and numerous contractors for carpentry, cement work, heating, lathing, masonry, plastering, plumbing, sewer and stone work, and even teaming, offered by Louis Hintz, 123 Prospect Avenue. By the time the directory was published, the building boom was over. Failure of the City-State Bank of Chicago left a ghost town in southeast Elmhurst, an area with several blocks of paved streets and sidewalks and imposing houses halted midway in their building. Land titles were tied up in endless litigation, and there was no demand for lots laid out in other subdivisions, some with sidewalks and no streets; some with streets and no sidewalks. As the Depression deepened, no one had money to buy or build.

However, many of the businesses listed in the 1928 directory survived the hard times just ahead. There were seven garages. A Studebaker could be bought from Douglas Chant, a Hudson or an Essex from Crandall Motor Car Co.; a Hupmobile or Packard from E.A. Langkafel, an Oakland or Pontiac from York Motor Sales, a Chevrolet from Anderson Chevrolet & Service, a Dodge from Bright Auto & Repair Co., a Ford from Elmhurst Motor Co., a Paige from Moller Motor Sales, or a Chrysler from Everett Motor Sales. More than half these cars are no longer made. Agencies have moved to areas that were far outside Elmhurst in those days.

There were seven groceries, five meat markets, and two bakeries and the only hint of chain-store supermarkets were the small stores of the Great Atlantic & Pacific Tea Co., and the National Tea Co. There were four drug stores. General stores had disappeared, as had most businesses offering a wide variety of divergent services. Other services no longer were in much demand: the coal yards of Davis Fuel Co., Rothmeyer Coal Co., Elmhurst Lumber & Coal Co., C.H. Casper & Sons, and Omer Rahm; and two laundries, Elmhurst Laundry, 155-161 West First Street and the Schriver Laundry, 107 West First Street. Rabe's Dairy was at 135 East First Street, and beside it Rabe's Field, here softball and other games were played. H.C. Hesse & Co., 105 West First Street, advertised suits with two pants, $25 to $50, and overcoats, $18 to $55. J.W. Ever sold dry goods and notions at 510 Spring Road, and McAllister Pittsfield, dry goods, was moving from 108 West Park Avenue to 136 North York Street.

In 1918, at the close of World War I, Philip Jacob Soukup, Sr., retired from a hardware business in Chicago and bought a house on Kenmore Avenue in Elmhurst. With the Soukup family came a history of interest in tools and hardware. Philip Sr.'s father, Rudolph Soukup, came to the United States from Bohemia about 1850. Rudolph was a blacksmith by trade. Two years after his arrival in Chicago, he began to forge tools such as pliers, screw drivers, and wrenches, making him the first hardware dealer in the family. His shop was on railroad property near where the Sox ballpark now is. Rudolph and his wife had five children, the oldest of whom was Philip Jacob Soukup. In 1905, Philip opened a hardware store on 40th Ct., which he operated for three years while building a hardware and furniture store on Crawford and 14th. In 1918 when Philip Jacob Soukup decided to retire, he sold his Crawford Avenue store to one of his five sons, Erwin. Two years after he retired, Philip Sr., decided he wasn't ready for retirement. Although he looked at new sites in Chicago, Philip Sr. decided to start a new hardware store in Elmhurst with his son Ray. Father, mother, and brother worked in the new store at 116 N. York Street while Philip Jacob Jr. was attending college. He worked in the store after school and on weekends.

Originally the Soukup store occupied only a small portion of what is Soukup's Elmhurst

The Asing store at 116 North York Street in 1913. The building is now occupied by Soukup's Hardware.

store today. The store was a small part of the first floor, and the second floor was a family apartment until 1927. It was then needed for the expanding business. By that time Philip Jacob Jr. had joined his brothers, Ray and Ted, full-time in the business. It was not long until the now well-known expansions of Soukup, or Soukup connected hardware stores began all over DuPage County. On the death of Philip Sr., Philip Jacob Jr. took over management of the Elmhurst store with the help and cooperation of Herb Weinbauer a brother-in-law. Ted and a nephew established a store in Glen Ellyn; Ray established a store in Hinsdale.

Philip Jr., had four sons. One son, David, is a Superior Court judge in Seattle. The other three sons followed the family tradition in business; stores were established by Jack in Geneva and then Aurora. In addition to these there is a store in Naperville, operated by a nephew Frank Lisjak and one in Wheaton which was started by Erwin Soukup, when he sold his Chicago store. This store is now operated by his son Vernon. The Elmhurst store, said to be the third largest hardware store in the state, celebrated its 50th anniversary in 1970. There are fifteen Soukup grandchildren, eleven of whom are boys, assuring continuances of the Soukup Hardware business for the foreseeable future.

THEATRES

In 1911 the first movie theatre in Elmhurst was established on the east side of South York Street next to the Heineman store. It cost five cents to watch the *Perils of Pauline* while sitting on a straight back chair. The Elms Theatre on First Street was started by Tom Hawkins who was then city clerk. John Deis of Wheaton managed the theatre for Mr. Hawkins from 1913 to 1918. Evelyn Davis added to the entertainment with piano accompaniment for the films.

The York Theatre was built in 1924 at 156 North York Street, winning over patrons of the Elms Theatre on West First Street. In the early days of silent films, Lew Harvey was featured at the organ and there were occasional stage shows. On Saturday afternoons long lines of youngsters crowded sidewalks waiting for doors to open to see westerns of Tim McCoy and Hoot Gibson and comedies of Charlie Chaplin. To keep crowds coming in Depression days there were bonuses of sets of books or dishes. George Kappus, who came to Elmhurst

The Elms Theatre, West First Street near York, showed only silent films.

as a pharmacist, was manager of the theatre for many years and still retained an interest in its ownership when he celebrated his 100th birthday in 1976.

WOMEN ORGANIZED

Characteristic of organizations that grew up in the early years of the 20th century was emphasis on cultural, educational, and philanthropic purposes and affiliation with national or international groups with similar purposes. An example is the Elmhurst Woman's Club, formed in 1913 in the home of Mrs. George Griffin, who became its first president. It has departments on home and education, community service, Americanism, literature, art, and music, thus combining what might have been a number of local clubs. It is affiliated with the General Federation of Woman's Clubs, and federations representing the State, Congressional District and DuPage County. The charter membership was 50, and meetings were held in private homes. As the club grew to 250 members, it required a larger meeting place; the First Methodist Church is used currently. The club backed programs for the city water supply, community high school, the Memorial Hospital, the Elmhurst Public Library, including a memorial book collection, and scholarships. Mrs. Oakley Morgan undertook a collection of slides of early Elmhurst, donated to the Elmhurst Historical Museum in 1954.

The Elmhurst Evening Woman's Club was originally the Junior Woman's Club, organized in 1926 with Hazel Stevens Dame as first president, sponsored by the Elmhurst Woman's Club and taking its present name in 1926. It built and equipped the Wilder Park Skating Rink, aided the fund for lighting athletic fields, built a stage and repaired the heating plant for the Elmhurst Youth Center, purchased the mobile bandwagon, and provided playground equipment for York Commons. It has a scholarship program and has given financial aid to many civic projects.

The Elmhurst Garden Club was originally the garden group of the Civics Department of Elmhurst Woman's Club, started in 1926 with Mrs. W.R. Corlett, chairman. Its first flower show opened September 14, 1927, under the chairmanship of Mrs. H.L. Breitenbach. The group was reorganized in 1929, under the presidency of Mrs. John A. Golden as the Elmhurst Garden Club, affiliated with the Woman's Club but responsible for its own finances and programs. It also affiliated with the Illinois Garden Club. It presented a memorial library of books on nature and gardening to the Elmhurst Public Library, and maintains flower and plant arrangements and Christmas decorations at the library. It also maintains gardens around railroad tracks and stations and highway interchanges. Many of the club's flowers and plants go to the Bensenville Home and the DuPage Convalescent and Nursing Center. A bird-feeding station is maintained in Wilder Park.

The Woman's Choral Group started in 1920 as a department of the Elmhurst Woman's Club with Mrs. Richard De Young as president. She served until 1925. Under directorship of Marian Ransteat and Helen Leefelt, and later Mr. Harry Walsh, and with Elsa Chandler Fischer as accompanist, the group of sixty singers sang annually for the Sunday Evening Club at Orchestra Hall, gave several concerts at the Chicago World's Fair of 1933-1934, and gave annual concerts in Elmhurst. The choral group was dissolved in 1956, leaving a fund for music scholarships to be administered by the Woman's Club.

PEO Sisterhood has three chapters in Elmhurst, FZ, founded in 1944 under the leadership of Mattie Anderson; HY, organized in 1952; and JU in 1961. PEO is a charitable and educational organization interested principally in bringing to women greatly increased opportunities for higher education. This is accomplished through three philanthropies - The PEO Educational Fund, the International Peace scholarship and the Cottey Junior College for Women in Nevada, Missouri.

PUBLIC HEALTH

A Board of Health was established under village government in 1896, consisting of Dr. George F. Heidemann, president; George W. Griffin, secretary; and Dr. F.H. Bates, commissioner. City government took over the board June 5, 1911, which at that time included Mayor Schumacher, Dr. F.H. Bates, L. Marks, Dr. E.W. Marquardt, and F.W. Sandiland. In 1923, Dr. L.H. Hills was commissioner, and Mrs. Ruby Seivers was employed as nurse for both public and parochial schools. In 1928 Miss Margaret Piggott was employed as nurse for north side schools. Dr. Frank D. Leahy became commissioner in 1929.

Mary C. Creighton, R.N. came to Elmhurst in 1932. She began as a school nurse, but after taking over as city nurse, she served in that position for more than 40 years. She was known to the police as the "one woman welfare department"; she gathered food, clothing and toys for needy families every Christmas. Her commitment to welfare and social work was lifelong for she worked for the City in the police department as a full-time matron. Mary Creighton received citations for outstanding work from the Elmhurst Police Department, the American Legion, the Lions Club, and Press Publications.

Dr. Franklin T. James was commissioner in 1931, with Dr. Harold Hague and Fred H. Gerberding on the board. Dr. A.L. Mathis was commissioner in 1933 with Dr. E.S. Watson, assistant; and Fred Runge, health officer. Dr. Leahy returned as commissioner in 1936 with Dr. H.L. Schultz as assistant. It was not until 1931 that birth certificates were issued by the board. Its duties were largely advisory, but in one respect the Board of Health was highly visible. In those days strict quarantine was enforced and a card of warning was tacked on every house where anyone was ill of diphtheria, scarlet fever, measles, chicken pox, mumps, or whooping cough, and that card could not be taken down until the house had been fumigated with formaldehyde. It was boasted in 1936 that Elmhurst had not had a case of small pox in many years, and that other diseases had been cut to a much lower rate. Innoculation against most of these diseases was a development during this period.

MEMORIAL HOSPITAL

A campaign for a hospital for Elmhurst was started in 1921 by Dr. Edward W. Marquardt,

Dr. E.W. Marquardt (1876-1958).

Ira A. Stone, and Julius Breuhaus, soon joined by Edwin F. Deicke, Alben F. Bates, and Fred B. Snite. In January, 1923, the Elmhurst Hospital board of directors was elected, including Otto W. Balgemann, Leo D. Canfield, Paul Dolle, Alonzo G. Fischer, William Hammerschmidt, A.L. Luessenhop, Henry C. Schumacher, Fred B. Snite, H.C. Wendland, Dr. C.F. Glasener, Dr. Henry F. Langhorst, Dr. J.H. Raach, Dr. Richard Schiele, and Dr. Marquardt. Construction started in 1925 and the building was dedicated October 10, 1926. It became Elmhurst Community Hospital, later Elmhurst Memorial Hospital, and as its field of service expanded it was renamed Memorial Hospital of DuPage County.

Dr. Marquardt, who had practiced in Elmhurst since 1905, was the prime mover in the hospital project. He served as president and chairman of its board, established the Marquardt Memorial Library in the hospital, and in his will left a legacy for the hospital's continuance.

The original building at Schiller Street and Avon Road is almost lost in the medical center with 451-bed capacity that stretches to Berteau Avenue and Third Street and well into Second Street and Elmhurst Avenue. Its emergency service system is among the most extensive and active in Illinois, fully staffed at all hours. Its

Original unit of Memorial Hospital, dedicated 1926.

South view of Memorial Hospital of DuPage County, 1966. The name was changed in 1948 from Elmhurst Memorial Hospital to Memorial Hospital.

basic services are general medical, surgery, pediatrics, obstetrics and gynecology. There are also an infectious disease facility, cardiac care unit, and intensive care unit. Memorial Hospital has pioneered in disaster preparedness. The hospital pharmacy maintains a community poison control center. The hospital employs 1,300 persons and its staff includes 200 physicians. It receives no tax support, operating as a nonsectarian not-for-profit corporation, governed by a volunteer board of directors.

The Stevens Renal Dialysis Unit was dedicated in 1975, honoring the hospital governor, Chris Stevens, and the Stevens family. A four-level Diagnostic and Treatment Center is scheduled for completion in 1978. Also planned are a 20-bed psychiatric unit and renovation of west and south wings.

The Elmhurst Memorial Hospital Guild was organized in 1929 with Mrs. Charles Larson as president. Membership totals 1,530 including the Elmhurst Junior Auxiliary and units in Villa Park, Lombard, Glen Ellyn, Wheaton, North DuPage, Addison and Oak Brook. Volunteers donate 45,000 hours' work a year to the hospital and fund-raising activities have netted nearly two million dollars. Mrs. Robert Terwedo helped organize the Hospital Gift Shop and was its manager for 22 years. The Pink Elephant Gift Shop in Villa Park has raised $105,000 for the hospital. An entertainment program "Cardiac Capers '76" was highly successful. The Guild Sewing Ladies make pink elephants called "Snuggles" as gifts for very young patients. Mrs. Dorothy Marquardt supervises the Remembrance Fund. Mrs. Marquardt (founder Marquardt's widow) received the Jaycees 1974 Distinguished Service Award for her untiring devotion to the hospital.

Mrs. Raphael A. Raab, daughter of past mayor, Henry Schumacher, and a long-time active member of the Memorial Hospital Guild succeeded Mrs. Marquardt as chairman of the Remembrance Fund.

DECADE OF STANDING STILL

The population of Elmhurst increased from 14,055 in 1930 to 15,458 in 1940, so slow a rate of increase as to seem standing still. In those years of the Great Depression, the entire country seemed to be standing still, if not moving backward. Building had stopped; carpenters, brick layers, plasterers, plumbers were idle. Real estate dealers could find no buyers for the many vacant lots around the city, and citizens were invited to plant gardens on them, both during the Depression and the shortages of the war years that followed. Mortgages were unpaid, and there was little point in foreclosing on them when there were no buyers. Taxes were unpaid, and parents rang doorbells selling tax anticipation warrants to keep the schools open. Jobless parents took in their jobless married sons and daughters, which may account for some of the small increase in population. In one such household, only one of five adults was employed, an unmarried daughter; her paycheck was minimal. Jobless executives peddled cakes and cookies, baked by their wives, or worked their vegetable gardens. Almost all of those who were working took a 10 per cent cut in pay.

Elmhurst was fortunate in the stability of its banks. While banks were tumbling all over Chicago and in western suburbs, Elmhurst had no bank failures. In 1930 the First National Bank took in the People's Trust & Savings Bank, and in 1931 merged with the Elmhurst State Bank and moved to the State Bank's new five-story building, built in 1927 at York Street and Park Avenue. Bank closings reached a crisis at the time of the inauguration of Franklin D. Roosevelt as President. One of his first acts was to declare a national bank holiday, closing all banks until they could be examined; when approved, deposits were insured by the Federal Deposit Insurance Corporation. The Elmhurst State Bank came through the crisis promptly, and in 1939 was federally chartered as the Elmhurst National Bank. Many attributed this to

The five-story Elmhurst State Bank Building, built in 1927 on the site of the private bank of Henry L. Glos, south east corner of York Street and Park Avenue.

German thrift and conservatism, and it may be. Henry C. Schumacher had succeeded Adam S. Glos as president in 1926. Albert Glos, nephew of Henry and Adam, became president in 1936 and served until 1952.

President Roosevelt was universally applauded during his first one hundred days for setting up federal agencies to handle the various economic problems. The Blue Eagle of the National Recovery Administration (NRA) was seen everywhere; in store windows, on packages, in advertising; until the Supreme Court put an end to the NRA in 1935. A Civilian Conservation Corps camp was established along Salt Creek near North Avenue; later a second camp was built farther down Salt Creek near the Graue Mill. The CCC was made up of jobless young men and war veterans, administered by the U.S. Army, which called up jobless Reserve Officers to help out. The CCC was used in reforestation, drainage and erosion control.

Edward H. Blatter was elected mayor of Elmhurst in 1931. Blatter was born in Olney,

Edward H. Blatter, mayor (1931-1933).

Illinois, June 16, 1880, but grew up in Chicago and was graduated from the International School of Sanitary Service. He was an undertaker in Forest Park for 18 years before retiring in 1928. He then moved to Elmhurst and opened a real estate office in Villa Park. He was elected on the Independent ticket and three aldermen of that party were elected with him. He named Walter Pflaume as chief of police.

The new administration immediately faced the problems of the depth of the Depression. In 1932 the Elmhurst Welfare Relief Committee was established, its chairman to be named by the Mayor and Council, and its membership to consist of one representative from each of the religious, social, and fraternal organizations. All funds collected were deposited with the City Treasurer and disbursed by him on the written order of the committee. Pay for relief workers was set at 30 cents an hour, raised to 40 cents by resolution of November 21, 1932. The Council on December 19, 1932, authorized expenditure of $500 for coal for the needy, to be distributed by the Welfare Relief Committee.

The pay of city employees was cut by 10 per cent by action of the City Council, March 13, 1933, with the further provision that all employees not on the city payroll in 1932 should be discharged and that no greater number should be employed than composed the staff in 1932. In May the Council borrowed money from the Special Assessment Fund to pay city employees. Tax anticipation warrants were issued by the City Council, December 3, 1934.

In 1933 the Elmhurst Unemployed Co-operative Association requested that the city give first consideration to men on relief for employment as city workers, to which the Council agreed. That spring the association adopted a gardens project and asked for the loan of the city's tractor. In 1935 the Elmhurst Workers Alliance asked the city to allow men on relief to work out the price of auto licenses, and this was granted. During the Depression, many men were put to work at tree trimming in parks and driveways; the collected dead wood supplemented the coal provided for winter heat, for in those days most people depended on hot air furnaces.

The City Council, December 3, 1934, applied for funds from the Federal Emergency Administration (FEA) to be used for work on water reservoirs and pumping equipment. An application for funds to build a swimming pool in East End Park was turned down. In 1935 the City Council accepted funds from the Works Progress Administration (WPA) for water mains and a sewage treatment plant, and in 1936 for storm sewers.

An organization peculiar to the Depression era was the Elmhurst Townsend Club, organized in 1935. It was the first in DuPage County. Its guidelines were the proposals of Dr. Francis E. Townsend of California for a $200 a month old-age pension to be spent within a limited period to aid the economy. When the Elmhurst club celebrated its tenth anniversary March 20, 1945, in Mahler Hall, membership was reported at 140, with a loss by death of 54 members. Among early officers of the club were Henry F. Hobein, John J. Lookabaugh, Mrs. Edna McGinnis, C.O. McGinnis, Mrs. Albert Peters, Mrs. A.L. Schafer, Emil J. Johnson, W.S. Clark, and Fred Stevens.

It is generally accepted that the Depression began when the stock market began its plunge, October 21, 1929, but when did it end? The Elmhurst National Bank's 60th anniversary booklet, *The Story of a Bank*, says that the Depression lasted five years, but we have overrun that period. It may have been pin-pointed by an Addison Avenue merchant early in 1939 who said, "A customer was in here this morning telling about his hard times back during the Depression. Is the Depression over?" Recovery came so gradually that no one could be sure.

POLITICAL PARTIES

Elmhurst being consistently Republican, had divorced its city government from national partisanship by forming local parties, which left few records as they came and went with little continuity as new issues arose or defeats became too discouraging. When Mayor Hammerschmidt was re-elected in 1913, he was endorsed by the Republican Party, the Democratic Party, and the Independent Citizens Party, an era of good feelings that may have marked the end of national parties on city election ballots. In 1919 the People's Party was founded and elected Otto Balgemann as mayor and Claude Van Auken as one of the aldermen. In 1933 the People's Party elected Van Auken to succeed Blatter as mayor. A short-lived Non-Partisan Party was defeated in the election of 1937. The Citizen's Party was organized in 1945, and in 1958 merged with the United Party, formed in 1937, as the Citizens-United Party.

Claude Van Auken, elected mayor in 1933, served continuously until 1945, through years of

Elmhurst City Council — 1941

Elmhurst City Hall, 134 Addison Avenue, 1941.

Claude L. Van Auken, mayor (1933-1945).

Depression and war. He was born in Delaware County, Ohio, in 1886, and grew up in Clinton, Iowa. He was graduated from the University of Wisconsin in civil engineering in 1910, worked for the North Western and the St. Paul railroads, and was editor and publisher of *Mass Transportation,* a trade magazine of the Kenfield and Davis Publishing Company. He moved to Elmhurst in 1918 and became active in civic and political affairs. He died June 16, 1976, in Salinas, California, at the age of 90.

During Van Auken's administration, George Kummerow was named Chief of Police. Police Headquarters had been moved to Addison Avenue in 1932 and a request for an addition to the

Elmhurst Fire Department Headquarters, 116 Schiller Street, 1940.

police station was denied because of lack of funds. However, the police department was authorized to purchase a Plymouth sedan for $495 in December, 1932. Chief Kummerow reported that during November, 1934, there were 21 men on the police force; and that they had responded to 314 calls, including 44 accidents, 30 arrests, 4 felonies, and 236 miscellaneous complaints.

In 1934 voters approved the creation of a Board of Fire and Police Commissioners to supervise the work of the two departments. The first board included Walter R. Youngberg, Matthew R. Thorneycroft, and Thomas E. McDonough. In 1942 Commissioner Thorneycroft was named chief of police in charge of administrative policies and Kummerow was promoted to captain, responsible for active operations. The police force then numbered ten men. The South Side Fire House, Vallette and Division streets, was built in 1941 to hold one piece of apparatus. The Police Pension Fund was established in 1944.

In 1936 the City of Elmhurst built an activated, mechanized sludge - sewage disposal plant on one and one-half acres of a five acre site south of St. Charles Road on Route 83. The cost was $450,000, federally financed for $250,000 over a twenty-year period with a bond issue covering the remainder. The Park District maintains a playground in front of the plant, including an ice skating rink.

Salaries for city officials, which had been nominal when city business was minimal, were raised in 1936: the mayor from $250 to $1,200 a year; the city attorney from $300 to $1,200; and aldermen, who had been paid $5 a meeting, were put on an annual salary of $300 a year.

ELMHURST CENTENNIAL

The Elmhurst Centennial was celebrated June 3 to 13, 1936, with a program of parades, pageants, sports, band concerts, a flower show, dancing in the streets, and contests. A bronze tablet marking the original site of Hill Cottage Tavern was unveiled by Martha Ibbetson Chapter, D.A.R., Mrs. Frank Thomas, chairman. Dr. Harlan Tarbell gave a magic show. The pageant, written by Mrs. Rosamond Du Jardin, had a cast of hundreds. A melodrama, *Gold in the Hills,* was given by the Community Players, Joseph Murray, director. Historical exhibits were in store windows. The huge parade hailed as the biggest ever staged by a Chicago suburb, included bands and drum and bugle corps from the Chicago area and many far-distant places. Souvenir badges were sold and a booklet, *100 Years of Elmhurst News*, was issued. The Elmhurst Centennial Commission, appointed by Mayor Van Auken, included Dr. J. Christian Bay, chairman; Otto W. Balgemann, A.D. Barnes, Alben F. Bates, H.H. Robillard, Mrs. Oakley V. Morgan, and Frank J. Maier.

HIGHLANDS CLUB

In 1932 residents of Berteau, Clinton, and Geneva avenues in northeast Elmhurst formed the Elmhurst Highlands Community Club. Seeking a challenging cause, members in 1938 suggested Halloween vandalism as a subject meriting attention. Halloween is a mysterious observance, its traditions passed on by generations of children with no reference to their elders. Only a boy knew how to make a tick-tack by notching a wooden spool, putting a stick through the hole, and wrapping the spool in a length of stout string. When the notches were placed against a window and the string jerked stoutly, a delightful noise was made. It was seldom that the window was broken, and that was not the intent.

Soaping windows was favored by Elmhurst children. On Halloween night York Street was thronged with boys and girls, each clutching part of a bar of Fels Naphtha laundry soap, seeking any vacancy where a final swipe could be given to a much-soaped window. Elmhurst merchants bowed to the inevitable and offered prizes for the best decorated glass, but it is not of record that any great artist was thus uncovered. No city could have been cleaner then Elmhurst on November 1 when all windows were washed - with plenty of soap.

These rites were relatively harmless, but with the obsolescence of wooden spools, the unavailability of corn and cabbages to be thrown on porches, and soap doomed in detergents, youngsters might find more destructive outlets for their energies. The Highland Club met the crisis head-on, and solved the problem. A huge parade was organized to wind through the three avenues, culminating at Rabe's Field on First Street where prizes were awarded for the most original costumes, and entertainment offered. By the time this was over, it was too late for the assembled and regimented urchins to do any extended damage to neighborhood property. The 1938 program was a huge success, and was almost immediately adopted by the entire city.

About this time another element, universally known as Trick or Treat, was added to Halloween tradition. The custom of giving eatables to masquers is as old as *La Gui-annee,* the New Year's festival of 18th century French settlers in Prairie du Rocher in southern Illinois, yet so new that Trick or Treat was sometimes denounced, circa 1938, as blackmail, extortion, and bribery. Yet so successful was this salutary phrase that the Trick alternative lost all meaning or connotation. Trick or Treat was hailed throughout Chicago and its metropolitan area as the solution to the Halloween problem - except in Elmhurst where the problem had been solved. The civic establishment, not daring to meddle in the traditions of childhood, each year solemnly proclaims the night preceding Halloween as Trick or Treat Night.

A more serious problem of public policy was faced by the Highland Club when it became a forum for discussion of a proposal offered by Hills Bros. Coffee Company for erection of a plant in Elmhurst. A petition was filed November 2, 1938, only two days after the Halloween parade, to rezone 37-1/2 acres for industrial purposes. This vacant area was north of the North Western tracks to about where Schiller Street would extend beyond Geneva Avenue, at that time the last street in town, and stretching on toward the Proviso yards, with the northern wye-track of the C. & N.W. within screeching distance. This field had a legend all its own that should be recorded. It is said that Charles Lindbergh's plane, *The Spirit of St. Louis,* had landed there and stayed several days. This was after the famous Lindbergh flight across the Atlantic, but long before the historic plane went to the Smithsonian Institution. The story was that a friend of Lindbergh's had borrowed the plane to visit Elmhurst. Children from Eugene Field School trooped to see it and maintained it was indeed *The Spirit of St. Louis,* but there seems to be no public record of the event.

President Hills of Hills Bros., presented his plan to the Highland Club, November 8. The surrounding area was to be landscaped, with tennis courts and other park facilities open to the public. In this Depression era, the taxes paid by an industry would have been useful, but one or two members from Geneva Avenue voiced opposition to a zoning change although the greenhouses of Wendland & Keimel Company, wholesale florists, faced the site just across the tracks. When it was proposed to take a vote, Mr. Hills demurred; if there was any opposition at all, he would withdraw the petition, which he did on December 12. An Elmhurst industrial park was postponed for three decades.

Ervin F. Wilson, a prime mover in organizing the Highland Club, was elected alderman in 1935, and E.A. Whitney, also active in the club, was elected alderman in 1939. This movement resulted in organization of the Citizens Party in 1945, when William H. Fellows was elected mayor to succeed Van Auken.

The business community remained fairly stable during the Depression years, perhaps because it had not expanded as rapidly as had the population during the previous decade. There were failures, of course, and a few successes. One example of both is a 1928 listing of Harry L. Ollswang, dry goods and general merchandise, 116-118 Park Avenue. Ten years later it was Ollswang's, Inc., Department Store, expanded to 106-118 Park Avenue, and eventually all the way to York Street. After the death of Mr. Ollswang, the business was taken over by his son-in-law, Richard Levinson. After Mr. Levinson's death, the store closed. Across the tracks on First Street, the Elm Department store started with a single store front and successfully expanded to its 1976 dimensions.

Irwin Ruby, who came to Elmhurst in 1943 began operating Ruby's Department store at 149 North York Street in 1947. Mr. Ruby, active in community affairs, aided in the Elmhurst Youth Center and served as President of the board. He was one of the founders of the Y.M.C.A., the Chamber of Commerce, and the Heart of Elmhurst Council. Ruby was responsible for the printing of the WPA *DuPage County Guide.*

ORGANIZATIONS OF THE 1930s

A necessity in early years of the Depression was some means of co-ordinating the work of various social, welfare, and charitable groups, especially in their fund-raising campaigns. Organization of the Elmhurst Community Chest, September 9, 1930, followed a national trend. The first directors were Mrs. George H. Johnston, Mrs. J.H. Earle, Mrs. Arden Nance, Mrs. D.H. Kinnett, Daniel D. Curtis, Ted Bright, Walter Beher, Claude L. Van Auken, and Lee E. Daniels. Elmhurst Community Chest now budgets $100,000 yearly to Boy Scouts, Campfire Girls, Catholic Charities, Community Nursing Service, Family Service Association of DuPage County, Girl Scouts, Ray Graham Association for the Handicapped, YMCA and YWCA.

The League of Women Voters of Elmhurst was organized November 16, 1932, by 21 charter members meeting in the home of Mrs. Edwin Koehler. The first money-raiser, a play given by Camp Fire Girls, netted $24 in 1935. The League's objective is to give voters factual and impartial information about candidates. Publications include *This Is DuPage,* about county government, and *Know Your Town,* about Elmhurst, first prepared in 1939. Observers attend meetings of local government units. The League supported a County Health Department, 1945; Elmhurst sewer separation, 1964; Elmhurst Human Relations Commission, 1967-68; recycling center, 1971; the Illinois Constitutional Convention, 1970; and Elmhurst underpass, 1974.

The Elmhurst Branch of the American Association of University Women was organized November 20, 1938, at the Congregational Church Community House with Mrs. Twitty Whaley as temporary chairman. Mrs. Carlyle Selden was elected president; other officers included Miss Louise Ruebling, Miss Edith Thompson, Mrs. Charles Berry, Miss Janet Nelson, and Mrs. Whaley. There were 56 charter members. The Association operated the Exchange Shop Retail Store from 1943 to 1945. A nursery school, Buttons and Bows, was founded in 1958 and expanded to four sessions at two locations. In 1971 the Educational Resource Volunteers project was formed to offer special knowledge and talents to school classrooms. Some 180 volunteers take part. District No. 205 supervises this program. An annual used book sale raises funds for the association's Educational Foundation. The Elmhurst Branch has also worked for establishment of the Prairie Path and the recycling center.

The Elmhurst Panhellenic was organized November 6, 1931, meeting in members' homes and making scrapbooks for the Illinois Children's Home and Aid Society. Since 1951 meetings have been held in the library of York High School. A scholarship program was started in 1933. Annual events include a Sorority Information Tea for high school seniors, Fall Scholarship Luncheon, September Potluck Supper, Winter Dance, March Card Party, and May Banquet.

The Elmhurst College Women's Auxiliary had its start December 29, 1919, at a meeting of faculty wives called by Mrs. H.J. Schick, wife of the college president. It has developed from "a women's sewing circle" to a service organization with membership of 280 individuals and 66 organizations. Annually it awards two $1,000 scholarships, offers two $250 grants-in-aid, and gives financial aid toward college facilities.

A new type of organization that developed in the early years of the twentieth century was that commonly known as the luncheon club. Membership was restricted to one representative of each business or profession, giving it a broad base of interests. As they adopted civic and charitable objectives, they also became known as service clubs.

The Kiwanis Club of Elmhurst was organized in 1931 under leadership of Mayor Edward Blatter. Its annual Pancake Day in Spring and Peanut Day in September help to support many programs: Little League Baseball, Hockey, and Football; three annual $350 scholarships, spastic research, Elmhurst College Speech Clinic; Ray Graham Rehabilitation Center, Boneparte School; sponsorship of a foster child in Ecuador, "Meals on Wheels" for aged and handicapped, and assistance to bed-ridden children and children with learning disabilities. The Kiwanis Club of Elmhurst sponsored organization of the Kiwanis Club of Greater Elmhurst, founded in 1956 with Howard A. Aldrich, president, and 35 charter members.

Elmhurst Lions Club, an affiliate of Lions International, was organized in 1940 with Miller Keyes as president and 46 members. It has grown to 75 active members. Its major effort is sight conservation and aid to the visually handicapped and those with hearing impairment. The club brings a Glaucomobile to Elmhurst annually and mans the S.O.S. (Save Our Sight) Clinic. Candy Days and Broom Sales aid in raising $8,000 to $10,000 yearly for these programs. The Elmhurst Lioness Club was organized in 1944 in the home of Dr. and Mrs. C.O. Evanson. The women send handicapped children to Camp Lions and assist in other activities of the Lions Club.

ELMHURST AND THE ARTS

THE AGE OF CARL SANDBURG

Carl Sandburg lived in Elmhurst from 1919 to 1930, his most productive years. When he arrived he was known as a poet, controversial because of his subject matter and because he was a leading practitioner of free verse. Forever after his Elmhurst years, he was to be remem-

Carl Sandburg (1878-1967).

bered primarily as the Lincoln biographer but also as a troubadour, a singer of folk songs, and as a writer of stories for children. Carl, christened Charles, was born in Galesburg, Illinois, January 6, 1878, the son of Swedish immigrants. His father, a blacksmith's helper in railroad shops, could and did read but never bothered to learn to write. Carl drove a milk wagon, shined shoes in a barber shop, and read poetry, biographies, and *Cyclopedia of Important Facts* and *A History of the World and Its Great Events*, which his mother bought for him from book agents. He traveled West as a hobo, enlisted in the 6th Illinois Infantry for the Spanish-American War, and attended Lombard College where he joined "Poor Writers Club" sparked by Professor Philip Green Wright. *In Reckless Ecstacy*, published in Galesburg in 1904, was a book Sandburg preferred to forget. He was secretary to the Socialist mayor of Milwaukee, 1910-12, then came to Chicago, wrote for *System* and N.D. Cochran's *Daybook*, and attained prominence in the free verse movement with *Chicago Poems*, 1915, and its perenially quoted lines on "Hog Butcher for the World..." *Cornhuskers* followed in 1918 by which time, Sandburg was employed by *The Chicago Daily News*. His reports on *The Chicago Race Riots* of 1919 were reprinted as a book.

Considering this background, conservative and Republican Elmhurst may have looked askance at the Sandburgs when they moved from Maywood to 331 South York Street, one of the city's oldest houses, built by Peter Torode in the 1850s. Fellow townsmen were disturbed by Carl's Socialist friends, Eugene V. Debs and Emil Seidel, and by his rebel and nonconformist free verse, further exemplified in *Smoke and Steel*, 1920, and *Slabs of the Sunburst West*, 1922. Yet is was noted that there was no hint of violence in anything he wrote.

Carl and Lillian Steichen were married in Milwaukee in 1908; her parents John P. and Mary Steichen lived at 245 South York Street, Elmhurst. Lillian's brother Edward was a famous photographer. Carl wrote about him in *Steichen the Photographer*, 1929, during the Elmhurst years, and collaborated with him in a "Road to Victory" exhibit shown at the Museum of Modern Art, New York, and across the country in 1932. Another Steichen exhibit, "The Family of Man," won wide acclaim in 1955. Steichen died March 25, 1973, in West Redding, Connecticut.

Happiness House, 331 South York Street, Carl Sandburg residence from 1919-1930.

Nearby families of Alexander Warren, Harry Grass, Sr., Lee Sturges, and Miles Sater found the Sandburgs good neighbors. The daughters Margaret, Janet, and Helga went to Hawthrone School and Mrs. Sandburg was active in the P.T.A. Their home, a little white house with a wooden fence around it, was dubbed *Happiness House*. Harry Hansen, book critic, wrote that Sandburg had hidden himself away in one of those wooded villages that has slipped out from under the pall of smoke and fumes that hovers over Chicago. Carl's second-floor back workroom had little square window panes looking out over a roof to trees and a barn. His flat-topped desk was flanked by pine shelves made by Carl and full of books. He had acquired army surplus metal record cans which he filled with notes and clippings. Nearby was a cot, covered with a Navajo blanket, on which he napped after working late. At hand was his guitar, for Carl had begun his exhibition tours as a singer of songs. Amy Lowell came by and wrote:

> Tonight I saw an evening moon
> Dodging between tree branches
> Through a singing silence of
>   of crickets
> And a man was singing songs
>   to a black-backed guitar.

One complaint of neighbors was that Carl kept them awake pounding his typewriter well into the night, then slept all morning. It might be wondered when he found time for his work at *The Daily News*. He wrote reviews of movies, but that lasted only a couple of years. At times he covered the labor beat and features on special assignment. Henry Justin Smith, managing editor, had a high tolerance for anyone he regarded as genius and came up with a feature called "Carl Sandburg's Notebook" which ran two or three times a week. When editor Don Russell moved the "Notebook" from the feature page to the editorial page, he was surprised at Carl's warm appreciation for getting a spot with more prestige.

Schlogl's Restaurant near the Daily News Building was a popular rendezvous, and Harry Hansen tells of Carl coming by one day with some stories he had been telling to his daughters and trying them out on Keith Preston, Henry Blackman Sell, Jerome Frand, and Carlton Washburne. They urged him to submit them to his publisher, and they became *Rootabaga Stories* in 1922, the first of his books for children, followed by *Rootabaga Pigeons*, 1923, and *Potato Face*, 1930. A collection of poems for children, *Early Moon*, was also published in 1930.

Karl Detzer, biographer, says that *Rootabaga Stories* was the only book for which Sandburg asked an advance on royalties. He wanted $600 to complete a deal to buy the lot next door to prevent having "a house we do not care to look at slammed close to us." Wrote Carl to Alfred Harcourt: "If you can find this $600 it will go into good land. It has two marvelous sugar maples in front. At the rear it has the biggest incomparable lilac bush in Northern Illinois. It is the only place I have ever found glow worms, I spaded it all and raised sweet corn year before last. Our cats have their kittens there in special sunny lying-in corners. So you see we know what we are getting." He got the money.

Abraham Lincoln: The Prairie Years, was published in two large volumes in 1926, about midway in his Elmhurst years. It was immediately acclaimed by critics as an outstanding biography. Part of the work on its sequel was done in Elmhurst, but *Abraham Lincoln: The War Years*, in four huge volumes, was not published until 1939. *The American Songbag*, a collection of the ballads and folksongs he sang with his guitar, appeared in 1927, and *Good Morning, America,* a book of poems, in 1928. *Abe Lincoln Grows Up,* 1928, was derived from

The Prairie Years, and an abridgement of it was published in 1929. In later years the Lincoln volumes were mined for other abridgements and combinations. There were also varied collections of poems. The autobiographical *Always the Young Strangers* and his only novel, came late, but it may safely be said that the bulk of his original work was pounded out on the typewriter upstairs on York Street. By 1930 he found Elmhurst growing too fast, traffic on York Street too frequent and too noisy and moved to Harbert, Michigan. Had he been patient, he might have found that Elmhurst was not destined to grow much more in a decade and a half of Depression and war. They moved to Harbert, Michigan, from which he commuted and Mrs. Sandburg started a goat farm. Later they moved to Flat Rock, North Carolina, where they called their home Connemara Farms. There he died July 22, 1967, at the age of 89.

The Sandburg house lasted a few years longer, but along with the incomparable lilac bush, the glow worms, and the lying-in corners for cats, it eventually gave way to a parking lot. When a Junior High School was being built in 1949, Fred C. Evers, collector and authority on Illinois and Elmhurst history, suggested that it be named for Sandburg, but at that time the suggestion was rejected. However, when a second junior high school was built, the old one at St. Charles Road near Poplar became the Sandburg Junior High School in 1960, belatedly, but while Carl could still know about it. He attended the school's rededication.

THOSE WHO CAME BY

Whether Elmhurst's tree lined streets actually stimulated creative talent might be questioned, but certainly a large number of writers, artists, and musicians lived here, worked here, or just came by and were noticed. Several have already been mentioned: Bonney of the *Banditti* who was postmaster, Jens Christian Bay, Mrs. Frances King, Frederick Conrad Koch, Thomas Nelson Page who came by to be married, and Ernest Thompson Seton who came by during Boy Scout beginnings. There is a tradition that Margaret Fuller spent a night at Hill Cottage Tavern although she did not mention it in her *Summer on the Lakes in 1843* in which she described "woods, rich in moccasin flowers and lupine" in northern Illinois. As a pioneer woman who demanded woman's liberation, she deserves remembrance.

There were many who came by to visit Sandburg besides Amy Lowell and Harry Hansen; among them: Sinclair Lewis author of *Main Street* and Lloyd Lewis author of *Sherman, Fighting Prophet;* Louis Untermeyer, Paul de Kruif, Fanny Butcher, Charles MacArthur, and Groucho Marx.

During the Sandburg days, *The Chicago Daily News* published daily on its editorial page a short story, light and bright, designed to attract women readers to that page; 800 words at $8, or one cent a word, a beginning rate for writers of that period. It developed a number of capable writers. One writer so completely caught the idea that one day Don Russell, the editor-in-charge, went to Rosamond du Jardin's Elmhurst home on Cayuga Street to tell her that *The Daily News* would buy all the stories she cared to write. At one time she counted her total of short stories at 75, most of them written for *The Daily News*. She also wrote 18 books for teenagers, among the titles; *Practically 17, Class Ring, Mercy Catches Up, Double Date, Double Feature, Double Wedding, Man for Marcy, Showboat Summer, Real Thing, One of the Crowd*, and *Young and Fair*. Mrs. Du Jardin later moved to Glen Ellyn, where she died in 1963.

Another writer of stories for the *Chicago Daily News* editorial page was Helen Tann Aschmann, then living on Washington Street in Elmhurst. She later moved to Itasca and was author of the prize-winning *Connie Bell, M.D.* Rosamond and Helen got together with Jane Durant and Viola Rowe and formed The Scribblers, a group that continues to study the problems of creative writing. Viola Rowe was author of *Oh! Brother, Girl in a Hurry*, and *Freckled and Fourteen*. Her books were translated into several languages.

THE SCRIBBLERS

Among the Scribblers have been Rosemary Musil, director of the Elmhurst Children's Theatre and author of many of its play: *Rip Van Winkle, King Arthur, Tad Lincoln in the White House, Quest of the Roaring Lion, Penrod*, and *Space Trip to the Moon*, and *The Ghost and Mr. Penny;* Dorothea Snow with 22 novels and Virginia Novinger with three books for children and many articles; Hazel Dame with *This Too Brief Moment*, a book of poems and *That Was*

Yesterday, a play based on Elmhurst history which was performed at the 10th Anniversary of the Elmhurst Community Theatre; Lucille Pannell, co-editor of *Holiday Roundup* and *My American Heritage;* Ann Seidel Armstrong, Katherine Carter, and Ruth Christensen.

A VARIETY OF WRITERS

Helmut Alan Berens, historian and author of *Elmhurst: Prairie to Tree Town,* was brought to Elmhurst at the age of two in 1887 when his father August came to be pastor of St. Peter's

Helmut A. Berens (1885-1964).

Church, and grew up under the influence of parents both of whom were writers. The Rev. August Berens published in 1889 a book of poems in German entitled *Fruhlingsboten.* Helmut Beren's notes give a picture of the village:

"I came to Elmhurst with my parents when my father was pastor at St. Peter's Church. When we arrived Mr. Brownell put us, bag and baggage, into a springless wagon and drove us up Cottage Hill Avenue to a new home behind St. Peter's Church. In 1887 there were not many elm trees but there were sidewalks, hedges, and fences. The side walks were board walks and when we lost pennies or Sunday School nickles through the cracks, we would crawl under and recover them."

Mr. Berens was educated in Elmhurst schools, was a graduate of Elmhurst College (then a two year school) in 1902 and the University of Chicago in 1904. He taught for forty years in Chicago schools. At Austin High School and Lewis Institute he pioneered in the teaching of journalism in secondary education.

After his retirement in 1950, he worked for the Chicago Historical Society as a director of their educational programs. Mr. Berens contributed enormously to the collection and preservation of local history in Elmhurst and Illinois. He was president of the DuPage County Historical Society. Mr. Berens was largely instrumental in organizing the Elmhurst Historical Commission and served as the director of the Elmhurst Historical Museum from its inception.

A history of a different sort came from the pen of Margaret Chant Papandreou. Margaret Chant, daughter of Mr. and Mrs. Douglas G. Chant, grew up on Clinton Avenue. Margaret spent Saturday mornings climbing to the top of a tall poplar tree to the chagrin of all boys in the neighborhood; she was never satisfied with less than the top. She was in public relations in Minneapolis as Chant, Inc., when she met Andreas Papandreou, associate professor of economics at the University of Minnesota. They were married in 1950 and went to Greece in 1961 where for a time Georgios Papandreou, father of Andreas, was premier; as he was a widower, Margaret was hailed as "first lady of Greece." That did not last long as Papandreou's leadership of the democratic opposition ended when a military junta seized control. Margaret Chant Papandreou's *Nightmare in Athens* is a frightening account of fascist excesses.

Werner Richter, a professor in Elmhurst College from 1939 to 1948, was an exile from Nazi Germany. He had been an undersecretary in the Prussian Ministry of Education during the Weimar Republic. He wrote *Re-educating Germany,* published in 1945.

Franz Heinrich Behnke, associated with the Lindlahr Sanitarium during his residence in Elmhurst, was author of *Weltwanderer und Gluckfucher,* an account in German of travels in Asia and Africa.

Joyce Van Norman has rounded up information on recent Elmhurst writers:

Alan Heimert grew up in Elmhurst and went to Harvard University for his Ph.D. He became a teacher there and specialist in colonial intellectual history. He is co-author with Reinhold Niebuhr of *A Nation So Conceived.* Reinhold Niebuhr is brother of H. Richard Niebuhr, a past president of Elmhurst College.

Elmhurst also claims several writers of murder and mystery novels. George Anderson is said to have written more mystery dramas than any other writer for radio. He is also author of a text for business training classes, *20 Point System for Sales Success*. His other books include *Magic Digest* and *Gambler's Digest*. Bishop Chandler Sterling, former, pastor of the Episcopal Church of Our Saviour in Elmhurst, is author of a mystery, the *Holroyd Papers*.

Harlan Tarbell, commercial artist and internationally known magician, was living on Cottage Hill Avenue when he wrote a six-volume course in magic with 5,000 of his own illustrations. The books explain tricks, offer lessons in psychology, and tell how to make people laugh and how to put on a magic show. Among those who benefitted from Tarbell's teaching were Houdini and Thurston, Harold Lloyd, Chester Morris, Warner Baxter and Orson Wells.

Clifford Hicks, special projects editor of *Popular Mechanics* is author of the *Alvin Fernal* series of books for children and maintains in his home an "inventing bench", similar to the one described in the series. A. Neely Hall has been mentioned for his "how-to" books for boys and his work for the Boy Scouts. His daughter Ruth Hall Smith is author of *Home Handicrafts for Girls*.

Colonel Robert Joseph Icks wrote *Tanks and Armored Vehicles* and six more books on the subject, as well as the *"Tank"* article in Encyclopedia Britannica. Laurence Seabright, chemical and metalurgical engineer, is author of a technical work, *The Selection and Hardening of Steel Tools*. Joseph Harrer of the staff of Argonne National Laboratory has written *Nuclear Reactor Control Engineering*, a compilation of technical know-how.

James M. Wall, editor of *Christian Century*, is co-ordinator for *Films Information*, a National Council of Churches publication on film reviews, and is the author of two books on motion pictures, *Church and Cinema* and *Three European Directors*. Thomas Willis, music critic of the *Chicago Tribune*, spent early years in Elmhurst.

Solveig Sveinsson (Mrs. Simon Sveinsson) lived in Elmhurst for several years. Born in Iceland, she was known for translation of Icelandic poetry, as a novelist, and a contributor of numerous articles to Canadian-Icelandic periodicals. She died June 13, 1976, in Blaine, Washington, at the age of 99, survived by two sons, 13 grandchildren, 32 great-grandchildren, 3 great-great-grandchildren, a brother and a sister.

J. Hart Rosdail, recognized as "the world's most traveled" man by the *Guinness Book of World Records*, recorded his travels in *Hiking Alone Around the World*, and *Adventures of a Globetrotter*. He also authored *The Sloopers*, a history of Norwegian immigration to America, and books on local history and geneology.

Don Russell is often consulted as authority on the American West. His *The Lives and Legends of Buffalo Bill* is in fourth printing. *The Wild West* is a history of Wild West shows. *Custer's Last* and *Custer's List* tell about and list a thousand pictures on the Custer fight. Other books are the *Adam Brandford, Cowboy* series of school readers, and *Sioux Buffalo Hunters*, translated into French, Spanish, and Italian. He has also edited several books, including *Trails of the Iron Horse* and Percival G. Lowe's *Five Years a Dragoon*, and has written numerous magazine articles, book reviews, and encyclopedia articles.

His son Jack Russell, a graduate of York Community High School, covered the Viet Nam War for two and one-half years for NBC and for many years since has broadcast news from Tokyo. Using his full name John Robert Russell, he is author of three science fiction original paperbacks: *Cabu, Sar,* and *Ta*.

WALTER BURLEY GRIFFIN

The only Elmhurst resident ever to be pictured on a postage stamp was Walter Burley Griffin. The stamp was issued by Australia in 1963 to mark the 50th anniversary of Canberra, its capital city, designed by Griffin. He was born November 24, 1876, in Maywood, the son of George Walter Griffin and Estelle Burley Griffin. They moved to Oak Park, where he attended high school. In 1893 the Griffins built a home at 223 South Kenilworth Avenue, Elmhurst. Walter was graduated from the University of Illinois in 1899 and opened an office as architect in Steinway Hall, Chicago. He was a draftsman for Frank Lloyd Wright for four years. There he met Marion Mahoney, an architect notable for her renderings of architectural plans in pen and ink, and in water color on satin. They were married June 29, 1911, and worked together on the Canberra plans. On May 23, 1912, Griffin was named winner of the international competition to design Australia's

Walter Burley Griffin (1876-1937).
An Australian stamp issued in 1963 to honor Griffin and the 50th anniversary of the founding of Canberra.

The Griffin residence, 223 South Kenilworth Avenue.

T.E. Wilder Stable, about 1902, designed by Walter Burley Griffin.

William B. Sloane house, designed by Walter Burley Griffin and built in 1909.

completing much of it. Canberra's central lake, formed by damming the Molongo River, was named Burley Griffin Lake. Griffin resumed private practice. He designed the University of Lucknow library in India; a fall from a scaffold there while he was supervising the project resulted in his death, February 11, 1937.

In addressing an Australian audience, Griffin once said that his first architectural design was for a $60 poultry house, and his second for a $300 stable. Elmhurst historians were unable to locate the poultry house, but deduced that the stable was the barn of Mrs. Filson, whose sister Mrs. Stone lived in the house afterward oc-

capital. The prize money was £1,750. He went to Australia the following year and was named Federal Capital Director of Design and Construction. However, the government was niggardly with funds and cut back on the plans; World War I further delayed the project. Years later Australia went back to the Griffin plan,

cupied by the Sandburgs. Mrs. Filson's house was that of the Grass family in Sandburg's day and the poultry house may have been there. Griffin also designed a stable-coach house for T.E. Wilder in 1902. It was gone before Elmhurst College took over the property. Griffin also designed the William Emery, Jr., house,

281 Arlington Avenue, in 1902; the William B. Sloane house, 248 Arlington Avenue, in 1909; "the Elm Street House," in 1911; and the original clubhouse of the Elmhurst Golf Club. Griffin's work elsewhere in Illinois includes landscaping the campus of DeKalb State Teachers College, and designing the Stimson Memorial Library at Anna, and a house for his brother Ralph D. Griffin at Edwardsville.

George Walter Griffin, father of the architect, was born in Haverhill, Massachusetts, March 20, 1851, and was married to Estelle Burley, October 20, 1875. He served on the Elmhurst village board during the presidency of Henry L. Glos. Mrs. Griffin was the first woman on the school board, the first president of the Elmhurst Woman's Club, an organizer of the Boys' Club, and was active in planning for the Elmhurst Public Library. She died June 20, 1927. Mr. Griffin died April 30, 1929. Their daughter Gertrude was married to Miles Sater in 1914, and they lived in the Griffin house, 223 Kenilworth Avenue, until 1941. Sater, previously mentioned as artist and lithographer, was born in Hamilton, Ohio, July 5, 1881. He came to Chicago and attended the Art Institute school for four years. He maintained his own studio and was never on any payroll. His commercial accounts included the 1915 Panama-Pacific Exposition, P.F. Volland & Co., Marshall Field & Co., and the Parker Pen Co. He was president of the Tree House Artists Guild, Chicago, 1924, and of the Elmhurst Art Guild, a predecessor of the Artists Guild, in 1934. He lived in Lombard from 1941 to 1946, then moved to Asheville, North Carolina, where he died. The Griffin-Sater home was torn down in 1969.

DRAMA, MUSIC, AND ART

The Elmhurst Children's Theatre has been mentioned in connection with the Rosemary Musil plays, more than 30, many of which have been produced by similar groups across the United States and in Great Britain. Mrs. Musil directed Children's Theatre from its founding in 1947 to her retirement in 1975. Three plays are given annually at the junior high schools and more than a hundred productions have been presented.

Elmhurst Community Theatre launched its first season in 1941 with a production of *The Male Animal*. It was the result of the enthusiasm of Professor C.C. Arends of Elmhurst College, who was its only director. By 1950 it was drawing an annual audience of 5,000 and was the largest nonprofessional summer theatre in the western suburbs. For its tenth anniversary, it presented an original play by a member, Hazel Dame, *But That Was Only Yesterday*, with the *Hill Cottage* of 1834 as its settings. Declining interest and lack of funds brought the Community Theatre to an end in 1966.

Rehearsal for "The Ghost of Mr. Penny," a Children's Theatre play written and produced by Rosemary Musil, 1974. Players (L to R) Kim French, Connie Booner, Rosemary Musil, and Scott Wilson.

Another drama group, The Masquers of Christ Church, had its beginnings in a tour of Europe conducted by the Rev. Fred Harrison. The group included Kenneth and Howard Larson, Phil Soukup, Dorothy Storm, Ethel Bosworth, and Florence Richards. After the tour, they met for play-reading sessions and dramatizations. In 1926, led by Hazel Stevens, The Masquers formally organized at a meeting in the home of F.O. Stevens. For several years, they put on one or two plays a year, some of them directed by Frances Hollinger, John Thorsen, and Mrs. John Watson.

The Elmhurst Symphony Orchestra grew out of the small group of musicians recruited to play for productions of the Elmhurst Community Theatre and was founded in 1961 with John Lazich as director. It plays three subscription concerts annually at Hammerschmidt Chapel of Elmhurst College; a Woman's Auxiliary sponsors a fund-raising "Pops" concert in March. The orchestra has grown to a membership of 90 directed by John Duckwall of Addison Trails High School. Free children's concerts are given in schools and a young artists contest is sponsored to encourage new talent.

Oldest of Elmhurst's musical groups is the Mannerchor or Men's Choir, which grew out of the Plattdeutsche Gilde, a mutual aid society.

The choir dates its formal founding to February 10, 1907, when it met in Mahler's Hall to perpetuate the traditions of German song. Early members were Oscar Irion, Otto Balgemann, Heinrich Schumacher, Alonzo Fischer, August Windrich, J.F. Weiser, and Michael Kross. The choir gives annual concerts in Elmhurst and takes part in song fests around the country. Scheduled for 1977 is participation in the National Concert of Singing Societies in Chicago.

The Elmhurst Ladies' Chorus or Damenchor was organized in 1936 by wives of the singers in the Men's Choir, meeting in the home of Mrs. Ella Drecoll. Anna Kamke was elected president. Mrs. Emma Reising has been social-financial secretary for 18 years and Mrs. Mildred Fletcher has been president since 1972. Members sang with the North American Singing Society in Milwaukee in 1974 and with the United Ladies Chorus of Chicago in 1975.

ELMHURST ARTIST GUILD

Miles Sater wrote in 1962:

> The idea of an artists guild in Elmhurst was first proposed by Karl Chworowsky in 1933 or 34.
>
> I went to Brown County, Indiana that fall for a week's sketching and when I returned I was told that I had been chosen President of the affair. Our next move was to find a meeting place; the old Griffin barn at 223 S. Kenilworth was revamped to suit the requirements. The renovation was done by members under the direction of Russell Daniels, using material donated by some generous Elmhurst citizens.
>
> There were no masterpieces produced, but the good times and good fellowship were enjoyed by all. Clarence Cole and Florence Fischer were probably the two best painters in the group. Norman Hall and Con Grange also painted with us. Con received one of the two special medals for special men issued by the British Army at the end of World War I.

Other artists mentioned in Mr. Sater's letter are: Emma Borms, Lee Sturges, Arthur Fraser, Caroline Wade, and Gertrude Griffin Sater.

The present day Elmhurst Artist's Guild was organized in Jane Duncan's Gift Shop in 1946. Mrs. Duncan served as the first president. Among the founders were Hildegard Horn, Alice Daniels, and Florence Horning. An Annual Member's Art Show is held each fall at the Elmhurst Public Library. With the Chamber of Commerce, the Guild co-sponsors the August Outdoor Art Fair. There is also an annual Art-Card Party. The 1976 president of the Elmhurst Artists Guild was Sophie Hermon.

Eleanor King (Mrs. Robert E. Hookham) whose paintings are shown annually in Paris, and who has been active in the Guild also heads the Foundation for the Fine Arts and Civic Center, organized in 1974 to plan for an art and community center at Cottage Hill Avenue and Virginia Street.

When the Elmhurst Artist's Guild held its 30th year celebration, these artists were named as honorary members: Lila Altendorf, Russell Bender, Alice Daniels, Dorothy Finch, Eleanor King Hookham, Hildegard Horn, Florence Horning, and Frieda Thoen.

Other noted Elmhurst artists include Eric Anderson, Charlotte Burgess, David Burnside, Tom Dunnington, Marge Ringhaver, and James Teason.

ELMHURST PUBLIC LIBRARY

An ordinance of July 8, 1912 provided an annual tax levy for support of a public library. Mayor F.W.M. Hammerschmidt appointed a library board including William E. Danforth, George A. Sorrick, William B. Pearn, W.J. Keimel, Alfred H. Fischer, Alonzo C. Fischer, Guy Cantwell, Paul Dolle, and E.J. Bunge. The board delayed action until tax funds accumulated. In 1916 a room was rented at $15 a month in the rear of the Glos Building, York Street and Park Avenue. Mrs. H.L. Breitenbach, a

Katherine Breitenbach, first librarian of the Elmhurst Public Library. (1916 to 1926).

graduate of the University of Wisconsin library school, was employed as librarian at a salary of

$15 a month. The board allotted $400 for books and $5 a month for janitor services. The Elmhurst Women's Club contributed $75 for purchase of children's books.

The Elmhurst Public Library opened its doors March 22, 1916, and despite a heavy snow storm, 100 patrons crowded into the room. Available were 830 volumes, part of them a gift from a discontinued boys' club. The books could be borrowed Wednesdays and Saturdays from 2 to 5 and from 7 to 9 p.m. The first annual report in July, 1917, reported 1,507 books and 12 magazines available to 643 registered borrowers. A story hour was offered to children of the third and fourth grades on Saturday afternoons in summer.

The will of Thomas Edward Wilder bequeathed the north six acres of his estate to the city, provided that a library be built there at a minimum cost of $35,000. The city accepted, but lack of funds to build the library necessitated return of the property. The Elmhurst Park Board was organized in 1920 and negotiated for the entire estate which was acquired and became Wilder Park. The Park Board offered the residence for use as a library, and the Library Board purchased the building and one acre of land. This is the house that was built by Seth Wadhams in 1868 and named *White Birch*, sold to Henry W. King in 1888, and acquired from the Francis Kings in 1905 by Wilder, who renamed it *Lancaster Lodge*.

The library was moved into the Wilder house during the summer of 1922. Only the first floor was used. Library hours were increased to three days a week, Monday, Wednesday, and Saturday. Story hours were held throughout the year. A new service added in 1925 was the "Reading with a Purpose" course offered by the American Library Association. It was announced March 1, 1926, that the library would be opened every day except Sundays, all day except for lunch and dinner hours. Mrs. Breitenbach resigned, feeling unable to devote this much time, and an open house was held March 3 to express appreciation for her ten years' service and to mark the formal opening of the library on an every day basis. In her final report she stated that the library had 6,975 books and 1,304 borrowers. Mayor Balgemann named Mrs. Breitenbach to the Library Board.

Miss Grace Murray, a graduate of the University of Illinois library school was named librarian. She undertook a public relations program. A telephone was installed to offer public information services. "Library Notes" appeared regularly in the *Elmhurst Press,* with such features as reports on books received, a summer reading program for children, and information about new services, including a rental collection of recent popular books, loans of books to schools for classroom use, and special loans of books for teachers.

A fire in the second and third floors of the building, January 26, 1930, caused $12,000 damage, mostly to two rooms on the second

Temporary quarters of the Elmhurst Public Library during remodeling of the Library in 1936.

floor occupied by the Infant Welfare Clinic. Students from nearby Elmhurst College carried out furniture, books, and records. No books or records were destroyed, and insurance covered other loss and damage.

East facade of the 1937 remodelled Elmhurst Public Library.

E. Norman Brydes, Elmhurst architect, designed plans for the modernization and renovation of the building, including an addition, at a cost of $20,000. The plans were adopted in February, 1936, by the Library Board. The cornerstone was laid June 6 in a program celebrating the Elmhurst Centennial and the twentieth anniversary of the library. The library was closed for the summer during the construction. An open house was held January 31, 1937, to show the changes made. Outside porches were replaced by a large portico with four white pillars, opening into a small vestibule. The large north room was unchanged structurally but was refurnished in eighteenth century English style furniture. In other rooms early American style furniture was used. A fireplace in the entry hall was removed and the charge desk built around the opening, with staff offices behind it. Shelf space was doubled. An addition at the south end provided space for a children's room. The second floor north room shelved adult fiction; the east room had display cases for exhibitions; and there were a periodical room, a board room, and an apartment for the caretaker. The refurnished rooms were named for contributors to Elmhurst and its library: the Wilder Room by Mrs. William Emery; the Ullman Room by the family of A. I. Ullman, early board member; the King Room by Mrs. Cyrus Bentley, daughter of the Henry W. Kings; and the Sturges Room by Mr. and Mrs. Lee Sturges.

Miss Murray resigned in 1938 to become librarian of Jacksonville Public Library. Miss Ruth Strand, who had been a part-time helper and since 1926 assistant librarian, was named head librarian in March of 1939.

During Miss Strand's tenure, an open line of cooperation with all educational facilities and civic organizations was emphasized.

By the time of the annual report for the 1945-46 year, the library reported a raise in the tax rate to two mills, the hiring of a children's librarian and the establishing of a small building fund. Borrowers now numbered 7,082 with 24,115 volumes, 108 out-of-town borrowers, 164 college cards. Services included classroom collections and class visits for reading and instruction, story hours and movies for summer programs, plus regularly scheduled exhibits, talks, booklists, etc. Curtailment of services was noted in the closing of the library during the month of August, and starting in September, 1946, the closing of the library on Wednesdays.

April of 1947 brought the news of the start of a circulating record collection with 380 classical selections as a basis, as part of the extras provided by the Friends of the Library organization. The following February the Great Books Foundation began its series of seminars.

The annual report of 1951 showed the library had 24,949 volumes, 9,000 borrowers, cost of an out-of-town card rose from $1.00 to $3.00, and a collection of first editions of works by Carl Sandburg, a former resident who lived at 331 South York Street, Elmhurst. In 1951, Mrs. Berens, president of the library board, received the Distinguished Service citation of the Trustees Section of the Illinois Library Association.

The Elmhurst Friends of the Library Association was organized March 23, 1941, marking the twenty-fifth anniversary of the library. The association sponsored a circulating collection of 380 classical records, presented in 1947. At the annual meeting May 20, 1935, the Alice Seton Berens Room in the lower level was dedicated, honoring Mrs. Helmut Berens who was a member of the library board for 35 years.

Miss Strand, after 14 years as librarian, resigned in 1953 to attend classes at Columbia University. Mrs. Lois Zimmerman was acting librarian until June when Mrs. H.M. McIntosh was appointed librarian, but she resigned after serving only a few months. In the fall of 1954, Miss Strand was asked to resume the post of librarian.

After a survey by Harold Lancour and Harold Goldstein of the Graduate School of Library Science, University of Illinois, showed inadequacies in space and services, Byron F. Stevens, president of the library board, asked the City Council to authorize building an addition and essential remodeling. Charles Cedarholm, Elmhurst architect, drafted plans calling for an expenditure of $546,275.70. The plan was submitted to a referendum and approved by voters April 16, 1963. Groundbreaking ceremonies were held April 11, 1964. During construction library services continued except for a few days of moving and reorganization of materials. The building was dedicated October 17, 1965.

The remodelled building housed several new rooms. The Glos Room furnishings were the gift of Mrs. Ione Glos in memory of her hus-

West facade of the 1965 addition to the Elmhurst Public Library.

band, Albert Glos. The Wilder Room furnishings were the gift of Mrs. William Emery in memory of her parents, Mr. and Mrs. T.E. Wilder. The Genevieve Gavin Art Room was the gift of Mr. and Mrs. Steve Gavin. The Clara Glos Bates Room was the gift of Alben Bates in memory of his wife. The Ruth Strand Room was given by the Friends of the Library recognizing her years of service as Librarian. The Library Garden was the gift of the Elmhurst Garden Club. The May Reed Wilson Center for student study was given by Ervin Wilson, Sr. in memory of his wife. The Alice Seton Berens Room was named by the Board of Directors for Mrs. Berens in recognition of her 35 years of service as member and president of the board. Two rooms of the original library were then given over to the Elmhurst Historical Commission. These rooms were originally furnished in honor of two Elmhurst pioneer families.... the Emery room by Edward Emery and the Cruger Room by Mrs. Harold Cruger. The Elmhurst Historical Museum occupied these rooms on the second floor of the old section, remaining there until it was moved to the Glos Mansion in 1975. Paintings by Elmhurst artists were donated and hung throughout the building. A program of art rentals of paintings was begun and rental of records and films expanded.

Miss Strand resigned in October 1969, after many years of service. She was awarded the Distinguished Service Award by the Jaycees in 1973.

Lawrence Knudsen was appointed librarian. A collection of 1,700 paperback books was added in 1971. The Regiscope, a new circulation system, was put into operation in 1970, requiring reprocessing of all library materials and reregistration of all borrowers for microfilming and punch-card processing. Later the Suburban Library System and Computer Library Service, Inc., completed installation of a fully automated circulation control system.

In 1972 the Elmhurst Public Library joined the Suburban Library System, giving borrowers access to the resources of 58 libraries, as well as the Chicago Public Library. Parking meters were installed and hours open increased to 68 a week. Elmhurst Friends of the Library Association donated two Speed-a-matic reading machines, a postage meter and envelope sealer, and two sets of art slides and records.

Mrs. Edith Gavin, a volunteer who worked many hours to establish a picture file collection, bequeathed to the library a restricted gift of $160,000, available in 1972, to continue and promote visual education. Another volunteer, Ralph Mahon, finished a project of indexing and abstracting the *Elmhurst Press* after years of work. He also donated a slide collection of travel pictures. Mrs. Lois Zimmerman, Children's Librarian, retired in 1972, after twenty-five years' service.

Rooms vacated by the museum in 1975 were remodeled for use of the periodicals section. Other remodeling included enclosing porticos at north and south entrances, enclosing the book drop, building a partition behind the circulation desk, and construction of two staff offices. An art print collection was started for the children's department.

ELMHURST HISTORICAL COMMISSION, MUSEUM AND SOCIETY

The Elmhurst Historical Commission was created in 1952 by the City Council and authorized to receive, classify, and store materials relating to the history of Elmhurst. This action was inspired by Helmut Berens. Early members were Joseph Reilly, Fred C. Evers, and William Pollock. Others were Mrs. Roy DeShane, Donald Carlson, Munson Emery, Mrs. Howard Herder, Mrs. George Larkin, Erwin Schuttler, Mrs. William Semple, Herbert C. Sinn, and H.K. Story. The present membership includes Warren Larson, Theodore Kross, Mrs. E.H. Droegemueller, Jack Davis, R. Bradner Hilliard, A.N. Hammerschmidt, Mrs. Harold Norlie, Miss Ruth Strand, Richard Weber and Mrs. George Kulton. Mrs. Wayne Harlan is Curator and Nancy Wilson, assistant. The commission directs the work of the Historical

Museum.

Many prominent citizens contributed time and service to the development of the Historical Museum. Playing an important role were Joseph Reilly, Mrs. George C. Larkin, Fred C. Evers, Munson Emery, James P. Cosgrove, and of course, Helmut Berens, who became the Museum director. Others who shared in the work were Donald Carlson, Karl Carlson, A.E. Montgomery, Earl Strand, Mrs. Roy DeShane and Mrs. William Semple.

January 13, 1956, the Museum was formally opened to the public on the third floor of the Municipal Building. There were 40 items - certainly humble beginnings. In October 1965 the Museum was moved to the second floor of the newly remodeled public library. By this time the Museum possessed furniture artifacts, books and historic papers, clothes and memorabilia, enough to fill three rooms and an attic. In the spring of 1974 the Glos Mansion,

Historic pieces as displayed when the museum was housed on the second floor of the Elmhurst Public Library

Glos Mansion in the mid 70s, now the home of the Elmhurst Historical Museum.

The Old Elmhurst Room established 1974 in the Historical Museum.

104 S. Kenilworth, was restored for Museum use, the City having moved their offices to Schiller Street a few years before. The plans for the remodelling of the building were drawn by architect Robert Schill. Elmhurst residents refurbished the rooms. The Old Elmhurst Room was furnished by Mrs. George Larkin in memory of her parents, Mr. and Mrs. Jacob Glos. This room contains original furniture of the Glos family. A large exhibit room was made possible by the Alben Bates and Clara Bates Foundation. Miss Lena Ahrens donated funds for the second exhibit room. The library and research room were furnished by Mrs. Albert Glos in memory of her husband, Albert H. Glos, and her parents, Dr. and Mrs. Ernest Davis. The Elmhurst Historical Society presented a micro-film reader printer, carpeting, and mannequins.

In 1971, the commission named a committee consisting of Mrs. Norlie, Miss Strand, and the late Dr. Robert C. Stanger to consider formation of a citizen's group to support the commission's work. Their recommendation resulted in the organization of the Elmhurst Historical Society in 1972. At a meeting November 19, officers chosen were: Royal V. Burtis, president; Raymond D. Maxson and Bruce A. Mahon, vice-presidents; Stephen F. French, treasurer; Ruth Stickle, recording secretary; Mrs. James C. Dawson, corresponding secretary, and Dr. Robert Stanger, representative of the commission. Charter membership totaled 226. Quarterly meetings offered programs on historical and educational themes. Officers in 1976 included George Vann, president; Ruth Stickle, vice-president, Stephen French, treasurer; Ann Grass, recording secrecary; and Waltie Incopero, corresponding secretary.

While the Historical Commission is the governing body of the Museum and its members (all on a voluntary basis) are appointed by the Mayor and the City Council, membership in the Historical Society is open to all citizens.

North facade of the Lizzadro Museum of Lapidary Art.

As a part of the Bicentennial and as a reminder of the simple joys of the early 1900s, the Elmhurst Historical Commission preserved *Big Rock* by relocating it on the Museum grounds. Originally this "skinny-dipping" rock was at the pictured site in Salt Creek in Graue's Woods.

THE LIZZADRO MUSEUM

The Lizzadro Museum of Lapidary Art in Elmhurst's Wilder Park has been called a "unique shrine to the splendor of the mineral kingdom," which is no exaggeration, for while many museums display gems and carvings, few are devoted solely to that purpose, and none can rival some objects in the Lizzadro collection. Among these are a screen presented in 1736 to the Chinese Emperor Ch'ien Lung, 13 feet long and 7 feet high with 10 panels of red cinnabar framed in rosewood. The panels are ornamented with reliefs of birds and flowers, carved from jade, jasper, lapis lazuli, ivory, and mother of pearl. Another is a set of two wine vessels, two candlesticks, and an incense burner of dark green jade mounted on gold and blue cloisonne bases, obtained from Peking in 1860.

The museum was opened November 4, 1962, as the gift of Joseph F. Lizzadro and his family to the Elmhurst Park District and the people of Elmhurst. Lizzadro was born July 24, 1898, in a village near Naples, Italy, and came to the United States with his family at the age of 11.

Young Students test their knowledge of fossils and minerals in educational displays.

He worked with his father, a shoemaker until he was 16, when he became an electrician's helper at the Meade Electric Company in Chicago. One cold night he returned to the plant to drain radiators of the company's trucks to prevent them from freezing. This came to the attention of Thomas Meade, the company's president, who promoted Lizzadro to foreman. He completed high school in night classes, then studied law, while advancing in the electric company, and when Mr. Meade died, his heirs chose Lizzadro to manage the business, which he did for for 58 years. His wife, Mrs. Mary Lizzadro, was born in Kearsarge in Michigan's Upper Peninsula copper country, and it was during a visit there that Lizzadro found an agate that turned his attention to lapidary art. He began his collection and soon his home was jammed with gems and carvings. By agreement with the Elmhurst Park District, the $300,000 museum was built at Lizzadro's expense in Wilder Park.

He also established the Lizzadro School of Lapidary Art at 558 South York Street. Mr. Lizzadro died in 1972. Directors of the museum are Mrs. Lizzadro and sons John and Joseph. Four daughters are officers of the museum.

YEARS OF WAR AND RECOVERY

World War II had more impact on local communities and governments than any war of the United States, before or since. Even before the war started, there was conscription, administered by local draft boards, and eventually 16,363,639 persons were enrolled in the armed forces, a considerable proportion of the total population. One of the earliest effects of war in the Pacific was a shortage of rubber, for almost the entire supply of this product, associated with the jungles of Brazil, came from Malaysia. Old tires were gathered in, the best of them recapped, the rest melted down for their rubber content. With no tires, and gasoline strictly rationed, driving of automobiles was reduced to dire necessity. Tin cans were gathered for their small tin content; iron and aluminum were conserved. Ration books with red and green points governed family allowances of meat, sugar, canned goods, and other foods. All of these programs were administered by local governments.

Civil Defense systems were organized in Elmhurst, as elsewhere, and while happily little needed during the war, became permanent organizations ready to serve in case of disaster. Dr. Max Klinghoffer planned and organized the emergency and disaster plan of the Elmhurst Hospital. Dr. Klinghoffer received the Jaycee Distinguished Service Award in 1952, and President Nixon commended Dr. Klinghoffer for his work in emergency and disaster relief organization. The Municipal Defense Council was created by Elmhurst ordinance of June 26, 1942. The preservation and protection of Victory Gardens was guaranteed by ordinance of September 8, 1942. Many such gardens were planted on vacant lots with consent of the owners.

Mayor Fellows began his three-year term as mayor in April, 1945. William Fellows, a native of Chicago, was married to Helen Rea, January 12, 1897, and they lived on the south side of Chicago until 1903. For 13 years he worked for Sprague Warner Corporation, wholesale grocers; then, from 1914 to 1925 he worked for the Carpenter Cook Company in Menominee, Michigan, where he was a lifetime member of the Masonic Lodge. After a year in Ravenswood they moved to 261 West North Avenue, Elmhurst, and for 26 years he was general sales manager for Squire Dingee Company, Ma Brown Products. He was a leader in fund raising campaigns for Memorial Hospital, the

William S. Fellows, mayor
(1945-1948).

Community Chest, the American Red Cross, and the March of Dimes. He was active in the Methodist Church. Fellows was alderman of the Second Ward for 11 years. He was treasurer of the DuPage County Housing Authority.

An outstanding problem at the close of the war was a housing shortage. Millions of young men were returning home, getting married, and seeking homes, but there had been little or no building during sixteen years of Depression and war. Elmhurst had maintained high standards in construction and resisted pressure for jerry-built houses. In June, 1946, Mayor Fellows appointed a 20-member Plan Commission with a four-year term of office and paid secretary.

Mayor Fellow's efforts to obtain housing for veterans and school teachers resulted in the

$3,000,000 project at St. Charles Road and West Avenue called the St. Charles West Apartments. On December 17, 1947, the street named Fellows Court, on the eastern boundary of the St. Charles West apartment complex, was named for Mayor Fellows.

During Mayor Fellows administration, new public health and public welfare methods were adopted, and school crossing watchmen were hired. John Martens was chief of police from 1945 to 1947.

Mayor Fellows died while in office, January 17, 1948. George Meister served as acting mayor until Ervin Wilson took office June 29 to serve the unexpired term.

Ervin Wilson, mayor (1948-1953).

Ervin F. Wilson was elected mayor in April, 1948, was re-elected in 1949, and served until 1953. He was born in Polk County, Nebraska, and was educated at the University of Nebraska. He was a research chemist in Chicago for six years. He then became a supplier of chemicals to industry, heading the E.H. Haines Distributing Company. He moved to Elmhurst in 1919. He was a founder and a member of the board of directors of the Elmhurst Federal Savings and Loan Association, and was active in the Elmhurst Masonic Lodge and the Knights Templar. He was an alderman from the third ward for eight years.

Under Mayor Wilson's administration, a survey of traffic problems was made in 1952. The Board of Local Improvements was organized to take charge of street resurfacings, road improvements, and an addition to the Sewage Disposal Plant. Also in 1952, the Civil Defense Department was organized as an independent unit.

After serving as Mayor, Ervin Wilson moved, in 1956, to Palo Alto, California. A son,

Elmhurst Sewage Disposal Plant at Rex Boulevard and Crescent as it appeared in 1941.

Ervin F. Wilson, Jr. remained in Elmhurst.

George Kummerow again served as chief of police from 1947 to 1952. At this time the force included two lieutenants, eight patrolmen, three deskmen, one special officer, and seven school crossing watchmen. A three-wheeled vehicle was purchased in 1948 to service parking meters. Wilbert Rusteberg became chief of police in 1952, serving until his death in 1959. The Juvenile Bureau was established in 1953 under the direction of Leander Anasse and Robert De Roech. The new police headquarters building on Schiller Street was completed in 1955.

ORGANIZATIONS OF POSTWAR YEARS

The Elmhurst Junior Chamber of Commerce was organized March 15, 1950, with Frank Rebek as president. It is affiliated with the national organization which had its beginnings in St. Louis in 1915 and as Junior Citizens became affiliated with the St. Louis Chamber of Commerce, an idea that spread rapidly across the country. However, the United States Junior Chamber of Commerce has ceased to be an arm of the United States Chamber of Commerce, but goes its own way to similar civic objectives as Jaycees. Membership is open to young men between 21 and 35 years of age. Elmhurst Jaycees have won many plaques and trophies for outstanding civic programs, as well as awards for its bowling team.

The Elmhurst Young Men's Christian Association had its beginning January 31, 1952 at a meeting in the Irving Park YMCA called by Irwin Ruby. A board of directors was elected including Alben Bates, Sr., chairman; Norman Hanson, president; Mrs. Joseph Ackerman, recording secretary; and Marvin Pollard, trea-

Years Of War And Recovery

South facade, Elmhurst Y.M.C.A., 109 W. First Street.

surer. A YMCA office was opened May 1 on the second floor of 109 West First Street by Keith Boys, executive director. Organization of the YMCA was the result of a two-year campaign, headed by Mrs. Ackerman of the Education Committee of the American Association of University Women, aided by Mrs. Lester Tripp and Mrs. Robert Bigler, backed by Mr. Ruby, owner of Ruby's of Elmhurst. At the end of the first year of organization there were 532 members, and it was decided that Elmhurst YMCA should serve Lombard, Addison, Itasca, Wooddale, Bensenville, Northlake, Villa Park, Berkeley, Hillside, Yorkfield, Timber Trails, and York Center.

The first Indian Guide Tribe was organized August 13, 1952, by six fathers and their sons meeting at the home of Lester Tripp, and perfecting their organization a week later at the home of Dr. Winfield Fisher. The Elmhurst Indian Guide movement became the largest in the Metropolitan YMCA of Chicago, and the largest in Illinois. The Indian Princess movement for fathers and daughters was formed in 1957.

In 1955 property on First Street between Maple and Elm avenues was donated by Mr. and Mrs. Alben Bates, Mr. and Mrs. Albert H. Glos, and Mrs. George Larkin as a site for a YMCA building. Ground was broken December 7, 1958, and the million dollar facility was dedicated May 1, 1960.

The YMCA staff includes 13 full-time and 71 part-time employees, led by a board of directors of 31 volunteers. It is estimated that 17,000 persons of all ages take part in programs, including gymnasium, swimming pool, ice skating, classes in ballet, art, crafts, adult social dancing, guitar, and weight control. Organizations for young people include Junior Leader Club, Model United Nations, and Youth in Government. Dennis Paulson became executive director in 1975.

Y-Knots, a group of women interested in learning "living skills," was organized in 1970, sparked by the leadership of Ruth Christensen. From the Y-Knot Center in the Presbyterian Church, 53 programs are directed for 500 women while caring for their 1,200 children. As the name of the organization is interpreted as "Why Not " the membership includes scuba divers, glider pilots, performing dancers, singers, guitarists, authors, artists, book illustrators, and business women.

The Elmhurst Safety Council was founded in 1945, the outgrowth of a school program started in 1938 by A.E. Hotle. Safety education was started at Lincoln School in 1945. Robert Bloedel devised a "Safety Joe" demonstration that attracted wide attention and was recognized by the National Safety Council in 1958. The council's program was featured by NBC television in 1950 and received the Automotive Dealers and Bankers award in 1973. Civic awards recognized the protective fence at the Salt Creek Disposal Center in 1962 and the bicycle paths program in 1974. The annual bicycle check began in 1947 and the automotive check in 1970. Edward H. Heller heads the 51 member council.

The Elmhurst Newcomers Club was organized in 1949 by thirty young women, and within a year reached a membership of 65, meeting in the Memorial Hospital auditorium. After membership grew to 160 meetings were held in the Congregational Church. Special interest groups include arts and crafts, a baby sitting co-op, book discussion, international dining, bridge, pinochle, bowling, and needlework. The club supports many civic programs and has won awards in the 1959 Float Competition, the Santa Lucia Float Competition, and trophies for Fourth of July parade entries.

The Welcome Wagon Luncheon Club of Elmhurst was organized in 1956 in the home of Mrs. Arnold Stender with the purpose of extending a friendly hand to newcomers in the city. Its membership grew from 18 to 140, meeting at the River Forest Country Club. A Christmas Walk and a Candlelight Bowling Part raise funds for philanthropic projects.

Tree Towns Business and Professional

Women's Club was organized at a meeting called by Mrs. G.F. Gould with the sponsorship of the Maywood club, and was chartered March 1, 1959. The club holds classes in practical politics and defensive driving, grants scholarships, and gives award dinners to outstanding women in the area, including Dr. Elizabeth Koppenaal in 1974.

The Elmhurst Auxiliary of the Illinois Children's Home and Aid Society was founded in 1959 as a privately supported child-placing agency. A January dinner dance and a spring "mini-benefit" raise funds for the foster care program and other child-family services. Leaders in the auxiliary include Mrs. George Scheppach, Mrs. William Ketelhut, and Mrs. Ralph Maxson.

Elmhurst Rotary Club was founded by John W. Marshall, Sr., and was admitted to Rotary International, January 26, 1955, with Alvin N. Hammerschmidt as president and a membership of 26, which has increased to 66. With the motto "Service Above Self," the present Rotary activities include support of the Rotary Foundation Scholarship program (the last two scholarships have been awarded to Japanese students who attend Elmhurst College); support and participation in the "Experience In International Living" program which brings foreign students to the United States for six weeks during the summer in which time they stay with various Rotary Club families; and on the local level, four or more scholarships, awarded each year to high school students for participation in college or trade school programs.

As Dr. Arthur Luchs, Rotary Club's 1976 president stated, "Rotary Club has a long history of continuing support for service programs beginning with Meals on Wheels, the Elmhurst College's Living Endowment program, the Y M C A , the Family Services Association, and programs for Senior Citizens.

CHURCHES OF WAR AND POSTWAR YEARS

Yorkfield Presbyterian Church

Yorkfield Presbyterian Church was organized September 26, 1943, by the Rev. Walter Reid of Bellwood Presbyterian Church at a meeting of 35 charter members held in a one-story, white frame schoolhouse. Lester J. Dacken took charge as student minister while he completed his training at Wheaton College and McCormick Seminary. He was ordained in 1949 and served as pastor until 1975. He was succeeded by the Rev. Randolph Coney. The first unit of the church was built in 1947 at 1099 South York Street. The manse was added in 1948 and an educational unit in 1953. The completed sanctuary was dedicated in 1959.

Immanuel Evangelical

Immanuel Evangelical Lutheran Church was long-established by 1940, close to celebrating 40 years of congregation, but it was in 1944 that the Rev. Carl Abel, third pastor of Immanuel Lutheran, retired. He had served the church since 1911. Under Pastor Abel, English services were introduced in 1912. 1914 saw the ground-breaking for a new school. In 1930 a new church was dedicated. The Rev. E.T. Lange was his successor. Under Lange's pastorate, dedication of the new school addition took place. The Rev. Walter F. Fischer held the pastorate in 1976.

Elmhurst Presbyterian Church

Elmhurst Presbyterian Church held its first service October 11, 1953 in Elmhurst College Chapel and was organized November 1, by Dr. Robert Lee Sawyer with 147 charter members. Christmas services were held in the church, 367 Spring Road, December 21, 1958, and the church was dedicated January 4, 1959. Dr. Clare E. Tallman served from 1956 to 1975, and during his ministry the sanctuary and educational buildings were completed. He was a leader in development of the Ray Graham Association. The Ray Graham Workshop for retarded children was opened in the church basement. Under Dr. Tallman the church became "The 7 Day a week Church" with a variety of programs. Meals on Wheels, aid to neighborhood houses in Chicago, the Y-Knot program, and the "Sheltered Workshop" all came about under Rev. Tallman's leadership. Housed in the church were the Family Service Association and the renal-dialysis unit. Dr. Tallman retired in 1975. He was succeeded by the Rev. William R. Hayes.

Bethel United Church of Christ

Bethel United Church of Christ was founded

under the Northern Illinois Synod April 23, 1953 with 48 members. The Rev. Merl Schiffman became pastor in 1954. The church at 315 East St. Charles Road was dedicated November 23, 1958. Rev. Schiffman retired in 1971. He had been very active in work with young people. The Rev. Edward W. Bergstraesser was installed in 1974.

Visitation Roman Catholic Church

Visitation Church was founded in 1953 with the Rev. John Podesta celebrating the first Mass in Yorkfield Public School. The church was built at York and Madison streets and the first service was a Midnight Mass, Christmas 1953 with a membership of 400 families. Ground was broken for Visitation School at 851 South York Street, and it was opened in September 1954. A convent was built in 1957 and an addition to the school was completed in 1960. A new church was dedicated in 1967. The Rev. Podesta held the pastorate in 1976.

Mary Queen of Heaven Roman Catholic Church

Mary Queen of Heaven, the third Roman Catholic parish in Elmhurst, was founded by the Rev. Thomas B. O'Keefe in 1956. Holy Mass was celebrated for the first time June 24 at the Emerson School for a membership of 225 families. Services continued in Emerson School while church and school were being built at 430 North West Avenue. Mary Queen of Heaven School opened in September, 1957, under the guidance of the Sisters of Mercy. Holy Mass was celebrated in the new church September 22, 1957. Father O'Keefe continued as pastor until 1964. His successor was the Rev. Stanley Orlikiewicz; the Rev. Paul J. Benson became his successor.

Christ Methodist Church

Christ Methodist Church at Swain and Van Buren was founded December 23, 1956, with 42 members. The Rev. Eugene H. Bonham arrived in May, 1957, to become the first full-time pastor. The first building, an A-frame unit, at Swain Avenue and Van Buren Street, was dedicated Easter Sunday 1960, with a membership of 343. An addition to the church was dedicated in October of 1976. The Rev. James Darby is pastor.

Crescent Avenue Baptist Church

Crescent Avenue Baptist Church, affiliated with the American Baptist Convention, was founded November 2, 1958, by the Rev. J.R. Hastings with 12 members. The Rev. C.F. Wagstaff became the first full-time pastor in June 1959. The congregation had no church building. The parsonage was at 410 East Crescent Avenue. Services were held at Jefferson School, and later at the Baptist Seminary in Oakbrook. The church had purchased three acres of land at Fern and Crescent avenues but built no church. Crescent Avenue Baptist Church was disbanded June 2, 1968.

Messiah Lutheran Church

Messiah Lutheran Church was organized in 1961 in affiliation with the English District of the Missouri Synod at a meeting held in Bryan Junior High School. The church is at 130 West Butterfield Road with the Rev. E.L. Sterz as pastor and 400 members. The Rev. Ewald Sterz became pastor in 1964.

Church of the New Covenant

The Church of the New Covenant was founded in 1966 as a protestant ecumenical group. Meetings were held in the Elmhurst College Chapel and at Bethel Church. Mission efforts include Ada McKinley Center and St. Leonard's House. The Church of the New Covenant is a member of the Chicago Metropolitan Association of the United Church of Christ.

Elmhurst Bible Church

Elmhurst Bible Church is a 1970 offshoot of North Elmhurst Community Apostolic Church, located at 825 North Van Auken Street. The Rev. David Getz is pastor.

Elmhurst Christian Reformed Church

Elmhurst Christian Reformed Church was the First Christian Reformed Church of Bellwood until it dedicated its new building at 905 Kent Street, Elmhurst, in 1964 with a membership of 78 families. Pastors serving Elmhurst Christian Reformed Church have been the Rev. J. DeVries, 1961 to 1966, and the Rev. G. Stoutmeyer 1967 to 1972. In 1974 the Rev. Wayne Leys became pastor.

Seventh Day Adventist

The Seventh Day Adventist Church of Elmhurst, at 243 West Butterfield Road was established in 1967. The original Italian American Seventh Day Adventist Church was established in Chicago in 1912. The Elmhurst church began its congregation with John Valcarenghi as pastor. The church building was completed in March of 1968. Dr. Robert T. Hirst succeeded Valcarenghi as pastor.

St. Demetrios Greek Orthodox Church

St. Demetrios Greek Orthodox Church of DuPage first opened its doors on February 1, 1967, after many long meetings and planning sessions. Rev. Father Denice Katsihtis was the first priest. The permanent board of St. Demetrios Church consists of Ted Dulles, founder and first president; Chris Stavros, second president, and George Koliveros, permanent member. Others who were active in establishment of the church were Katherine Anagost, legal advisor, and George Pappa, secretary. On February 21, 1970, the church was heavily damaged by a fire. Immediate help was offered by all churches in the area, and temporary housing was given in the building of Immanuel United Church of Christ. The 1971 Parish Council, headed by Phil Manolis, president and George Cotsirilos, vice-president undertook the task of finding a new permanent location for the church. The old Churchville Jr. High located at 890 Church Road, Elmhurst, was purchased in 1972. Part of this building is used as the St. Demetrios Educational Center; services are also held in the Center. The congregation of St. Demetrios hopes to build a new church in Elmhurst on Route 83 between North Avenue and Lake Street where property has been purchased. The Very Reverend Peter Malamis succeeded Katsihtis as pastor.

Bethel Assembly of God

Bethel Assembly of God was organized in 1960 under the guidance of Wesley E. Butler and moved to North and West Avenues in 1961. The church building was completed in 1964. The Rev. A.M. Johnson assumed the pastorate in 1964.

Timothy Christian School

Timothy Christian School at 188 West Butterfield Road, Elmhurst, includes grade school, junior high, and high school. It is a private school, maintained by a society, members of which must be affiliated with an Evangelical Church.

WORLD WAR II ROLL OF HONOR

Elmhurst men who gave their lives during World War II include:

Wilbert A. Backhaus
John E. Bleiler
Earl Boldebuck
Fred H. Bucholz
Henry W. Bucholz
William J. Callow
A. Atwood Colwell
William B. Davis
James John Dezutel
Robert Thomas Duncan
Edward Fred Egan
Richard W. Fellows
Glenn A. Fister
Willis Flannery
Ralph LeRoy Glatfelter
John W. Graybill
Ralph W. Gregerson
Martin Hammerschmidt, Jr.
Donald W. Hill
Archie Iman
Richard Jernegan
William Kapp
Warren Charles Karas
Edward Ladwig
Erwin M. Licht
Nathan Manning
Charles Miller
Richard E. Miller
John R. Parsons
Vernon Patzer
David Peirce
Donald Remic
Joseph Ricker
Frederick Saint
William Samuel
Richard J. Schmitt
Eugene J. Schumacher
Harry L. Seavey
Kurt Speckmann
Peter A. Trick
William O. Uhlir
Donald W. Waddell
Philip Welsher
Harry J. Weidenbeck
Walter Williamson
Norman Woeller
Robert C. Zawne
Alfred Zwicky

THE BOOMING 1950s

The population of Elmhurst grew from 15,458 in 1940 to 21,273 in 1950, most of the increase coming in the five years after the end of the war in 1945. It was apparent that this growth would continue, in accordance with the huge spread of suburban development throughout the Chicago area, and that municipal government could no longer be carried on as a part-time, after-working-hours avocation. Earl Ogden was

Earl Ogden, mayor (1953-1957).

elected mayor in 1953. By special ballot, the city manager form of government, strongly backed by the Jaycees and other civic groups, was adopted.

Robert Palmer was installed as city manager

Robert T. Palmer, City manager (1953-   ).

August 5, 1953. A graduate of the University of California in civil engineering, he worked for the Minnesota Department of Highways in 1939, served in the U.S. Army Corps of Engineers during the war, and became assistant city manager for South Haven, Michigan, in 1946. He was city manager for St. Johns, Michigan, from 1947 to 1953.

The Elmhurst city manager is responsible for the Building Department, Water Department, Department of Public Works, Public Highways, Finance, Sewage Treatment, and Police and Fire Departments. Palmer continued to serve through several administrations. Of him Dr. R.C. Stanger said, "Robert Palmer is a unique person, the essence of efficiency, honesty, and integrity."

During Mayor Ogden's administration bond issues were approved of $225,000 for water and sewer system improvements in 1953 and of $350,000 for building a sewage disposal plant at Illinois Route 83, south of St. Charles Road in 1954. City ordinances were codified and application was made for a special census to increase receipts from the state motor tax fuel fund. A bond issue of $175,000 for a new fire station was approved in 1954. There was an increase in fire department personnel, and a firemen's pension fund was established.

Streets were paved in Emery Manor subdivision, in north Elmhurst, developed by Munson Emery, grandson of William Emery, Sr., original owner of the property, and Joseph Pollock. The Parkview subdivision and the Brynhaven subdivision were also developed during this period. A bond issue in 1956 provided for widening streets and blacktop paving. Rezoning for the Youth Center was approved. A city garage was built. The Elmhurst-Villa Park Water Commission was formed.

In 1955 the city was divided into seven wards, with two aldermen representing each ward. Another governmental change was the abolition of justice of the peace courts. By state law county judges took over the duties of magistrates.

An indication of expansion in city government as compared to village government is shown in the expenditure of the taxpayer's dollar in 1955. The police department took 21 cents; maintaining state road, 19; street and bridge fund, 15; rubbish disposal, 13; administration, 13; pensions, 5; public lighting, 4; fire protection, 4; library, 4; and public health, 2. The dollar was raised from real estate taxes, 38 cents; motor fuel taxes, 19; service charges, 14; building permits, 8; vehicle taxes, 7; other licenses, 8; fines and penalties, 3; miscellaneous, 3.

Local political parties continued their confusing comings and goings, and in the election of 1957 there were three of them. Benjamin D. Allison of the People's Party was elected mayor, defeating Mayor Ogden of the United Party and Thor Holter of the Citizens' Party. Mayor Allison served until 1961. He was an electrical engineer for the Chicago & North Western Railroad and lived in Elmhurst for 25 years, serving as an alderman from the Third Ward from 1953 to 1957. He was on the board of Grace Bible Church.

During Mayor Allison's term the sewage

Ben Allison, mayor (1957-1961).

treatment plant was expanded. Three overhead water pumps were built and storm pumps were installed. The Plan Commission under the successive chairmanships of Howard Willman, Donald Toeppen, and Roger Creighton, sought a long-range plan for the rapidly growing city, and in 1958 employed Evert Kincaid & Associates to survey Elmhurst's needs in zoning changes and in helping the central business district to compete with shopping centers growing up on the fringes of the city. The Elmhurst Master Plan was adopted October 20, 1958 and an underpass study commission was appointed. Also, under Mayor Allison's administration, Florence Gradolph was elected City Clerk. She was the first woman city clerk and served from 1957-69.

The Elmhurst Chamber of Commerce had a leading part in city planning. In 1947 it set up permanent offices at 105 South York Street, and in 1954 employed Howard Wendt as first full-time executive manager. His successors have been Harry Weeks, Kenneth Brace, Robert Haehl, and Rollin C. Smith. Offices were moved to 111 South York Street in 1957. The

Typical Farmers Market Day.

Alben F. Bates, Sr., as honorary Market Master.

Chamber of Commerce sponsored free parking areas and facilities for downtown music for shoppers. It took the lead in the program for Christmas street decorations and each year since 1968 has provided an office for Santa Claus, who is photographed with children and gives them coloring books and other gifts. Since

1975 the Chamber of Commerce has sponsored, with the cooperation of several organizations, the Festival of the Elms - an old-fashioned giant-size block party for all Elmhurst residents. In 1976 the Farmer's Market was established with great success.

THE CHANGING BUSINESS COMMUNITY

The middle years of the twentieth century were marked by the growth of chain stores, branch stores, and franchised stores, representing nationally owned corporations. Among those that have been in Elmhurst for many years are the Singer Sewing Center, Fannie May candies, Goodyear and Firestone Tire, and General Finance Corporation. Not all have been successful and many have come and gone. F.W. Woolworth Five and Ten Cent stores were a national institution in the early years of the century, and for sixty years after their beginning in 1879 found thousands of items that could be sold at those modest prices. Inflation doomed Elmhurst's Five-and-Ten although many Woolco stores carry on but not at five-and-ten prices. W.T. Grant moved its Chicago Loop store to Elmhurst, but eventually closed. John M. Smyth, maintained an Elmhurst branch for many years. Sears, Roebuck and Company closed its Elmhurst outlet in 1976.

Family-owned groceries gave way to supermarkets that strangely recall the general stores of Elmhurst's beginnings, as do Walgreen's Drug Store and Korvettes. National Tea Company started in 1924 with a small store at 125 West First Street. Its major shopping centers at North Avenue between York and Addison, and at Butterfield Road closed in 1976 when National withdrew from the Chicago area. Others that have come and gone are Kroger and High-Low. The Great Atlantic & Pacific Tea Company had five stores in Elmhurst in 1928, later consolidated at 131 Addison Avenue. A & P then built across the street at 178, only to sell out to the Market Place. Jewel Food Stores started with a small store at 157 North York Street, moved to the building in Schiller Street now occupied by City Hall, then built the large combination with Osco Drugs at 153 Schiller Street. Another Jewel store is at 1042 South York Street.

HALF CENTURY VETERANS

Many Elmhurst businesses have been thriving for a half century and more, and many others are approaching that veteran status.

One survivor of individualism is Otto's Quality Meat Market, 125 Addison Avenue, started in 1926, at which time fresh-killed rabbits and poultry were frequently seen in the window or hanging from the outside awning. There have been several owners, and the shop draws business from surrounding communities.

Nearly 50 years ago, The Palace Meat Market opened on First Street. Three years later the market was moved to 124 N. York Street and became Mannebach Foods. Throughout the next 25 years, Mannebach's served the community at that location with Victor Tarabilda managing the meat shop. For a time Krogers had the grocery concession. Approximately three years before moving, the grocery concession was dropped. Since Mannebach's was moved to 149 Addison Avenue in 1947, Mr. Tarabilda has continued its management.

Christian Pfund came to the United States from Switzerland in 1887. He and his wife Bertha moved to Elmhurst in 1913 and started a nursery on Lake Street in 1914. Several members of the family were in the flower business, Christian and Robert M. as florists; Ernest R., Liebhart, and Paul in the nursery. Lee Pfund opened the Pfund Elmhurst Flower Shop, 130 Addison Avenue, in 1926. It was moved to the northeast corner of York and Schiller streets, becoming Pfund & Clint. When Lee Pfund retired in 1952, Nels Clint became owner. The florist and gift shop later moved to 123 North York Street, former location of the Miller Keyes Funeral Home.

At least two Elmhurst real estate offices survived the Depression and were to round out a half century, W.S. Weller established real estate and insurance offices at 186 North York Street and there has been no change in location although the name of his son Bert Weller is now on the door. Thomas O. Myers, Sr., operated real estate offices in several locations, at one time advertising three, one of them at 600 East Lake Street, ready to greet newcomers as they drove into Elmhurst. The firm at 419 North York Street, still has the same name although it is Thomas O. Myers, Jr., who is the present manager.

The York State Bank and Trust Company was founded in 1927 at 529-629 South York Street and later moved across the street to 536

South York.

Davis Fuel Company, 137 West Vallette Street, started in 1926, advertising "Coal Business Exclusively". Retailing of fuel oil was added in 1950; an automobile service station in 1961, and a car wash operation in 1968.

As the central business district became crowded, auto dealers moved to outlying areas. The Bright Auto & Repair Company was in business for 57 years at 131 Schiller Street under the guidance of George Bright, Sr., then George Bright, Jr., and Ralph Mears, and then David Bright and David Mears. In 1952 it moved to 150 West Grand Avenue, becoming the Elmhurst Lincoln Mercury, Inc.

The Elmhurst Apartments, 203 South York Street is the red brick house built by Dr. Frederick Fischer as a residence. It has been variously known as the York Manor Private Hotel, York Manor Hotel, and Elmhurst Hotel, and has been operated by the Crane family since the closing of the Crane Sanitarium.

The Gibbons Robillard Funeral Home, 134 South York Street, is successor to the undertaking establishment started in 1910 by Harrison H. Robillard. Thomas Gibbons took over the business in 1960. Mr. Robillard died in 1975.

Lund Hardware was founded by Henry Lund in 1927 at 512 South York Street, later moving to 132 Addison Avenue, where it is operated by Raymond Lund, son of the founder.

J.C. Licht Company, which has paint and wallpaper stores in several suburbs, opened its Elmhurst store in 1926 at 170 North York Street and subsequently moved around the corner to 111 West Second Street.

Elmhurst Plumbing & Heating Company opened in 1921 at 152 East Park Avenue.

The Cottage Hill Cafe, for many years a meeting place for Elmhurst college students and business men's luncheon clubs, was founded in the 1920s at 117 West First Street by Chris and Peter Stevens, who later established the Stevens Steak House at York and Lake. The Cottage Hill Restaurant is now managed by two nephews of the founders.

Keeler's Candy Shop was opened in 1927 at 118 North York Street by Marvin H. Keeler. In 1931 it was sold to Frieda Knicker, who subsequently moved it down the street to 164 North York Street. Notable for making its chocolate candies on the premises, it is also a restaurant and ice cream and snack shop. Chipain's fruit and vegetable store, started in 1926 at 126 North York Street, became a liquor store after the repeal of Prohibition, and since 1947 has become a sporting goods store.

Harry C. Hesse started his men's clothing store in September, 1925, at 105 West First Street, later moving to 130 North York Street, and finally to 118 North York Street. When Mr. Hesse retired in 1951, the store was sold to C. Arthur Maxey, and subsequently to Albert Fine.

Jack Moeck, the tailor, would still be at his shop at 133 East First Street if the bulldozers making room for the railroad underpass had not leveled the building, which once had served as Rabe's Dairy. Jack Moeck started a few doors away in 1927. With his son William Moeck carrying on, the tailoring business has moved to Villa Park to start a second half century.

The Ramsey family started the newspaper distribution business known as the Elmhurst News Agency in 1926 and many generations of youngsters have traveled newspaper routes, at first from a small office at 127 West First Street, and later from 130 West Park Avenue, which was at one time the butcher shop of Henry G. Fritz.

Hammerschmidt and Franzen, millwork shop at 516 South York Street, and Elmhurst Peoples Coal and Material Company, 512 South York Street, both derive from the Hammerschmidt & Franzen coal, feed, and lumber yard which occupied a tract along the Chicago & North Western tracks west of the downtown area at the beginning of the century.

Other businesses more than a half century old have been discussed previously. The Elmhurst-Chicago Stone Company was started in 1883 by Adolph Hammerschmidt and Henry Assman. The Hammerschmidt name is still associated with this industry. Elm Lawn and Arlington cemeteries, both on East Lake Street, had their beginnings prior to 1910. The Soukup Hardware Store opened in 1920. The Elmhurst Press had its start before the turn of the century and has been published by the Cruger family since 1923.

The Elmhurst National Bank traces its beginnings to the private bank opened by Henry L. Glos in 1894. It assumed its present name in 1939, following the Depression mergers. Henry Schumacher was president from 1926 to 1935. Albert Glos, a nephew of Henry and Adam

The Booming 1950s

Glos, was president of the bank from 1936 to 1952. Edward Krell served as Executive Vice-President from 1939 to 1952. Donald Carlson has been president of the Elmhurst National Bank since 1952.

The bank operates a drive-in facility at Addison Avenue and Second Street and in 1975 opened a new structure with six drive-in and six walk-up windows at 145 S. York Street, south of the main bank building.

Closely associated with the history of the bank is Alben Bates, Sr. who retired in 1975 as Chairman of the Board and is now Emeritus Chairman. He had been a director of the bank since 1909 and during much of its history had

To the north of the new bank building are located two cut stones which were parapet decorations on the private bank of Henry L. Glos founded in 1904. The private bank ultimately became the Elmhurst National Bank and was located on the present site of the 5 story bank building. The new bank opened in October 1975.

also served as the bank attorney. He was succeeded as Chairman of the Board by his son Alben Bates, Jr. in 1975.

Alben Bates Sr., is the son of Dr. Frederick H. Bates, pioneer Elmhurst physician, and grandson of Gerry Bates, who built *Hill Cottage*. Mrs. Alben Bates, Sr. was Clara L. Glos, daughter of Jacob Glos and niece of Henry L. and Adam S. Glos. Mrs. Glos died June 10, 1965.

Alben F. Bates, Sr., attended Elmhurst schools and was graduated from Lake Forest College. He received a law degree from Northwestern University, and was admitted to the bar in 1911. He was Elmhurst city attorney from

Alben S. Bates Sr., Grandson of Gerry Bates, founder of Elmhurst.

1913 to 1938. He negotiated the acquisition of the Elmhurst Spring Water Company for the city. He has been awarded honorary law degrees from Lake Forest and Elmhurst colleges. He has been a member of the board of directors of the Elmhurst Memorial Hospital and of the board of directors of the YMCA. He was a charter member of the Elmhurst Chamber of Commerce. He is a member of the First Congregational Church and served for a time as moderator. His sons Alben, Jr., and Henry are active in civic affairs.

THE TURBULENT 1960s

Charles Weigel, Jr., was elected mayor in 1961 by the combined Citizens-United Party; he was re-elected by the Independent Party in 1963 and remained in office through a decade of

Charles Weigel, Jr., Mayor (1961-1973).

rapid expansion. He was born in Chicago and attended Steinmetz High School there, the University of Wisconsin, and the University of Illinois. He was manager of a small manufacturing company in Addison, and headed the Addison Industrial Association. He served on the Elmhurst Plan Commission, 1953-1957; was alderman from the third ward, 1957-1961 and was chairman of the Health and Sanitation Committee.

During Mayor Weigel's administration the land use report of the City Planning Commission was accepted. Expansion of the sewage system and the sewer separation projection were undertaken. The Elmhurst Youth Court was established. A referendum for the Elmhurst Public Library expansion was approved.

City Manager Robert T. Palmer in 1971 proposed $2,400,000 improvements for the city's sewage treatment plant. In 1972 a design study was received which recommended changes in the water distribution, supply source, and storage. This report focused on the use of "potable" water reservoirs (under-

Elmhurst City Hall, 119 Schiller Street, converted from Jewel Store in 1970.

ground in location). The "storm" run-off problem was solved by the sewer separation system.

Mrs. Dorothy Lentz was elected city clerk in 1969, succeeding Florise J. Gradolph. George N. Bathum, who had served as chief of police since 1959, was succeeded in 1963 by Victor E. Maul, who retired in 1968 after twenty years service. William T. Payne previously of Chicago, became chief in 1968. At this time the department manned ten patrol cars, four ambulances, and one unmarked car.

James D. Samuelson became the first full-

Central Business Districts Develpoment Plan of 1962 being discussed by (L to R) J.C. McCarthy, Kenneth S. Jacobs, Sr., Don G. Prindle, Robert E. Costigan, and George W. Unverzagt.

The Turbulent 1960s

time fire chief in 1967. Neil Fulton was employed in 1970 as fire protection consultant. An addition to the Schiller Street fire house was completed in 1970 and a new fire house was built on North York Street in 1972. The three stations housed eleven pieces of apparatus, a light wagon, and a Civil Defense trailer. The Elmhurst Fire Department includes fire chief, three captains, six lieutenants, 27 paid firemen, and 25 volunteer firemen.

Also under Weigel's administration, a Recycling Center, co-sponsored by the Elmhurst Environmental Committee, Inc., and the city, was established in 1972, and after a six months trial period in which the Center showed a profit, it was continued.

Charles Weigel, Jr., was awarded the Distinguished Citizen's Award by the Elmhurst Jaycees in 1972.

ELMHURST INDUSTRIAL PARK

A need to broaden the tax base was the reason given for the establishment of the Elmhurst Industrial Park, zoned for light industry in 1956. Tracts stretching to Grand Avenue were annexed in 1962 for a total of 600 acres, including a 200-foot lot at Lake Street and Myrtle Avenue, purchased from E.F. Boeske; 17 acres

Elmhurst Industrial Park, photographed in 1966, looking northwest from York Street north of the Eisenhower expressway.

at Interstate 294 and Factory Avenue, purchased from Caroline Blecke; and lots at Lake Street and Oaklawn Avenue, purchased from Enrico Gaetano. Within a few years 120 companies were located in the industrial park.

ORGANIZING TO MEET NEW PROBLEMS

The Elmhurst Unit of the DuPage County Homemakers Extension Association was organized September 19, 1961, at the home of Mrs. Perry Gatso with 15 members, and has grown to 68 members. Programs include craft workshops, clothing construction, consumer education, and food preservation, and sponsorship of a needy family.

The Elmhurst Unit of the Community Nursing Service of DuPage County was organized in 1963 with Mrs. George Scheppach as president. It holds an annual card party and luncheon benefit, conducts volunteer service workshops and has programs on health education, safety, rehabilitation, and new health services.

The Elmhurst Family Campers Club was organized August 15, 1964, by 19 families at Butterfield Park Field House. It took part in Operation Clean Sweep and Litter Pick-Ups. It is affiliated with the National Campers and Hikers Association and the Illinois state association. Co-presidents are Jack and Mary Sanborn.

Tree Towns Chapter No. 163, Parents Without Partners was chartered October 27, 1965, under sponsorship of the Oak Park Chapter. Members from Elmhurst, Villa Park, Lombard, Glen Ellyn, and West Chicago elected Don Erickson as president. It seeks to aid in solving the problems of single parents. Dolores Bonfield heads the group of 140 members.

The Elmhurst FISH, Inc., was organized May 1, 1969 by Shirley Flaherty to "serve the emergency needs of individuals not served by the state or county agencies" on a 24-hour call basis in such ways as delivering meals or driving patients to doctors' offices. There are 140 members. Jerome A. Urbik is executive director.

Elmhurst Chapter No. 1007, American Association of Retired Persons was organized in 1971 by Ida M. Goss, president, with 80 members. Its objective is to aid members' social, physical, economic, and intellectual needs, including adequate housing and public transportation. The 1976 membership is 160.

The Elmhurst Environmental Committee, Inc., was formed in 1971 at a meeting in the home of Bruce Mahon, and was supported by the Elmhurst City Council in opening a recycling center January 8, 1972. The purpose is to conserve resources by recycling paper, aluminum, glass, and tin cans. Thirty organizations assist in manning the center. Proceeds provide fencing and signs for the center, books for the library, aid the Illinois Prairie Path, and assist the programs of the DuPage Environmental Council and the Salt Creek Watershed Committee.

The Elmhurst Well Child Conference was organized in 1972 by 15 women meeting at the First Baptist Church to provide free or low cost medical care for children of indigent families, including monthly physical checkups. The group also assists a Vietnamese family and several foster children. The 20 members meet second Wednesdays at Redeemer Lutheran Church. Mrs. Frank Troost is president.

The Ray Graham Association for the Handicapped was formed in 1971 by a merger of the Ray Graham Association and the Community Welfare Association. The movement had its beginning in 1960 in a pilot program for handicapped children in a Baptist Church in LaGrange. In 1952 the group moved to Glen Ellyn in a vacant one-room school with "Bonaparte" over the door, and Bonaparte School became the permanent name of the project. Mrs. Ethel Kopecky was teacher and director. In 1956 'Bonaparte School' moved to Bensenville where the Community Welfare Association for Retarded Children provided three buses to bring 45 students and five teachers from 35 communities to the special education center. Office space was rented on York Road in Elmhurst, with a library manned by parents. The Ray Graham Workshop was started in the Elmhurst Presbyterian Church for older students, some over 23 years old. In 1958 nursery programs were set up in Elmhurst, Bellwood, and West Chicago.

Bonaparte School, with an enrollment of 125, a director, eight teachers, and a volunteer aide, moved to Addison Village Hall in 1958. Proviso Association for Retarded Children was founded in 1962, taking in Cook County students from Bonaparte and the Bellwood nursery class.

Bonaparte School continued to grow, having five classrooms, a practical life area, a craft room, ten teachers and two full-time volunteers. Mrs. Jeri Kelsey became director in 1970.

After the 1971 merger, Bonaparte School was continued for students from 2 to 14 years of age, while the Ray Graham Rehabilitation Program served those 14 years of age and older. Bonaparte School students come from school district referrals; children who do not meet public school standards. The staff includes director, program co-ordinator, 3 infant teachers, 2 teachers of ambulatory children, 9 teachers of non-ambulatory children, occupational therapist, physical therapist, a psychologist, physical education instructor, speech pathologist, and secretary. One of the original teachers of Bonaparte School, Marie Ekberg, is still teaching two-year-olds.

VIETNAM WAR

The first United States troops arrived in Viet Nam February 7, 1962 and a cease-fire went into effect January 27, 1973. During that period of nearly eleven years, many young men from Elmhurst served in the armed forces, of whom ten were killed in action and two were killed in vehicle accidents while in service. Those who died were: David R. Burkes, Jr., Steven J. Churchill, John Curtin, James T. Cummings, Jr., Thomas L. Leston, Thomas A. Mitchell, Larry Ray Palmer, Lawrence C. Rose, Jack A. Schneider, David Schulze, Kenneth E. Steinhebel, and Ronald L. Surges.

Listed as missing in action were: Robert L. Bennett, William B. Caldwell, Jack D. Demers, John R. Graf, Charles Ingels, William J. Kipp, John Eugene Krause, Edward J. Kunzer, Jr., John L. Schlener, Woodrow D. Schnitzius, Donald H. Shiley, Frederick J. Sibley, and Richard Wallen.

CITY OF THE 1970s

The population of Elmhurst in 1970 was 50,547, a large increase over the 36,991 of 1960, and more than doubled in two decades. The 1970 census figures show that Elmhurst retained its character as a city of homes. There were 14,594 housing units, of which 12,277 were occupied by their owners. The median number of rooms was 5.7 although 1,580 houses had 8 or more rooms. The median value was $28,600, with 544 houses valued at $50,000 or more, and only seven at less than $5,000.

Ray W. Fick, Jr., was elected mayor in 1973 on the Peoples Party ticket. Educated at the

Ray W. Fick Jr., mayor (1973-1977).

University of Illinois and Northwestern University, he was an attorney, and partner in the Chicago law firm of Herrick, McNeill, McElroy, and Peregrine. A resident of Elmhurst for fourteen years, he was a member of the Zoning Board of Appeals, was active in the campaign for the College of DuPage, and was a member of the Speakers Bureau for the Illinois Constitutional Convention. Mayor Fick also served on the Community Welfare Association Board and the Ray Graham Association Board. He was a past president of the Elmhurst Jaycees, and has served on the Elmhurst Presbyterian Church Board.

During his administration, the Senior Citizen's Commission was strengthened, and cab fares for senior citizens subsidized. Study and planning for changes in water distribution, storage and supply continued. In 1974 the design study report and recommendation of sites for the "potable" reservoirs was received and work began on redistribution of water supply. Progress was made in the long-continuing program to obtain Lake Michigan water for Elmhurst use. Designs of city engineers for reservoirs were approved in 1976 and acquisition of three sites was undertaken.

Neil Fulton was named assistant city manager in 1974 to succeed Anton Hartung who served from 1971 to 1973.

The major undertaking of Mayor Fick's administration was final approval of plans for an underpass under tracks of the Chicago & North

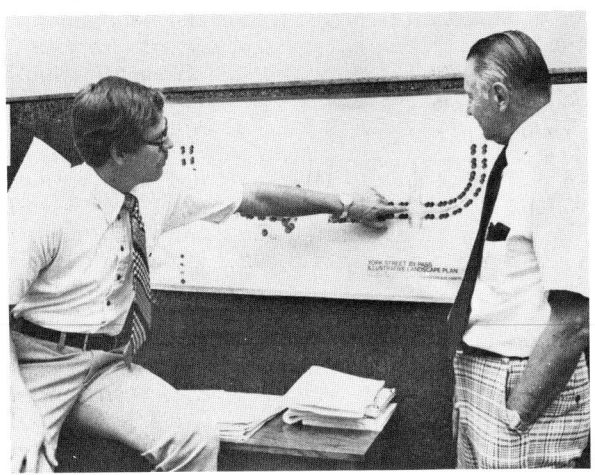

Robert Palmer, city manager, and Thomas Borchert, director of Public works examine landscape plans for the Elmhurst underpass.

Western Railroad, and beginning of its construction. The problem of getting across the tracks had plagued Elmhurst for decades, and became intensified with completion of the railway's Proviso yards in the 1920s, the increased length of freight trains for reasons of economy, and the vast increase in auto traffic during the rapid growth of the city. Over the years numerous plans for overpasses and underpasses were offered, all increasingly expensive. The plan adopted was estimated to cost $6,000,000, with the city's share about $1,000,000; the state's grade crossing protection fund providing $800,000, and the rest provided by the federal government. Early in 1976 the city began buying the necessary 26 parcels of land from South York and Marion streets north along Kenilworth Avenue to Second Street, then back to York Street. Ground breaking ceremonies August 6, 1976, started work on twelve-foot travel lanes, separated by a four-foot median. At the same time the railway built temporary tracks on Park Avenue, to be used until the underpass was completed.

Richard R. Swanson was named fire chief in 1976, succeeding James E. Samuelson. In 1977 Abner Ganet was elected mayor.

BICENTENNIAL CELEBRATION

Elmhurst celebrated the American Revolution Bicentennial with a festival week, beginning June 27, 1976, with entertainment, contests, and activities in city parks, a pioneer picnic, the traditional Fourth of July Parade on Saturday, July 3, and a bicentennial party Monday, July 5, at Wild Meadows Trace where Mayor Fick presided at ceremonies dedicating the Bicentennial Fountain, designed by landscape architect Dan Schourek.

In 1976 to celebrate the nations bicentennial, the citizens of Elmhurst contributed funds to build a fountain on South York Street in Wild Meadows Trace. Part of the funds were collected by asking citizens to send an additional seventy-six cents to city hall with their water bill payment.

Great Western passenger station, located in Wild Meadows Trace east of York Street, was restored in 1976 by the Park District as a museum, available to community groups as a meeting place.

CONCLUSION

What next? Every nation, every community, every person is a product of a past that inevitably shapes its future. This record shows that in many ways Elmhurst is very much like all other cities, but it also shows that in many ways Elmhurst is unlike any other community anywhere. It is the differences that make it worth while to delve into the past to better understand the present. In the future it is unlikely that Elmhurst will continue the rate of growth that has marked its recent decades. Its physical expansion is halted as it approaches in all directions the boundaries of neighboring communities. Projections indicate that Elmhurst will not long continue to be the largest city in DuPage County. But because of what has gone before, and because of what exists here, Elmhurst will retain a civic character that no computer can measure.

It is hoped that this history of the City of Elmhurst will be more than an incentive to the local pride of its citizens, that in showing in some detail one small part of the world in which we live, we will gain greater understanding of where we are, and where we are going.

ELMHURST CHRONOLOGY

1673 - Discovery of Illinois country by Jolliet and Marquette
1800 - Formation of Indiana Territory, including Illinois
       Inhabited at the formation by Indian tribes - Potawatomi, Ottawa, and Illinois
1809 - Achievement of territorial status for Illinois
1818 - Granting of statehood to Illinois
1830 - Beginning of forty years of pioneer immigration to Illinois
1833 - Signing of Treaty of Chicago by Indians, giving northeastern Illinois to the United States
1834 - Arrival of pioneer families in York Township (Atwater, Eldridge, Talmadge, Thurston)
1834 - Arrival of Frederick Graue family in Addison Township, settlement in Graue woods.
1835 - Final great war dance of Potowatomi before leaving area
1836 - Arrival of Torode family from Isle of Guernsey, settlement in Spring Road area
1837 - Settlement of Glos family on St. Charles Road, Cresent Park area
1837 - Opening of Frink & Walker Stage Lines on St. Charles Road
1839 - Organization of DuPage County, February 9, 1839
1842 - Purchase of land at $1.25 per acre on St. Charles Road by Gerry Bates
1843 - Construction of Hill Cottage Tavern
1845 - Establishment of Cottage Hill Post Office
1847 - Arrival of Edward Bonney, author of *Banditti of The Prairie*, in Cottage Hill
1849 - Occupation of new home at York Street and Park Avenue by Gerry Bates family
1849 - Opening of Bingham's Tavern on St. Charles Road
1849 - Routing of Galena & Chicago Railroad through Cottage Hill
1850 - Organization and naming of York Township
1850 - Organization of Public School District No. 1
1854 - Opening of Ludwig Graue store on First Street
1854 - Platting of lots in "Original Cottage Hill" by Gerry Bates
1856 - Purchase of 1000 acres in Cottage Hill by Thomas Barbour Bryan
1857 - Population - 200
1857 - Purchase of land at Prospect Avenue and St. Charles Road by Lucian Hagans and family
1857 - G.P.A. Healy purchases *Hill Cottage* and renames building *Clover Lawn*.
1860 - Settlement of land on South York Street by John R. Case, Sr. and family, planting of 1,000 cherry trees and 600 apple trees
1861 - First volunteer in the Civil War from Cottage Hill and Chicago, Cyrenus Litchfield
1861 - Eruption of Mammoth Spring on Talmadge Farm
1861 - Leadership of Civil War welfare effort by Thomas B. Bryan
1862 - Formation of first Protestant congregation in Cottage Hill - non denominational - meeting in Bryan's Bowling Alley
1863 - Construction of St. Mary's Church - first Catholic church
1864 - Construction of first brick building in Elmhurst - second Graue store
1864 - Construction of *Byrd's Nest Chapel*
1867 - Planting of elm trees on Cottage Hill Avenue by Lathrop, Bryan, Wadhams, and others
1869 - Changing the name of the village of Cottage Hill to Elmhurst
1870 - Population - 329
1871 - Arrival in Elmhurst of refugees from the Chicago fire
1871 - Founding of Elmhurst College as Melanchton Seminary
1872 - Platting of Emerson subdivision
1876 - Organization of St. Peter's Church - establishment of first parochial school
1879 - Establishment of Immanuel Lutheran School

1879 - Granting of franchise by Chicago Telephone Company, installation of first telephone in Elmhurst in Glos Building
1880 - Population - 723
1881 - Incorporation of the Village of Elmhurst
1882 - Election of Henry Glos as first village president
1883 - Founding and organization of Elmhurst-Chicago Stone Quarry
1884 - Construction of Village Hall on south side of City Road (renamed Schiller Street, 116 Schiller)
1886 - Granting of right of way through Elmhurst to Great Western Railroad
1887 - Election of Peter Wolf as village president
1888 - Construction of original Hawthorne School
1889 - Purchase of Wadhams Farm in south Elmhurst for subdivision by William H. Emery
1889 - Founding of Elmhurst Spring Water Company
1889 - Founding of Elmhurst Electric Light Company
1890 - Population - 1050
1892 - Installation of electric power in Elmhurst
1892 - Appointment of Thomas B. Bryan as vice-president of the Columbian Exposition
1893 - Laying of first sewers
1893 - Adoption of first health ordinance
1893 - Establishment of volunteer fire department
1894 - Founding of the *Elmhurst News*, first weekly newspaper.
1896 - Organization of health department
1899 - Establishment of St. Mary's Catholic School
1900 - Population - 1728
1900 - Founding of Elmhurst Golf Club (land later used for York High School)
1902 - Election of Edwin Heidemann as village president.
1902 - Routing of Chicago, Aurora & Elgin Railroad through Elmhurst
1903 - Organization of the Elmhurst State Bank
1903 - Granting of gas franchise to H.W. Darling
1905 - Election of Henry C. Schumacher as village president
1907 - Opening of Cherry Farm subdivision
1908 - Election of C.J. Albert as village president
1910 - Population 2360
1910 - Adoption of *city* form of government.
1910 - Election of Henry C. Schumacher as first city mayor
1912 - Election of F.W.M. Hammerschmidt as mayor
1913 - Organization of Elmhurst Woman's Club
1914 - Organization of Boy Scouts in Elmhurst
1916 - Establishment of Elmhurst Public Library
1917 - Destruction by fire of original Hawthorne School
1917 - Organization of Camp Fire Girls in Elmhurst
1918 - Organization of Elmhurst Boosters Club
1918 - Establishment of York Community High School
1919 - Organization of Girl Scouts in Elmhurst
1919 - Organization of the Peoples Party
1919 - Organization of the American Legion Post
1919 - Election of Otto Balgemann as mayor
1919 - Holding of first service, January 5 - First Church of Christ, Scientist
1920 - Population - 4594
1920 - Establishment of the Elmhurst Park District
1924 - First Special Zoning Commission - recommendation for creation of Board of Appeals
1925 - Organization of the Elmhurst Police Department
1926 - Organization of Elmhurst Hospital, building of first unit
1926 - Publication of first zoning ordinance
1926 - Relocation of city offices to 134 Addison Avenue
1926 - Organization of Elmhurst Boosters Club as Elmhurst Chamber of Commerce
1928 - Organization of Elmhurst Garden Club
1930 - Population - 14,055

1931 - Election of Edward Blatter as mayor
1931 - Establishment of the Veterans of Foreign Wars organization
1932 - Organization of the League of Women Voters in Elmhurst
1933 - Election of Claude Van Auken as mayor
1933 - 35 - Depression years
1934 - Organization of Board of Fire & Police Commissioners
1936 - Celebration of Elmhurst Centennial
1938 - Organization of American Association of University Women, AAUW, in Elmhurst
1939 - Organization of United Party
1940 - Population - 15,458
1940 - Organization of Elmhurst Community Theatre
1945 - Election of William S. Fellows as mayor
1945 - Organization of Elmhurst Safety Council
1945 - First meeting of Elmhurst Plan Commission, February 26
1946 - Relocation of city offices to Glos Mansion in April
1946 - Incorporation of Elmhurst Artist Guild
1947 - Organization of Elmhurst Children's Theatre
1948 - Completion of Mayor Fellows term by Ervin Wilson
1949 - Organization of Newcomers Club
1950 - Population - 21,273
1951 - Election of Ervin F. Wilson as mayor
1952 - Adoption of *council - manager* form of government
1952 - Organization of Elmhurst YMCA
1952 - Creation of Elmhurst Historical Commission
1953 - Election of Earl Ogden as mayor
1953 - Employment of Robert Palmer as city manager
1953 - Initiation of services by YMCA on First Street
1953 - Platting of Emery Manor subdivision
1954 - Platting of Brynhaven subdivision
1955 - Identification of first Dutch elm disease in Elmhurst
1956 - Planning and establishment of Elmhurst Industrial Park
1957 - Election of Benjamin Allison as mayor
1957 - Initiation of services by Elmhurst Historical Museum, 3rd floor, Glos Mansion
1957 - Suspension of services by Chicago, Aurora & Elgin Railroad
1959 - Organization of Elmhurst Business and Professional Women
1960 - Population - 36,991
1960 - Celebration by Elmhurst of fifty years of city form of government
1961 - Election of Charles Weigel as mayor
1961 - Construction of Lizzadro Museum of Lapidary Art
1961 - Dedication of YMCA building
1965 - Dedication of addition to Elmhurst Public Library, relocation of Elmhurst Historical Museum to second floor of library
1968 - Dedication of Berens Park as observance of Illinois Sesquicentennial Celebration
1970 - Population - 50,547
1970 - Relocation of city offices to 119 Schiller Street
1972 - Establishment of Elmhurst Recycling Center
1973 - Election of Ray W. Fick, Jr. as mayor
1974 - Organization and approval of Unit School District No. 2, June
1974 - Broadcasting of first programs by Elmhurst radio station WKDC, October 10
1975 - Relocation and dedication of permanent home of Elmhurst Historical Museum in Glos Mansion, May 18
1976 - Celebration of American Bicentennial by Elmhurst with dedication of fountain and restoration of railway station
1977 - Election of Abner Ganet as mayor

ELMHURST OFFICIALS

VILLAGE OFFICIALS

1882 - 1883

President - Henry L. Glos

Trustees

Peter A. Wolf
Christian Blievernicht
George Sawin
Ernst Balgemann
Henry Hohmann, Sr.

Village Clerk - William H. Litchfield
Treasurer - George F. Heidemann

1883 - 1884

President - Henry L. Glos

Trustees

Peter A. Wolf
Christian Blievernicht
George Sawin
Ernst Balgemann
Henry Hohmann, Sr.

Village Clerk - William H. Litchfield
Treasurer - George F. Heidemann

1884 - 1885

President - Henry L. Glos

Trustees

Peter A. Wolf
Christian Blievernicht
George Sawin
Ernst Balgemann
Henry Hohmann, Sr.

Village Clerk - William H. Litchfield
Treasurer - George F. Heidemann

1885 - 1886

President - Henry L. Glos

Trustees

Peter A. Wolf
Ernst Balgemann
George Sawin
Henry Hohmann, Sr.

Village Clerk - F.H. Bates
Treasurer - George F. Heidemann

1886 - 1887

President - Henry L. Glos

Trustees

Peter A. Wolf
Henry Hohmann, Sr.
Ernst Balgemann

F.H. Bates
Samuel G. Taylor

Village Clerk - William H. Litchfield
Treasurer - George F. Heidemann

1887 - 1888

President - Peter A. Wolf

Trustees

Henry L. Glos
Henry Hohmann, Sr.
Ernst Balgemann

Samuel G. Taylor
Albert S. Brownell

Village Clerk - William H. Litchfield
Treasurer - George F. Heidemann

1888 - 1889

President - Henry L. Glos

Trustees

Peter A. Wolf
Ernst Balgemann
Henry Hohmann, Sr.

Samuel G. Taylor
Albert S. Brownell
William Hanebuth

Village Clerk - William Litchfield
Treasurer - George F. Heidemann

1889 - 1890

President - Henry L. Glos

Trustees

Peter A. Wolf
Ernst Balgemann
Henry Hohmann, Sr.

Albert S. Brownell
Sanuel G. Taylor
William Hanebuth

Village Clerk - William Litchfield
Treasurer - George F. Heidemann

1890 - 1891

President - Henry L. Glos

Trustees

Peter A. Wolf
William Hanebuth
Allen S. Ray

Ernst Balgemann
Philip Hohmann

Village Clerk - August Baeder
Treasurer - George F. Heidemann

Elmhurst Village Officials

1891 - 1892

President - Henry L. Glos

Trustees

Peter A. Wolf
William Hanebuth
Allen S. Ray

Ernst Balgemann
Philip Hohmann
Henry Hoehne

Village Clerk - August Baeder
Treasurer - George F. Heidemann

1892 - 1893

President - Henry L. Glos

Trustees

Ernst Balgemann
Philip Hohmann
John D. Keiler

William Hanebuth
Allen S. Ray
John Langguth

Village Clerk - August Baeder
Treasurer - George F. Heidemann

1893 - 1894

President - Henry L. Glos

Trustees

Ernst Balgemann
John D. Keiler
Albert H. Fischer

William Hanebuth
John Langguth
John Mueller

Village Clerk - August Baeder
Treasurer - George F. Heidemann

1894 - 1895

President - Henry L. Glos

Trustees

Ernst Balgemann
Albert H. Fischer
F.H. Bates

John Langguth
John Mueller
H.A. Christy

Village Clerk - August Baeder
Treasurer - George F. Heidemann

1895 - 1896

President - Henry L. Glos

Trustees

Ernst Balgemann
John Mueller
H.A. Christy

John Langguth
F.H. Bates
H.G. Struckmann

Village Clerk - Henry C. Schumacher
Treasurer - George F. Heidemann

1896 - 1897

President - Henry L. Glos

Trustees

Edwin F. Heinemann	Ernst Balgemann
Charles W. Bates	John Mueller
Lee L. Bettinger	Henry Struckmann

Village Clerk - Henry C. Schumacher
Treasurer - George F. Heidemann

1897 - 1898

President - Henry L. Glos

Trustees

Edwin F. Heinemann	John D. Keiler
Charles W. Bates	John Mueller
Lee L. Bettinger	Herman Cordt

Village Clerk - Henry C. Schumacher
Treasurer - George F. Heidemann - Nov. 6, 1897
Otto H. Stange - appointed

1898 - 1899

President - Henry L. Glos

Trustees

John D. Keiler	Charles J. Marhoefer
John Mueller	George W. Griffin
Herman Cordt	Henry Blecke

Village Clerk - Henry C. Schumacher
Treasurer - Otto H. Stange

1899 - 1900

President - Henry L. Glos

Trustees

Charles J. Marhoefer	John D. Keiler
George W. Griffin	Albert F. Ohlerich
Henry Blecke	Ernst Balgemann

Village Clerk - Henry C. Schumacher
Treasurer - Otto H. Stange

1900 - 1901

President - Henry L. Glos

Trustees

John D. Keiler	Henry Blecke
Albert F. Ohlerich	George W. Griffin
Ernst Balgemann	Fred Schroeder

Village Clerk - Henry C. Schumacher
Treasurer - Otto H. Stange

Elmhurst Village Officials

1901 - 1902

President - Henry L. Schumacher

Trustees

Henry Blecke
George W. Griffin
Fred Schroeder

Philip Hohmann
John D. Keiler
Ernst Balgemann

Village Clerk - Henry C. Schumacher
Treasurer - Otto H. Stange

1902 - 1903

President - Edwin F. Heidemann

Trustees

Philip Hohmann
Fred H. Goltermann
John D. Keiler

Ernst Balgemann
Emerson H. Brush
Charles J. Marhoefer

Village Clerk - Henry C. Schumacher
Treasurer - Otto H. Balgemann

1903 - 1904

President - Edwin F. Heidemann

Trustees

Fred H. Goltermann
Emerson H. Brush
Charles Marhoefer

William J. Meyer
R. Hammerschmidt
Carl Fielitz

Village Clerk - Henry C. Schumacher
Treasurer - Albert F. Ohlerich
(elected for 2 terms)

1904 - 1905

President - Edwin F. Heidemann

Trustees

William J. Meyer
R. Hammerschmidt
Carl Fielitz

George F. Rosche
William Beutjer
John Mueller

Village Clerk - Henry Schumacher
Treasurer - Otto H. Balgemann

(Aug. 20, 1903, John Mueller elected president protem in place of Heidemann who resigned)

1905 - 1906

President - Henry C. Schumacher

Trustees

George F. Rosche
William Beutjer
Oscar G. Fischer
Fred H. Mahler
Fred C. Haas
John Mueller

Village Clerk - Lorenz P. Wolf
Treasurer - Otto W. Balgemann

1906 - 1907

President - Henry C. Schumacher

Trustees

Oscar G. Fischer
Fred H. Mahler
Fred C. Haas
Charles J. Marhoefer
John Mueller
George F. Rosche

Village Clerk - Lorenz P. Wolf
Treasurer - Edwin Fiene

1907 - 1908

President - Henry C. Schumacher

Trustees

Charles J. Marhoefer
John Mueller
George F. Rosche
Fred C. Haas
C.J. Albert
Oscar G. Fischer

Village Clerk - Lorenz P. Wolf
Treasurer - Edwin Fiene

1908 - 1909

President - Henry C. Schumacher

Trustees

Fred C. Haas
C.J. Albert
Oscar G. Fischer
Louis Stromberg
Fred H. Golterman
Charles J. Marhoefer

Village Clerk - Ray R. Osborne
Treasurer - Edwin Fiene

1909 - 1910

President - C.J. Albert

Trustees

Louis Stromberg
Fred H. Golterman
Charles J. Marhoefer
A. Julius Breuhaus
Edwin F. Balgemann
Richard M. Hanson

Village Clerk - Ray R. Osborne
Treasurer - George W. Thoma

Elmhurst City Officials

CITY OFFICIALS

1910 - 1911

Mayor - Henry C. Schumacher

Alderman

C.J. Albert
Charles J. Marhoefer
William J. Meyer

John Mueller
George F. Rosche
Gottfried Weber

City Clerk - Julius J. Braun
Treasurer - R. Hammerschmidt
City Attorney - F.C. Harbour

1911 - 1912

Mayor - F.W.M. Hammerschmidt

Aldermen

W.J. Meyer
G.F. Rosche
G. Weber

J. Mueller
H.E. Egolf
W.B. Pearn

City Clerk - Thomas Hawkins
Treasurer - Julius J. Braun
City Attorney - Charles S. Williston

1912 - 1913

Mayor - F.W.M. Hammerschmidt

Aldermen

J. Mueller
H.E. Egolf
W.B. Pearn

G. Meyer
O.H. Stange
H.H. Putnam

City Clerk - Thomas Hawkins
Treasurer - Julius J. Braun
City Attorney - Charles S. Williston

1913 - 1914

Mayor - F.W.M. Hammerschmidt

Aldermen

J. Mueller
H.E. Egolf
W.B. Pearn

G. Meyer
O.H. Stange
H.H. Putnam

City Clerk - Thomas Hawkins
Treasurer - Fred H. Mahler
City Attorney - Alben F. Bates

1914 - 1915

Mayor - F.W.M. Hammerschmidt

Aldermen

J. Mueller
H.E. Egolf
W.B. Pearn

O.H. Stange
H.H. Putnam
H.F. Hobein

City Clerk - Thomas Hawkins
Francis N. Neumann - Mar. 1, 1915 to Apr. 31, 1915
Treasurer - Fred H. Mahler
City Attorney - Alben F. Bates

1915 - 1916

Mayor - F.W.M. Hammerschmidt

Aldermen

J. Mueller
H.E. Egolf
W.B. Pearn

O.H. Stange
H.H. Putnam
H.F. Hobein

City Clerk - Arthur H. Kochaisky
A.G. Radenzel
Treasurer - Julius J. Braun
City Attorney - Alben F. Bates

1916 - 1917

Mayor - F.W.M. Hammerschmidt

Aldermen

J. Mueller
H.E. Egolf
W.B. Pearn
A.G. Bauersfeld

O.H. Stange
H.H. Putnam
H.G. Hobein
J. Randolph

City Clerk - Francis N. Neumann - May 1, 1916
Treasurer - Fred H. Mahler
City Attorney - Alben F. Bates

1917 - 1918

Mayor - F.W.M. Hammerschmidt

Aldermen

J.O. Eis
W.R. Cadwell
J. Mueller
V.M. Ollier

O.H. Stange
H.H. Putnam (A.C. Warren)
A.G. Bauersfeld
H.F. Hobein

City Clerk - Francis N. Neumann
Treasurer - Charles F. Hess
City Attorney - Alben F. Bates

Elmhurst City Officials

1918 - 1919

Mayor - F.W.M. Hammerschmidt

Aldermen

J.O. Eis	C.E. Kersten
W.R. Cadwell	R.H. Fluegge
J. Mueller	H.F. Hobein
V.M. Ollier	A.C. Warren

City Clerk - Francis N. Neumann
Treasurer - Charles F. Hess
City Attorney - Alben F. Bates

1919 - 1920

Mayor - Otto W. Balgemann

Aldermen

J. Mueller (C.L. VanAuken)	C.E. Kersten
W.R. Cadwell	R.H. Fluegge
G.R. Chapman	H.F. Hobein
G.J. Scott	A.C. Warren

City Clerk - Francis N. Neumann
Treasurer - W.S. Weller
City Attorney - Alben F. Bates

1920 - 1921

Mayor - Otto W. Balgemann

Aldermen

C.L. VanAuken	C.E. Kersten
W.R. Cadwell	R.H. Fluegge
G.R. Chapman	H.F. Hobein
G.J. Scott	A.C. Warren

City Clerk - Francis N. Neumann
Treasurer - W.S. Weller
City Attorney - Alben F. Bates

1921 - 1922

Mayor - Otto W. Balgemann

Aldermen

G.J. Scott	C.E. Kersten
W.R. Cadwell	R.H. Fluegge
C.L. VanAuken	H.F. Hobein
G.R. Chapman	A.C. Warren

City Clerk - Francis N. Neumann
Treasurer - L. Brodt
City Attorney - Alben F. Bates

1922 - 1923

Mayor - Otto W. Balgemann

Aldermen

G.J. Scott
W.R. Cadwell
C.L. VanAuken
G.R. Chapman

C.E. Kersten
E. Schuttler
H.F. Hobein
H.T. Richards

City Clerk - Francis N. Neumann
Treasurer - L. Brodt
City Attorney - Alben F. Bates

1923 - 1924

Mayor - Otto W. Balgemann

Aldermen

G.J. Scott
E.W. Bosworth
C.L. VanAuken
G.R. Chapman

C.E. Kersten
E. Schuttler
H.F. Hobein
H.T. Richards

City Clerk - Francis N. Neumann
Treasurer - Louis W. Holle
City Attorney - Alben F. Bates

1924 - 1925

Mayor - Otto W. Balgemann

Aldermen

G.J. Scott
E.W. Bosworth
C.L. VanAuken
G.R. Chapman

W. Youngberg
E. Schuttler
H.F. Hobein
H.T. Richards

City Clerk - Francis N. Neumann
Treasurer - Louis W. Holle
City Attorney - Alben F. Bates

1925 - 1926

Mayor - Otto W. Balgemann

Aldermen

W.R. Gernon
E.W. Bosworth
C.L. VanAuken
G.R. Chapman

W. Youngberg
E. Schuttler
H.F. Hobein
H.T. Richards

City Clerk - Francis N. Neumann
Treasurer - Alexander H. Miller
City Attorney - Alben F. Bates

Elmhurst City Officials

1926 - 1927

Mayor - Otto W. Balgemann

Aldermen

W.R. Gernon
E.W. Bosworth
C.L. VanAuken
G.R. Chapman

W. Youngberg
E. Schuttler
M. Maffit
H.T. Richards

City Clerk - Francis N. Neumann
Treasurer - Alexander H. Miller
City Attorney - Alben F. Bates

1927 - 1928

Mayor - Otto W. Balgemann

Aldermen

B.A. Schumacher
J. Cronin
B. Simmons
J. Morrell
W. Burdsall

W. Youngberg
W.J. Reinhold
M. Maffit
H.T. Richards
M.J. Gara

City Clerk - Francis N. Neumann
Treasurer - Louis W. Holle
City Attorney - Alben F. Bates

1928 - 1929

Mayor - Otto W. Balgemann

Aldermen

B.A. Schumacher
J. Cronin
B. Simmons
J. Morrell
W. Burdsall

W. Youngberg
W.J. Reinhold
A.J. Bartusch
H.F. Richards
M.J. Slavik

City Clerk - Francis N. Neumann
Treasurer - Louis W. Holle
City Attorney - Alben F. Bates

1929 - 1930

Mayor - Otto W. Balgemann

Aldermen

B.A. Schumacher
J. Cronin
B. Simmons
G.L. Meister
W.R. Burdsall

W. Youngberg
W.J. Reinhold
A.J. Bartusch
H.T. Richards
M.J. Slavik

City Clerk - Francis N. Neumann
Treasurer - Alexander H. Miller
City Attorney - Fred C. Harbour

1930 - 1931

Mayor - Otto W. Balgemann

Aldermen

B.A. Schumacher
J. Cronin
B. Simmons
G.L. Meister
W.R. Burdsall

W. Youngberg
W.J. Reinhold
A.J. Bartusch
A.J. Breuhaus
M.J. Slavik

City Clerk - Francis N. Neumann
Treasurer - Alexander H. Miller
City Attorney - Fred C. Harbour

1931 - 1932

Mayor - Edward H. Blatter

Aldermen

R.B. Hilliard
W.S. Weller
P.J. McGary
G.L. Meister
S.T. Bennett

W. Youngberg
M.M. Slocum -
   To fill one year vacancy
   created by resignation of
   Wm. J. Reinhold
A.J. Bartusch
A.J. Breuhaus
M.J. Slavik

City Clerk - Francis N. Neumann
Treasurer - John M. Boardman
City Attorney - Charles M. Haft

1932 - 1933

Mayor - Edward H. Blatter

Aldermen

R.B. Hilliard
W.S. Weller
P.J. McGary
G.L. Meister
S.T. Bennett

W. Youngberg
M.M. Slocum
A.J. Bartusch
A.J. Breuhaus
M.J. Slavik

City Clerk - Francis N. Neumann
Treasurer - John M. Boardman
City Attorney - Charles M. Haft

1933 - 1934

Mayor - Claude L. Van Auken

Aldermen

A.J. Strand
H.H. Brodt
L.W. Holle
G.L. Meister
R.T. Butts

W. Youngberg
M.M. Slocum
A.J. Bartusch
A.J. Breuhaus
M.J. Slavik

City Clerk - Francis N. Neumann
Treasurer - Frank J. Maier
City Attorney - Fred C. Harbour

Elmhurst City Officials

1934 - 1935

Mayor - Claude L. Van Auken

Aldermen

A.J. Strand
H.H. Brodt
L.W. Holle
G.L. Meister
R.T. Butts

J.W. Vogel
W.S. Fellows
J.L. Glass
A.J. Breuhaus
M.J. Slavik

City Clerk - Francis N. Neumann
Treasurer - Frank J. Maier
City Attorney - Fred C. Harbour

1935 - 1937

Mayor - Claude L. Van Auken

Aldermen

J.W. Vogel
H.H. Brodt
J.L. Glass
G.L. Meister
W.R. Carpenter

R.C. Hickey
W.S. Fellows
E.F. Wilson
A.J. Breuhaus
H.A. Webb

City Clerk - Francis N. Neumann
Treasurer - John F.X. Hennessy
City Attorney - Fred C. Harbour

1937 - 1939

Mayor - Claude L. Van Auken

Aldermen

J.W. Vogel
H.H. Brodt
J.L. Glass
G.L. Meister
W.R. Carpenter

R.C. Hickey
   Resigned Dec. 20, 1937
   Jarrel A. Burrow Elected Feb. 19, 1938
W.S. Fellows
E.F. Wilson
A.J. Breuhaus
H.A. Webb
   Resigned Dec. 20, 1937
   Howard C. Willman Elected Feb. 19, 1938

City Clerk - Francis N. Neumann
Treasurer - Frank J. Maier
City Attorney - Fred C. Harbour to May 1, 1935
Lawrence C. Traeger June 6, 1938
to Nov. 1, 1947

1939 - 1941

Mayor - Claude L. Van Auken

Aldermen

B.F. Stevens
H.H. Brodt
E.F. Wilson
E.A. Whitney
H.C. Willman

J.W. Vogel
W.S. Fellows
J.L. Glass
G.L. Meister
W.R. Carpenter

City Clerk - Francis N. Neumann
Treasurer - Frank J. Maier
City Attorney - Lawrence C. Traeger
Police Magistrate - C. Andy Anderson

1941 - 1943

Mayor - Claude L. Van Auken

Aldermen

J.M. Burrow
W.S. Fellows
W.O. Sanford
G.L. Meister
M.J. Slavik

H.C. Willman
H.H. Brodt
B.F. Stevens
E.F. Wilson
E.A. Whitney

City Clerk - Francis N. Neumann
Treasurer - J.W. Vogel
City Attorney - Lawrence C. Traeger
Police Magistrate - C. Andy Anderson

1943 - 1945

Mayor - Claude L. Van Auken

Aldermen

B.F. Stevens
H.H. Brodt
N.A. Ulseth
E.A. Whitney
H.C. Willman

M.J. Slavik
G.L. Meister
W.O. Sanford
J.M. Burrow
W.S. Fellows

City Clerk - Francis N. Neumann
Treasurer - John W. Vogel
City Attorney - Lawrence C. Traeger
Police Magistrate - C. Andy Anderson

1945 - 1947

Mayor - William S. Fellows

Aldermen

R.L. Yeisley
Harry A. Roe
W.O. Sanford
G.L. Meister
M.J. Slavik

B.F. Stevens
H.H. Brodt
N.A. Ulseth
E.A. Whitney
H.C. Willman

City Clerk - Francis N. Neumann
Treasurer - Frank J. Maier
City Attorney - Lawrence C. Traeger
Police Magistrate - Alfred E. Watts

1947 - 1949

Mayor - William S. Fellows (deceased 1-17-48)
Ervin F. Wilson (6-29-48 unexpired term)

Aldermen

E.W. Dornoff
H.H. Brodt
N.A. Ulseth
W.C. Block, Jr.
H.C. Willman

R.L. Yeisley
H.A. Roe
W.O. Sanford
G.L. Meister
M.J. Slavik

City Clerk - Francis N. Neumann
Treasurer - Frank J. Maier
City Attorney - Lawrence C. Traeger
November, 1947 Michael Kross
Police Magistrate - Alfred E. Watts

Elmhurst City Officials

1949 - 1951

Mayor - Ervin F. Wilson

Aldermen

W.C. McHugh
H.A. Roe
R.M. Buswell
W.C. Block, Jr.
A.W. Sorenson

E.W. Dornoff
H.H. Brodt
N.A. Ulseth
G.L. Meister
H.C. Willman

City Clerk - G. Clifton Prager
Treasurer - Earl W. Ogden
City Attorney - George Billett
Police Magistrate - Roswell Eaton

1951 - 1953

Mayor - E.F. Wilson

Aldermen

E.R. Dornoff
H.A. Roe
T.J. Woeller
W.C. Bloch, Jr.
A.W. Sorenson

W.C. McHugh
G.W. Unverzagt
R.M. Buswell
G.L. Meister
C.O. Tilly

City Clerk - G. Clifton Prager
Treasurer - Earl W. Ogden
City Attorney - George Billett
Police Magistrate - Roswell Eaton

1953 - 1955

Mayor - Earl W. Ogden

Aldermen

J. Van Gorkom, Jr.
G.W. Unverzagt
T.J. Woeller
J. VanSlyke, Jr.
H.J. Miller

B. Allison
W.C. Block, Jr.
C.O. Tilly
E. Goldthorpe,
    Resigned 7-1954
B. Atwood

City Clerk - Barthel Nelson
Treasurer - W.C. Schaefer
City Attorney - George Billett
Police Magistrate - Alfred E. Watts

1955 - 1957

Mayor - Earl W. Ogden

Aldermen

Thomas M. Strane
John Van Slyke, Jr.
Henry J. Miller
T.J. Woeller

B. Allison
Clarence Reichold
William J. Collins
Benton Atwood
James Palmquist

City Clerk - Barthel Nelson
Treasurer - W.C. Schaefer
City Attorney - George Billett
Police Magistrate - Alfred E. Watts

1957 - 1959

Mayor - Benjamin D. Allison

Aldermen

Thomas M. Strane - First Ward
Chas. R. VanSlyke - First Ward
Jack Knuepfer - Second Ward
Frank Rebek - Second Ward
   (Resigned 11-17-58)
T.J. Woeller - Third Ward

Gary Garrett - Third Ward
Clarence Reichold - Fourth Ward
William J. Collins - Fourth Ward
James E. Palmquist - Fifth Ward
Charles Weigel, Jr. - Fifth Ward

City Clerk - Florise J. Gradolph
Treasurer - Robert H. Long
City Attorney - George Billett
Police Magistrate - Henry F. Marquard

1959 - 1961

Mayor - Benjamin D. Allison

Aldermen

Charles R. VanSlyke - First Ward
John M. Armstrong - First Ward
Don G. Prindle - Second Ward
Daniel J. Lenane - Second Ward
Gary Garrett - Third Ward
Herbert G. Rosback - Third Ward
William J. Collins - Fourth Ward

George F. McGregor - Fourth Ward
Charles Weigel, Jr. - Fifth Ward
Naneth R. Tilly - Fifth Ward
James E. Palmquist - Sixth Ward
   (Resigned 9-1-59)
Henry T. VandeKerkhoff - Sixth Ward
Max L. Bedell - Seventh Ward
James T. Cummings - Seventh Ward
Robert E. Costigan - Sixth Ward
   (Special Election 10-18-60)

City Clerk - Florise J. Gradolph
Treasurer - Robert H. Long
City Attorney - George Billett
Police Magistrate - Henry F. Marquard
(Deceased 12-21-59)

1961 - 1963

Mayor - Charles Weigel, Jr.

Aldermen

John M. Armstrong - First Ward
   (Resigned 2-5-62)
Kenneth S. Jacobs, Sr. - First Ward
Don G. Prindle - Second Ward
Daniel J. Lenane - Second Ward
Herbert G. Rosback - Third Ward
Geo. W. Unverzagt, Jr. - Third Ward
   (Resigned 2-18-63)
George F. McGregor - Fourth Ward

William C. Sanford - Fourth Ward
Naneth R. Tilly - Fifth Ward
Hugh H. Drake - Fifth Ward
Henry T. VandeKerkhoff - Sixth Ward
   (Resigned 6-19-61)
Robert E. Costigan - Sixth Ward
Max L. Bedell - Seventh Ward
John C. Endahl - Seventh Ward

City Clerk - Florise J. Gradolph
Treasurer - Robert H. Long
City Attorney - George Billett
Police Magistrate - Marvin E. Johnson

Elmhurst City Officials

1963 - 1965

Mayor - Charles Weigel, Jr.

Aldermen

Kenneth S. Jacobs, Sr. - First Ward
   (Resigned 1-20-64)
James S. Weldon - First Ward
Daniel J. Lenane - Second Ward
Carl Lundgren - Second Ward
Donald C. Ames - Third Ward
William P. Butler - Third Ward
George F. McGregor - Fourth Ward
William C. Sanford - Fourth Ward

Hugh H. Drake - Fifth Ward
John H. Carnell - Fifth Ward
Robert E. Costigan - Sixth Ward
John H. Carnell - Fifth Ward
   (Resigned 1-31-65)
Robert E. Costigan - Sixth Ward
Philip M. Sullivan - Sixth Ward
John C. Endahl - Seventh Ward
Robert R. Nelson - Seventh Ward

City Clerk - Florise J. Gradolph
Treasurer - Robert H. Long
City Attorney - George Billett
Police Magistrate - Marvin E. Johnson

1965 - 1967

Mayor - Charles Weigel, Jr.

Aldermen

James S. Weldon - First Ward
Thomas D. Kennedy - First Ward
Carl Lundgren - Second Ward
Robert J. Haehl - Second Ward
Donald C. Ames - Third Ward
Lyle J. Hope - Third Ward
George F. McGregor - Fourth Ward

Frank J. Zink - Fourth Ward
Robert E. Kett - Fifth Ward 4 yr.
Terence F. Leen - Fifth Ward 2 yr.
Philip M. Sullivan - Sixth Ward
Edward J. Jungles - Sixth Ward
John C. Endahl - Seventh Ward
Robert R. Nelson - Seventh Ward

City Clerk - Florise J. Gradolph
Treasurer - Robert H. Long
City Attorney - George Billett

1967 - 1969

Mayor - Charles Weigel, Jr.

Aldermen

James S. Weldon - First Ward
Thomas D. Kennedy - First Ward
*Carl Lundgren - Second Ward
Robert J. Haehl - Second Ward
Donald C. Ames - Third Ward
Lyle J. Hope - Third Ward
Frank J. Zink - Fourth Ward

Marvin J. Voelz - Fourth Ward
Robert E. Kett - Fifth Ward
John H. Carnell - Fifth Ward
Edward J. Jungles - Sixth Ward
Timothy Mogan - Sixth Ward
John C. Endahl - Seventh Ward
   (Resigned 1-31-68)
Sanford H. Steward, Jr. - Seventh Ward

City Clerk - Florise J. Gradolph
Treasurer - Robert H. Long
Attorney for the City - George E. Billett

*Resigned 1-20-69
Effective 4-27-69

1969 - 1971

Mayor - Charles Weigel, Jr.

Aldermen

James S. Weldon - First Ward	George W. Timmer - Fourth Ward
Thomas D. Kennedy - First Ward	John H. Carnell - Fifth Ward
Robert J. Haehl - Second Ward	Paul R. Bees - Fifth Ward
Neil D. French - Second Ward	Edward J. Jungles - Sixth Ward
Donald C. Ames - Third Ward	*Timothy Mogan - Sixth Ward
John E. Kasperski, Jr. - Third Ward	Sanford H. Steward, Jr. - Seventh Ward
Marvin J. Voelz - Fourth Ward	Allen H. Rank - Seventh Ward

City Clerk - Dorothy Lentz
Treasurer - Robert H. Long
Attorney for the City - George E. Billett

*Resigned effective March 8, 1970   Peter W. Ernst - Apptd. 8-'72

Harry D. Nelson elected 6-16-70 to replace Mogan

1971 - 1973

Mayor - Charles Weigel, Jr.

Aldermen

John J. Carroll - First Ward	George W. Timmer - Fourth Ward
*Marilyn Ferrara - First Ward	Paul R. Bees - Fifth Ward
Robert J. Haehl - Second Ward	James M. Graham - Fifth Ward
Arnold O. Makela - Second Ward	Edward J. Jungles - Sixth Ward
John E. Kasperski, Jr. - Third Ward	J.C. McCarty - Sixth Ward
John P. Vernon - Third Ward	Allen H. Rank - Seventh Ward
Marvin J. Voelz - Fourth Ward	Frank J. Gaudio - Seventh Ward

City Clerk - Dorothy Lentz
Treasurer - Robert H. Long
Attorney for the City - George E. Billett

*Elected for two year term to replace Kennedy who resigned.

1973 - 1975

Mayor - Ray W. Fick, Jr.

Aldermen

John J. Carroll - First Ward	William A. Kroeplin - Fourth Ward
Marilyn Ferrara - First Ward	James M. Graham - Fifth Ward
Arnold O. Makela - Second Ward	Doris Kahler - Fifth Ward
Don W. Feeley - Second Ward	J.C. McCarty - Sixth Ward
John P. Vernon - Third Ward	*John Julian - Sixth Ward
Glenn S. Ryburn - Third Ward	Frank J. Gaudio - Seventh Ward
Marvin J. Voelz - Fourth Ward	John Jordan - Seventh Ward

City Clerk - Dorothy Lentz
Treasurer - Alfred C. Nowaczyk
Attorney for the City - Peter W. Ernst

*Resigned 4-14-75 - effective immediately;
Edward Jungles appointed by Mayor 4-21-75

Elmhurst City Officials

1975 - 1977

Mayor - Ray W. Fick, Jr.

Aldermen

Marilyn Wiencek - First Ward
John J. Carroll - First Ward
Don W. Feeley - Second Ward
Joseph T. Cesario - Second Ward
Glenn S. Ryburn - Third Ward
John R. Hazelton - Third Ward
William A. Kroeplin - Fourth Ward

Jeanne Stuart - Fourth Ward
Doris Kahler - Fifth Ward
Richard DeVita - Fifth Ward
Edward J. Jungles - Sixth Ward
Frank N. Capparelli - Sixth Ward
Frank J. Gaudio - Seventh Ward
John Jordan - Seventh Ward

City Clerk - Dorothy Lentz
Treasurer - Alfred C. Nowaczyk
Attorney for the City - Peter Ernst

1977 - 1979

Mayor - Abner Ganet

Aldermen

John Carroll - First Ward
Florence Aldred - First Ward
Joseph T. Cesario - Second Ward
Glen Kistner - Second Ward
John R. Hazelton - Third Ward
Glenn S. Ryburn - Third Ward
Jeanne Stuart - Fourth Ward

William A. Kroeplin - Fourth Ward
Richard DeVita - Fifth Ward
John A. Magnetta - Fifth Ward
Frank Capparelli - Sixth Ward
Patricia Larson - Sixth Ward
Frank J. Gaudio - Seventh Ward
Robert J. Antonio - Seventh Ward

City Clerk - Dorothy Lentz
City Treasurer - Kenne Bristol
Attorney for City - Peter Ernst

BIBLIOGRAPHY

The collections and files of the Elmhurst Historical Museum provide most of the essential sources for Elmhurst history including the scrapbooks and occasional publications of organizations, churches, schools, and other institutions. Among reminiscences of early citizens, the letters of Wilbur Hagans were of special value. The City of Elmhurst Council Minutes and the annual reports of the City of Elmhurst have been consulted. Oral history has not been neglected, and many long-time residents have contributed their recollections. Incomplete files of the Elmhurst Press are available at the Elmhurst Public Library and at the offices of the Elmhurst Press, Inc.

All photographs not otherwise credited were furnished by the Elmhurst Historical Museum and interested friends.

Books and pamphlets listed relate directly to Elmhurst and DuPage County. Omitted are biographies of notable residents such as Carl Sandburg and W.P.A. Healy, and much collateral material concerning Chicago and Illinois.

Angle, Paul M., editor, *The Great Chicago Fire*, Chicago: Chicago Historical Society, 1946

Armstrong, Ann, *Story of a Parish*, Elmhurst, 1966

Bates, Dr. Frederick H., *"Old Elmhurst," Being the Personal Recollections of a Native*, Elmhurst: Elmhurst Historical Commission, second printing, 1973

Bateman, Newton, and Paul Selby, editors, *Historical Encyclopedia of Illinois and History of DuPage County*, two volumes, Chicago: Musell, 1913

Berens, Helmut Alan, edited by Virginia B. Novinger, *Elmhurst: Prairie to Tree Town*, Elmhurst: Elmhurst Historical Commission, 1968

Blanchard, Rufus, *History of DuPage County*, Chicago: Baskin & Co., 1882

City Directories of Elmhurst, Lombard, and Villa Park, Illinois, 1928-1929 edition, Chicago: Smith Directory Co., 1928

City Directory, 1938, Elmhurst, Villa Park, Lombard, Illinois, Neenah, Wisconsin: Directory Service Co., 1938

Elmhurst: Origin of Names, Streets, Schools, Parks, and Landmarks, Elmhurst Branch, American Association of University Women, 1976

Elmhurst-Chicago Stone Company: 75 Years of Progress, 1883-1958, Elmhurst: 1958

The Elmhurst Story... Biography of Progress, 1910-1960, published by The Elmhurst Story Steering Committee, 1960

Fischer, Howard C., editor, *100 Years of Elmhurst News, 1836-1936*, Elmhurst Centennial Historical Committee, 1936

Knobloch, Marion, editor, *DuPage County: A Descriptive and Historical Guide, 1831-1939*, American Guide Series compiled and written by workers of the Federal Writers' Project of the Works Progress Administration in the State of Illinois, re-edited for publication in 1948, Elmhurst: Irvin A. Ruby, 1948

Portrait and Biographical Record of DuPage and Cook Counties, Illinois, Chicago: Lake City Publishing Co., 1894

Bibliography

Quaife, Milo M., *Chicago's Highways Old and New,* Chicago, D.F. Keller & Co., 1923

Richmond, C.W., and H.F. Vallette, *A History of the County of DuPage, Illinois,* Chicago: Scripps, Bross & Spears, 1857

Schmidt, Royal J., *Bugles in a Dream: DuPage County in the Civil War,* Elmhurst: Historical Society of DuPage County, 1962

The Potawatomie Indians of DuPage County, Wheaton: DuPage County Historical Society, 1974

Stanger, Robert C., *Elmhurst College, 1871-1971, The First One Hundred Years,* Elmhurst College Magazine, Volume IV, Number 3, 1971.

St. Peter's United Church of Christ, Elmhurst Illinois, Centennial, Elmhurst: 1976

The Story of a Bank, 60th Anniversary, Elmhurst National Bank, Elmhurst, 1954

Thompson Bros. & Burr, *New Combination Atlas, DuPage County, Illinois,* 1874

INDEX OF INDIVIDUALS

City officials designated by *

Abel, Rev. Carl	132
Ackerman, Mrs. Joseph	130,131
Adams, Charles	89
Adams, "Fuzz" Victor	92
Addy, Rev. A. Roy	103
Ahrens, Otto	14
Ahrens, Lena	126
Ahlf, Gunther	88,93
Albanese, Pat	92
Albert, Christopher J.	40,55,68,71*
Albert, Mrs. C.J.	71,72
Albert, Eugene Pauley	71
Aldis, Owen	16
Aldred, Florence	*
Aldrich, Howard A.	114
Alexander, Melvin	87
Allen, Raymond	87
Allison, Benjamin D.	102,136*
Altendorf, Lila	122
Ames, Donald G.	*
Anagost, Kathrine	134
Anasse, Leander	130
Anderman, "Pee Wee"- George	92
Anderson, C. Andy	*
Anderson, Mrs. Ben O.	84
Anderson, Rev. Charles P.	22
Anderson, Ed	91
Anderson, Eric	122
Anderson, George	119
Anderson, Mattie	106
Antonio, Robert	*
Arends, Clifford C.	121
Arlt, H.	41
Armstrong, Ann Seidel	118
Armstrong, John M.	*
Arthur, Rev. John	73
Asche, "Norm" Norman	88
Asche, William	34
Aschmann, Helen Tann	117
Asing, Henry	75
Assman, Henry	47,48,138
Atwater, Jesse	12
Atwood, Benton	*
Babcock, Grover C.	100
Backhaus, Bob	88
Backhaus, Wilber T.	134
Baeder, August	*
Baeder, Frank	49
Baethke, Bernice	89
Baethke, Ed	53,75
Baethke, Hannah	75
Baethke, William	8
Balgemann, Bill	88
Balgemann, Edwin F.	154
Balgemann, Ernst	43,50,56,149,150,151,152,153
Balgemann, Ewald	87
Balgemann, George	81
Balgemann, Louis A.	51,52,53,56,99
Balgemann, Otto W.	89,99,107,111,112,122,123*
Ball, Leroy	88
Banser, Henry	89
Barbee, Grace	96
Barge, John	50
Barnes, A.D.	112
Barr, Rev. T.E.	55
Bartman, Emma	75
Bartman, John	75
Bartusch, Alfred J.	*
Bartusch, Walter	83
Bates, Ansel	33
Bates, Alben F. Sr.	55,64,107,112,126,130,131,136,139*
Bates, Alben Jr.	139
Bates, Mrs. Alben	64,126,131,139
Bates, Capt. Benjamin	15
Bates, Charles W.	152
Bates, Elvira	19
Bates, Dr. Frederick H.	3,20,43,50,51,53,60,63,76,83,106,139*
Bates, Gerry	13,15,16,17,18,19,34,49,50,136,139
Bates, Georgia Smith (Mrs. Gerry Bates)	15,50
Bates, Harold	88
Bates, Henry	139
Bathum, George	140
Battermann, Henry	50
Baucke, Chester	92
Baucke, Wallace	92
Bauer, Carl	40,41,49
Bauersfeld, Albert G.	*
Baumann, Rev. A.	55
Bay, Jens Christian	68,69,112
Bayer, Albert	89
Beck, Christian	73
Becker, Rev. Charles	23
Beckman, Elmer	88
Beckman, William	16,17
Bedell, Max L.	*
Bees, Paul R.	*
Beetlestone, H.	64
Beetlestone, Mrs. H.	64,138
Beetlestone, Robert	64
Beher, Walter	113

Index Of Individuals

Behnke, Franz H.	118
Bender, Russell	122
Benedetto, Arthur	88
Bennett, Robt. L.	142
Bennett, Sherman T.	*
Bennett, "Vince"	88
Benson, A.	88
Benson, Ed	72
Benson, Rev. Howard	74
Benson, Rev. Paul J.	133
Bentley, Elizabeth King (Mrs. Cyrus Bentley)	36,124
Berens, Alice Seton (Mrs. Helmut Berens)	83,124,125
Berens, August	23,24,118
Berens, Clara (Mrs. August Berens)	23,24,118
Berens, Helmut	24,68,83,101,102,118,125
Berg, Ray	90
Bergstraesser, Rev. Edward W.	133
Beringer, C.	83
Berry, Mrs. Charles	114
Bierlein, Herbert	91
Bettinger, Lee L.	152*
Beutjer, William	*
Bigalke, Richard	88
Bigler, Mrs. Robert	131
Billett, George	*
Black, Phillip	91
Black Hawk	5
Black Hawk War	12
Blaine, Mrs. Emmons	16
Blair, Thomas S.	80
Blatter, Edward H.	110,111,114*
Blau, Mrs.	76
Blau, Frank	50
Blecke, Caroline	141
Blecke, Henry	*
Bleich, Harry	91
Bleiler, John E.	134
Blievernicht, Christian	43,49,149
Block, W.C. Jr.	*
Bloedel, Robert	
Boardman, John M.	*
Boeber, Rev. Frederick W.	23,24
Boeger, Art	87
Boeger, Russ	141
Boeske, Edwin F.	88
Boettcher, Henry	50
Bohassek, Charles	74
Boke, Robt. "Bob"	89
Boldebuck, Earl	134
Boldt, Rev. Wm. J.	103
Boltman, Frederick	33
Bonfield, Dolores	141
Bonham, Rev. Eugene	133
Bonney, Edward	17,26,117
Booner, Connie	121
Borchert, Thomas	143
Borms, Emma	122
Bornemann, Rev. George W.	
Bosworth, Ethel	121
Bosworth, Ernest W.	81*
Bourke, Richard	35
Boys, Keith	131
Brace, Kenneth	136
Brandt, Berkeley	55
Brandt, Mrs. Berkeley	55
Braun, Julius J.	72*
Breitenbach, Henry L.	41
Breitenbach, Mrs. H.L.	106,122 pic
Brethauer, Monte	92
Brettman, Paul	88
Breuhaus, A. Julius	107*
Brice, Mrs. William	84
Bright, David	138
Bright, George, Jr.	83,138
Bright, George, Sr.	83,138
Bright, Mrs. George	82
Bright, Ted	87,113
Bristol, Kenne	*
Brodt, Herman	40
Brodt, Hugo H.	87*
Brodt, Lem	87
Brodt, Lothar W.	*
Brown, Elias	19
Brownell, Albert S.	43,118*
Brownell, Harry G.	55
Brumm, Jack	88
Brumme, Rev. Howard L.	104
Brush, Emerson H.	80*
Bryan, Charles Page	26,58,60,61
Bryan, Jenny	19,25,61
Bryan, Daniel	25
Bryan, Thomas Barbour	16,18,22,25,26,28,33,39,44,55,58,60,61,68,78,101
Bryan, Mrs. Thomas (Page, Jane Byrd)	25,30
Bryant, Rev. Harry	103
Brydges, E. Norman	113,114
Bucholz, Fred	91,92,134
Bucholz, Henry	134
Bucholz, Mrs. Henry	16
Buck, Kingsley	94
Buckner, Warren	60
Buehler, A.C.	97
Buley, James S.	64
Bunge, Ernest J.	122
Burdsall, Walter R.	*
Burgess, Charlotte	122
Burke, Bill	87,88
Burke, Mildred	93
Burke, "Pat" Patricia	93
Burke, Red	92
Burke, Wm.	88
Burkes, David R. Jr.	142
Burmeister, Gustav L. "Shorty"	87
Burmeister, Gustav S.	72,76
Burns, James	83
Burnside, David	122
Burrow, Jarrel A.	*
Burrows, Rev. Joseph	74
Burtis, Royal V.	126
Busch, Don	92
Buschbauer, Hans	22
Buswell, Robt. M.	*
Butler, Rev. Wesley E.	134
Butler, William P.	*
Butts, R. T.	*
Cadwells,	81

Cadwell, William R.	100*
Caldwell, Wm. B.	142
Callow, Wm. J.	134
Canfield, Leo D.	107
Cantwell, Guy	122
Capparelli, Frank	*
Carlson, Beda	84
Carlson, Donald	125,126,139
Carlson, Karl Henning	96,126
Carlson, Margaret	84
Carlson, Miriam	84
Carnell, John	*
Carney, June	89
Carpenter, William R.	*
Carroll, John J.	*
Carter, Katherine	118
Case, Mrs. John Sr.	17
Case, John R. Sr.	32,54,80
Case, John R. Jr.	16,17,32,55,61,79,80
Case, Mrs. John R. Jr.	31
Casper, C.H.	104
Cedarholm, Charles	124
Cesario, Joseph T.	*
Challacombe - House	71,96
Challacombe, George	97
Chant, Douglas	104
Chant, Margaret (M.C. Papandreou)	118
Chapman, George R.	*
Chipains family	77
Christensen, Ruth	118,131
Christy, H.A.	*
Churchill, Steven J.	142
Churchill, W.	13
Chworowsky, Karl M.	103,122
Claridge, Thomas W.	102
Clark, George Rogers	8
Clark, W.S.	110
Clint, Nels	137
Cobb, Zerais	13
Cohrs, Ralph	90
Colby, Marge	93
Cole, Clarence	122
Collins, William J.	16*
Colwell, A. Atwood	134
Commare, "Art"	88
Condon, John	35,62
Coney, Rev. Randolph	132
Coney, George	31
Conrad, Vern	87
Cooley, F.W.	55
Cooney, Warren	89
Cooper, Donald	89,90
Cordt, Herman	*
Corlett, Mrs. Walter R.	106
Corneille, Louis	101
Corrigan, "Ed"	62
Cosgrove, James P.	126
Costigan, Robert E.	140*
Cotsirilos, George	134
Countryman, Rev. Frank	74
Courdt, Hattie	63
Crane, D.E. Riley	85,86
Crane, D.E. Milo	85,86
Crann, James Harry	93
Creighton, Mary	106
Creighton, Roger	136
Criswell, George	88
Cronin, James	*
Cronin, Dr. Richard	62
Cruger, Harold	64,95,138
Cruger, Mrs. Harold	125
Cruger, John Wesley	64,138
Cruger, Melvin J.	64,138
Crumpton, Robt.	87,88
Crusius, Paul N.	41,96
Cummings, James T.	142*
Cunningham, Doug	93
Curtin, John	142
Curtis, Daniel D.	113
Curtiss, John	28
Dacken, Rev. Lester	132
Dagley, Jack	89
Dame, Hazel Stevens	106,117,121
Dammeier, Amanda	63
Dammeier, Wm.	87
Danforth, Rev. W.C.	55,74,122
Daniels, Alice	122
Daniels, Lee D.	113
Daniels, Russell	122
Daniels, Seth F.	33
Darby, Rev. James	133
Darling, Harry	66
Davenport, Norma	102
Davis, Bert, Sr.	104
Davis, Mrs. Bert, Sr.	84
Davis, Dr. Ernest	126
Davis, Mrs. Ernest	126
Davis, Evelyn	105
Davis, Fran	93
Davis, Rev. J.W.	74
Davis, Jack	125
Davis, Lawton	88,91
Davis, William	87
Davis, Wm. B.	134
Dawson, Mrs. James	126
Day, Winfield S.	62,102
Dehling, Otto	34
Deicke, Edwin F.	107
Deis, John	105
Demers, Jack D.	142
Deniz, A.M.	64
Deniz, Louis A.	63,64
DeRoech, Robert	130
DeShane, Mrs. Roy	125,126
DeVita, Richard	*
DeVries, Rev. J.	133
DeYoung, Mrs. Richard	106
Dezutel, James J.	134
Dezutel, "Jo" Josephine	89
Dickson, John	88
Dietzel, Fred	78
Dinkmeyer, Rev. Henry W.	97
Discher, Mrs. Elton	84
Dixon, Al	87
Dixon, Byron	93
Dobbeck, Albert	92

Index Of Individuals

Dolberg, Edward 50
Dolle, Paul 107,122
Dornoff, E.W. ....*
Drake, Hugh H. ....*
Drecoll, Ella 122
Drews, Rev. Richard D. 103
Droegemuller, Mrs. E.H. 125
Duckwell, John 121
duJardin, Rosamund 112,117
Dulles, Ted 134
Duncan, Jane 122
Duncan, Robt. T. 134
Dunklee, Ebenezer 20
Duncklee, Hezekiah 12,20
Dunnington, Tom 122
Durant, Jane 117
Durham, Robert P. 16
Earle, Mrs. J. Harold 113
Eaton, Roswell ....*
East, Clarence 93
Eastham, Marge 93
Edwards, Rev. John Herbert 22
Egan, Ed. Fred 134
Eggert, Walter A. 89
Egolf, Homer E. 83*
Ehlers, Kay 89
Eis, J.O. ....*
Ekberg, Marie 142
Eldridge, Edward 12,18,102
Emery, Alben 54,55
Emery, Edward 125
Emery, Grace (Mrs. Berkeley Brandt) 55
Emery, Harrison 83
Emery, Ida (Mrs. Albert Ullman) 55,73
Emery, Jack 83
Emery, James 54,55
Emery, John 55
Emery, Mary Adelea Toby (Mrs. W.H. Emery) 55
Emery, Munson 83,125,126,135
Emery, William H. Sr. 23,54,55,135
Emery, William H. Jr. 55,60,120
Emery, Mrs. Will H. Jr. 55,124
Endahl, John ....*
English, Don 89
Enlow, Tom 90
Erickson, Don 141
Ermisch, Charles "Nick" 90
Ernst, Rev. Eldon Gerald 103
Ernst, Fritz 72
Ernst, Peter ....*
Ervendberg, Rev. L.C. 21
Evanson, Mrs. Charles 114
Ever, J.W. 104
Evers, Fred C. 117,125,126
Ewald, "Lefty" Herman 88
Ewan, Mrs. Philip T. 84
Falck, Grace 96
Farrell, "Ed" 88
Fawell, Harry 88
Feeley, Don W. ....*
Fellows, Helen Rea (Mrs. Wm.) 129
Fellows, Richard W. 134
Fellows, William H. 113,129,130*

Ferguson, Ruth 89
Ferrara, Marilyn (M. Wiencek) ....*
Fick, Ray W. Jr. 143,144*
Fiebrandt, August 19,77
Fiebrandt, Donald 77
Fiebrandt, Edwin 77
Fiebrandt, Raymond 77
Fieldler, William 90
Field, Florence, Mrs. Henry Field (Florence Lathrop)
27
Field, Henry 30
Field, Minna 28
Fielitz, Carl ....*
Fiene, "Ed" 88,93,154
Fiene, Henry A. 75
Filson, Mrs. 120
Finch, Dorothy 122
Fine, Albert 138
Finnemore, Wray 83
Fiorelli, Fred 92
Fischer, Albert H. ....*
Fischer, Alonzo 64,80,107,122
Fischer, Alfred H. 122
Fischer, Alphonse 78
Fischer, August H. 32
Fischer, Conrad 101,102
Fischer, Elsa Chandler 106
Fischer, E.W. 72,77
Fischer, Florence 122
Fischer, Frederick 24,37,78
Fischer, Dr. Frederick 32,43,85,86,138
Fischer, Oscar G. ....*
Fischer, Otto 78
Fischer, Rev. Walter F. 132
Fish, Elisha 12
Fisher, Dr. Winfield 131
Fister, Glenn 134
Fitch, Rev. Elmer F. 103
Flaherty, Shirley 141
Flannery, Willis 134
Fleege, Marvin 93
Fletcher, Mrs. Mildred 122
Fluegge, Robert H. ....*
Flynn, Ed 100
Foley, Rev. John 33,103
Foster, Rev. Thomas 73
France, Frank 90
Franzen, Gustav 72
Franzen, John Henry 14
Fraser, Arthur Valair 69,122
Frega, "Norm" Norman 93
Freimuth, Jack 88
French, Kim 121
French, Neil D. ....*
French, Stephen Jr. 126
Frendreis, John 81
Frick, Dr. Ivan 97,98
Friedli, Alfred 97
Frink, John 16
Fritz, Henry G. 75,138
Frobenius, Rev. Reno R. 103
Froeming, Harvey 87
Froeming, Leonard 87

Fuller, Benjamin	12
Fuller, Charles	100
Fulton, Neil	141,143
Gaare, Jack	88
Gabelman, James	90
Gaetano, Enrico	141
Galbraith, Dr. Thomas B.	76
Gallagher, G.K.	81
Gallup, Mrs. Charles	84
Ganet, Abner	144*
Gara, Martin J.	*
Garbi, Mrs. Love	84
Garrett, Gary	*
Gatso, Mrs. Perry	141
Gaudio, Frank J.	*
Gauger, Herman	87
Gavin, Edith (Mrs. Steve)	125
Gavin, Genevieve	125
Gavin, Steve	125
Gehrke, Henry	50
Gerberding, Fred H.	106
German, Rev. Edwin	103
Gernon, W.R.	*
Getz, Rev. David	133
Gibbons, Thomas	78,138
Giese, Irving W.	95
Giese, William	52
Gillespie, William S.	64
Glass, James L.	*
Glatfelter, Ralph L.	134
Glasener, Dr. C.F.	107
Glos, Adam	78,109,139
Glos, Adam M.	14
Glos, Adam S.	24,43,45,49,66,109,139
Glos, Albert	89,124,126,131,139
Glos, Mrs. Albert	124,126,131
Glos, Catherine (Mrs. August Timke)	14
Glos, Clara (Mrs. Alben Bates)	64,126,131,139
Glos, Henry L.	14, 19,24,37,43,45,47,49,70,99,109,121,139,149,150,151,152,153
Glos, Mrs. Henry (Lucy Schween)	45,81
Glos, Jacob	126,139
Glos, Mrs. Jacob	126
Glos, John, Sr.	13,14,49
Glos, John, Jr.	13,20
Glos, Lucy Schween (Mrs. Henry Glos)	45
Glos, Mabelle (Mrs. George Larkin)	84,125,126,131
Glos, Mary (Mrs. Gustave Fischer)	14
Goebel, Rev. Peter	40,41
Goetschel, "Howie"	88
Goff, Rev. Charles Ray	74
Golden, Mrs. Gertrude John	84,106
Goldthorpe, E.	*
Goltermann, Frederick H.	52*
Golub, Emil	89
Goss, Ida M.	141
Gould, Mrs. G.F.	132
Gradolph, Florise J.	136,140*
Grady, Frank	92
Graf, John R.	142
Graham, James J.*	*
Grass, Ann	127
Grass, Harry, Sr.	63,116,120
Graue, Albert	14
Graue, August	14,34,49
Graue, Diedrich	14
Graue, Frederick, jr.	14,18
Graue, Frederick, sr.	14
Graue, Fremont	14
Graue, Henry	14
Graue, Julius	14,49
Graue, Lucie	14,49
Graue, Ludwig (Louis)	14,18,34,49
Graue, Wilhelmina	14
Graue, William	14,49
Gray, Joseph, Jr.	83
Graybill, John W.	134
Greaves, J.L.	73
Greenlee, Isabel	28
Greenlee, W. Brock	28
Gregerson, Ralph W.	134
Griffin, Gertrude (Mrs. Miles Sater)	121,122
Griffin, Mrs. George	100,105,119,121
Griffin, Walter, Burley	71,80,119,120
Griffin, Mrs. Marion Mahoney (Mrs. Walter)	119
Griffin, George Walter	106,119,121*
Griffith, "Hub"	88
Grimshaw, Earl	90
Haack, Otto	91
Haak, Richard	87
Haas, Fred C.	*
Haehl, Robert J.	136*
Haft, Charles M.	*
Hagans, Anne	19,26
Hagans, Elisha	18,19,26
Hagans, Lovela (Mrs. Lucian)	26,27,28,61
Hagans, Lucian	17,26,27,58,61,68,80
Hagans, Wilbur	19,20,26,28,30,59,60,61,62,66,80
Hagermann, "Red" Ed	87
Hague, Dr. Harold	106
Hahn, Johanna (Mrs. John Hahn)	50
Hahn, John	50
Hain, "Ron"	90
Hale, Robert	96
Hall, A. Neely	83,119
Hall, Norman P.	122
Hall, Ruth (Mrs. Robt. Smith)	119
Hammerschmidt, Adolph	47,48,138
Hammerschmidt, Alvin N.	125,132
Hammerschmidt, S.W. Max	48,60,64,72,111,122*
Hammerschmidt, Louis M.	97
Hammerschmidt, Martin Jr.	134
Hammerschmidt, Richard	72*
Hammerschmidt, William	107
Hanebuth, William	50*
Hanscom, Alfred	83
Hansen, Emil	41
Hansen, Kurt "Pat"	92
Hansen, Evelyn	84
Hansen, Margaret	84
Hansen, Waldo	83
Hanson, Charley "Snipe"	88
Hanson, Norman	83,130
Hanson, Richard M.	154
Harbour, Fred C.	72*
Harbour, Irving " Red "	92

Index Of Individuals

Harbour, Marge	93
Harding, Mrs. G.	84
Hargreaves, Vivian	89,163
Harlan, Mrs. Wayne	125
Harrer, Joseph	119
Harris, Mrs. Montgomery	84
Harrison, Rev. Fred	74,121
Hartung, Anton	143
Harvey "Lew"	105
Haskell, Harriet	28
Hastings, Rev. J.R.	133
Hawk, R.	91
Hawkins "Augie"	88
Hawkins, Thomas	105*
Hayes, Rev. William R.	132
Hazelton, John R.	*
Healey, George Peter Alexander	15,16,18,19,26
Heegard, Julius	49
Heidemann, C.	87
Heidemann, Edwin	70*
Heidemann, Mrs. Edwin	70
Heidemann, Dr. George	31,35,45,70,106*
Heidemann, George F.	149,150
Heimert, Alan	118
Heinberg, Dorothy	89
Heine, Arthur	83
Heinemnn, Amanda	63
Heinemann, Anna	63
Heinemann, Cramer	53
Heinemann, Edwin	75
Heinemann, Louis H.	75
Heinemann, Lydia	63
Heinke, Art	89
Heinke, Elmer	88
Heinke, Grace	87
Heller, Edward H.	131
Helmick, Homer	96
Hennessy, John F.	*
Hennessy, Rev. P.H.	103
Henning "Bud" Al	88
Heper, Otto	102
Herder, Mrs. Howard	125
Hermansen, John	90
Hermon, Sophie	122
Hersch, Dr. Thomas B.	103
Hertzfeld, Herman	87
Hess, Charles F.	77*
Hesse, Harry C.	104,138
Hesterman, Frank	87
Hesterman "Joe"	88
Hesterman, Ralph	87
Hickey, Ralph C.	*
Hicks, Clifford	119
Higginson, George M.	39,68
Higginson, Anna E. (Mrs. George M. Higginson)	39
Hild, Rev. John	56
Hild, "Mickey" Milton	88,91
Hild, Paul	87,91
Hild, Walter	87,91
Hill, Donald W.	134
Hilliard, Bessie	75
Hilliard, R. Bradner	83,125*
Hilliard, William J.	83
Hills, Dr. Lester H.	51,106
Hinkley, John P.	69
Hintz, Adolph	87,91
Hintz, Alvin	87
Hintz, Anton	91
Hintz, Arthur	91
Hintz, Bruno	91
Hintz, Herbert	87
Hintz, John	87
Hintz, Louis	104
Hintz, Richard	91,94
Hintz, "Zan"	87
Hirst, Dr. Robert T.	134
Hobein, Henry F.	110*
Hobein, Josephine	93
Hobson, Bailey	6,12
Hoehne, Henry	*
Hoffman, Francis Arnold	20,21,22,78
Hoffman, Frieda	21
Hoffman, Paul	33
Hohman, Adam	88
Hohmann, "Eddie" Edward	91
Hohmann, Caroline	102
Hohmann, Henry C. Sr.	45,99,149,150,151
Hohmann, Mary (Mrs. Henry C. Schumacher)	71
Hohmann, Philip	150,151,153
Holle, Louis W.	*
Hollinger, Frances	121
Holtdorf, Rev. Edward Theo.	103
Holter, Thor	136
Hooker, Rev. Robt. L.	103
Hookham, Eleanor King	122
Hope, Lyle J.	*
Horn, Hildegard	122
Horning, Florence	122
Hotchkins, Mrs. C.S.	67
Hottle, Antone E.	131
Hough, Bert	90
Houghteling, James L.	16
Housley, Guy	69
Housley, Mrs. Guy	84
Hovey, John L.	15,16,18,34
Howard, Mrs. J.L.	75
Howe, Charles	16
Hultquists,	81
Hunter, Rev. Paul	104
Huntzinger, Rev. Ernest, Jr.	74
Icks, Col. Robert Joseph	119
Iman, Archie	134
Incopero, Waltie	127
Ingels, Charles	142
Irion, Rev. Daniel	23,40,41,95,96
Irion, Oscar	122
Irvin, Rev. Karl E.	103
Jacobs, Kenneth Sr.	140*
Jaeger, Herman	87
James, Dr. Franklin T.	106
Jeggle, Father Meinrad	22
Jepson, "Bill"	91
Jernegan, Richard	134
Johnson, Rev. A.M.	134
Johnson, Charles	52,89
Johnson, Christian	33

Johnson, Emil J.	110
Johnson, George	92
Johnson, Herbert	64
Johnson, Ken	93
Johnson, Marvin	*
Johnson, Ronald	102
Johnston, Mrs. George H.	113
Johnstone, Gladys	84
Jordan, John	*
Jordan, Ray	92
Josephson, Dr. Clarence	97
Julian, John	*
Jungles, Edward J.	*
Kabat, "Ed"	88
Kahler, Doris	*
Kamke, Anna	122
Kapp, Wm.	134
Kappus, George	105
Karas, Warren C.	134
Kasperski, John E. Jr.	*
Katsihtis, Rev. Father Denice	134
Keeler, Marvin H.	138
Kehler, Philip	33
Keiler, John D.	50*
Keiler, Stephen	33
Keimel, Wm. J.	77,102
Keir, "Bud" Norman	88
Keller, Albert	91
Keller, Ann	84,93
Keller, Mrs. Norman	84
Kelsey, Mrs. Jeri	142
Kennan, Dr. R.R.	74
Kennedy, G.F.	81
Kennedy, Jack	92
Kennedy, Sue	81
Kennedy, Thomas D.	*
Kenney, Terence	23
Kentgen, Al	89
Kersten, Charles E.	*
Kester, A.A.	55
Ketelhut, Mrs. William	132
Kett, Robert E.	*
Keuchen, Rev. Emil	23
Keyes, Miller	114,137
Kidder, Walter	83
Kindl, Harry	93
King, Eleanor (Mrs. Robert Hookham)	122
King, Francis	16,36,123
King, Mrs. Francis	117
King, Henry W.	15,16,31,123,124
King, Mrs. Henry W.	36
King, Louisa Yeomans (Mrs. Frances King)	36,37
Kinnett, Mrs. David	84,113
Kinnett, Frances	84
Kipp, Wm. J.	142
Kirch, "Irv"	89
Kiting, Henry	87
Kistner, Glen	*
Klaeren, "Al"	92
Klasen, "Wally"	89
Kleckner, Dr. Donald C.	97
Klinghoffer, Dr. Max	129
Knicker, Frieda	138
Knudsen, Lawrence	125
Knuepfer, John (Jack)	*
Koch, Adheleid	38
Koch, Carlotta	3,21
Koch, Rev. Edwin	103
Koch, Dr. Fred Conrad	38,117
Koch, Dr. Frederick	37
Koch, Louise Fischer	37,39
Kochaisky, Arthur H.	*
Koehler, Mrs. Edwin	114
Koliveros, George	134
Kolvitz, Viola	89
Kopecky, Mrs. Ethel	142
Koppenaal, Dr. Elizabeth	132
Korthauer, Henry	32
Koval, Frank	67,68
Koxing, Henry	33
Krage, Martin F.	53
Krage, Mathilda	53
Kramer, Rudolph	43,49
Kranz, Carl F.	40
Kraus, August	87
Krause, Dorothy Bethke	75
Krause, John Eugene	142
Krause, Marion	89
Krause, Michael	91
Krell, Edward	139
Krieter, Erwin	92
Krisch, Ray	87
Krisch, Stanley	91
Krischak, George	91
Kroeplin, William A.	*
Krom, Myron	92
Kross, Michael	122*
Kross, Theodore	51,125
Kruckow, Emil	87
Krueger, "Bill"	90
Kruse, "Bill"	88
Kruskow, George	91
Kulek, "Tom"	90
Kulton, "Fran" (Mrs. George)	89,125
Kulton, George	87,89,91,92,93
Kummerow, George	100,111,112,130
Kunzer, Edward J. Jr.	142
Laaser, Rev. Robert O.	103
Laatz, Henry	75
Ladwig, Edward	134
Lange, Rev. E.T.	132
Langguth, John	*
Langhorst, Dr. Henry	66,76,108
Langhorst, Oliver ("Pete")	96
Langkafel, E.A.	82,104
Lapp, Henry	33
Larkin, Mrs. George	84,125,
Larkin, Mrs. George (Mabelle Glos)	84,125,126,131
Larson, Mrs. Charles	107
Larson, Howard	121
Larson, Mrs. Howard	84
Larson, Kenneth	121
Larson, Patricia	*
Larson, Warren	125
LaSpisa, Jim	90
Lathrop, Barbour	29

Index Of Individuals

Lathrop, Bryan 28,29
Lathrop, Florence (Mrs. Henry Field)
  (Mrs. Thomas Nelson Page) 28,29,30
Lathrop, Jedediah 28,29,68,80,85
Lauerman, John 33
Lawson, John 87
Lazich, John 121
Leahy, Dr. Frank 106
Leefelt, Helen 106
Lean, Terence F. ....*
Leeseberg, Ray 91
Lehmann, Rev. Timothy 96,97
Lehmann, Mrs. Timothy 96
Lenane, Daniel J. ....*
Lentz, Dorothy 140*
Leonhardt, Rev. Robert 96
Lesney, "Ted" 92
Leston, Thomas L. 142
LesVesconte, Mrs. Lester 84
Levinson, Richard 113
Leyden, "Luke" 88
Leyes, Rev. Wayne 133
Licht, Erwin N. 134
Licht, J.C. 138
Lind, Harold 88
Linder, Mrs. C.A. 84
Lindlahr, Henry 84,85
Lindlahr, Victor 85
Linneweh, Louis G. 102
Lisjak, Frank 105
Litchfield, Cyrenus, Wirt 32
Litchfield, Wm. H. 22*
Lizzadro, John 128
Lizzadro, Joseph 128
Lizzadro, Joseph F. 127,128
Lizzadro, Mary (Mrs. Joseph) 127
Lloyd, Frank 100
Long, Robert H. ....*
Lookabaugh, John J. 110
Luce, W.R. 59
Luchs, Dr. Arthur 132
Luehring "Hal" 88
Luessenhop, A.L. 20,107
Lund, Henry 138
Lund, Raymond 138
Lundgren, Carl ....*
Lusk, James 16
McArthur, John 93
McCarty, J.C. 140*
McClurg, General Alexander Caldwell 16
McCrae, Leon 92
McDaniels, "Michie" Rosemary 89
McDonald, Alexander 62
McDonald, Rev. David L. 81,103
McDonald, Rev. Jack 103
McDonough, Thomas E. 112
McGary, Paul J. ....*
McGinnis, C.O. 110
McGinnis, Mrs. Edna 110
McGregor, George F. ....*
McHugh, W.C. ....*
McIntosh, Mrs. H.M. 124
McIntyre, Lyle 88

McNally, Andrew 68
McPartland, O. 88
McPartland, E. 88
McQuillan, Emmett M. 100
McVey, Rev. John I. 74
Maffit M. ....*
Magers, Harry 99,100
Maggio, Frank 90
Magnetta, John A. ....*
Maher, Rev. Arthur 103
Mahler, Fred H. 76*
Mahler, Frieda 76
Mahler, William 76
Mahon, Bruce 126,141
Mahon, Ralph 125
Mahoney, "Joe" 90
Mahoney, Marion (Mrs. Walter B. Griffin) 119
Maier, Frank J. 112*
Makela, Arnold O. ....*
Malamis, Rev. Peter 134
Malecha, Elmer 89
Maloit, Alvin 91
Maloit, Frank 91
Malone, Julia 63
Mann, "Joe" 89
Manning, Nathan 134
Manolis, "Phil" 134
Mardaga, William A. 77
Marhoefer, Charles J. 72*
Marks, George 68
Marks, L. 106
Marguard, Henry F. ....*
Marquardt, Dorothy (Mrs. E. Marquardt) 108
Marquardt, Dr. Edward W. 77,106,107
Marrs, "Joe" 90
Marshall, John W. Sr. 132
Martens, John 100,130
Mathis, Dr. Alvin 106
Maul, Victor 140
Maxey, C. Arthur 138
Maxson, Mrs. Ralph 132
Maxson, Raymond D. 126
May, Roy 88
Mears, David 138
Mears, Ralph H. 83,138
Melgard, Warren 88
Meister, George 60,130*
Mensching, "Ray" 88
Metz, Clyde 89
Metz, Logan "Bud" 88
Meyer, Alfred 24
Meyer, H.F. 60
Meyer, William J. 72,77*
Miche, D. Benjamin 49
Mielke, Harold 91
Miller, Alexander H. ....*
Miller, Charles 134
Miller, Harold 91,92
Miller, Henry J. ....*
Miller, Richard E. 134
Mitchell, Arthur 62
Mitchell, Thomas A. 142
Mittelhauser, "Del" 88

Moeck, Jack	138
Moeck, William	138
Moeller, "Skim" Emil	87
Moeller, Fred	93
Moeller, Henry	49
Moen, Mrs. Marcus M.	84
Mogan, Timothy	*
Mong, Diedrich	34
Montgomery, Alvin E.	126
Morey, Samantha	19
Morgan, George C.	58
Morgan, Mrs. Oakley V.	105,112
Morrell, John	*
Morris, Frank	92
Morrison, Mrs. Herbert	84
Morton, Luther	12
Morewitzer, Henry	50
Most, Charles	43,49
Most, "Dick"	87
Most, William	49
Mottashed, Ralph	88
Mowers, Willard	83
Mueller, Edward	76
Mueller, John	72*
Mueller, Theophil W.	96,97
Muench, Philip F.	40
Mundt, E.E.	89
Murphy, N.W.	62
Murray, Grace	123
Murray, Joseph	112
Musil, Rosemary	74,117,121
Myers, Thomas O. Sr.	137
Myers, Thomas O. Jr.	137
Nagle, Tom	92
Nance, Mrs. Arden	113
Naper, John	6,12
Naper, Capt. Joseph	6, 12
Nelson, Albert	100
Nelson, Andrew	29
Nelson, Mrs. Anton	100
Nelson Barthel	*
Nelson, Harry D.	*
Nelson, Janet	114
Nelson, Robert R.	*
Nelson, Swain	31
Neltor, John	63
Nemitz, Otto	87
Neumann, Francis N.	52*
Newell, "Bill"	89
Newlander, "Wally"	88,92
Newman, Andrew	33
Newman, Frank Wm.	100
Niebuhr, H. Richard	96,97,118
Nielson, Rev. G.D.	74
Nieman, Blanche	89
Nieman, Fred	89
Niemeyer, Art	88,89,90
Niemeyer, "Hutch" Hugo	88
Niemeyer "Irv"	88
Nissen, Norman	92
Nordmeyer, Florence	63
Norlie, Mrs. Harold	125,126
Novinger, Virginia	117
Nowaczyk, Alfred C.	*
Nowak, "Ed"	92
Obert, Rev. Carl H.	103
Ochefski, Samuel	87
Oehlerking, Louis	88
Ogden, Earl W.	135,136*
Ogden, Mahlon	15,16
Ohlerich, Albert F.	*
Ohlschefski, John	47
O'Keefe, Rev. Thomas B.	133
Oleschlaeger, Mrs. J.	82
Oliva, "Tom"	89
Ollier, Valentine M.	*
Ollswang, Harry L.	113
Olson, Clara	76
Olson, Don	89,92,93
Olson, Myrtle	83
Olson, Roger	83
O'Regan, Frank	88
Orlikiewicz, Rev. Stanley	133
Osborne, Ray R.	154
Osmanski, "Ed"	90
Ostrum, Martha (Mrs. Edwin Heidemann)	70
Otto, Emil	40,41
Overkamp, Herman	59
Paddock, H.C.	63
Page, Jane Byrd (Mrs. Thomas B. Bryan)	25
Page, Thomas Nelson	30,117
Page, Mrs. Thomas Nelson (Lathrop, Florence)	28,29,30
Paine, Christopher	6
Palmer, Augustus	34
Palmer, Rev. Joseph	103
Palmer, Larry Ray	142
Palmer, Robert	135,140,143*
Palmquist, James	*
Pannell, Lucile	118
Papandreou, Margaret Chant	118
Pappa, George	134
Parsons, John R.	134
Parson, Rev. W. Ridley	73
Patton, Ruth	84
Patzer, Vernon	134
Pauley, Lily (Mrs. C.J. Albert)	71,72
Paulson, Dennis	131
Payne, Mrs. John Barton (Jenny Bryan)	22
Payne, William T.	140
Pearn, W.B.	122*
Pearn, William Jr.	83
Pearson, Edward	88
Peck, Sheldon	13
Peddle, Clara	28
Pederson, Vernon	78
Pierce, David	134
Pentecost, Mildred	71
Perry, Russ	93
Peters, Mrs. Albert	110
Peters, "Frank"	88
Peter, Nicholaus	49
Pflaume, Walter	110
Pfund, Christian	137
Pfund, Bertha	137
Pfund, Ernest	137
Pfund, Lee	88,137

Index Of Individuals

Pfund, Paul	137
Pfund, Robert	137
Phillips, Owen	87
Pickell, James	90
Pierce, "Bob"	88
Pierce, Harold	88
Piggott, Margaret	106
Pillatt, Harold "Shorty"	88,91
Pladna, Lyle	88
Plankey, Rev. James	73
Plunkett, Rev. Wm. J.	102,103
Podesta, Rev. John	133
Pollard, Marvin	130
Pollock, William J.	125,135
Pope, Mick	102
Porter, Gilbert	80
Potter, Rev. J.A.	22
Poulos, Chris	75
Poulos, James	75
Prager, G. Clifton	*
Prindle, Don G.	140*
Putnam, H.	*
Raab, Mrs. Raphael A.	84,108
Raach, Dr. J.H.	107
Rabe, George H.	77
Radenzel, A.G.	*
Raese, "Bill"	89
Ragland, Chester	100
Rahm, Omer	104
Rakow, Louis	49
Ramsey family	138
Rand, William	68
Randolph, Blanche	84
Randolph, John	*
Ranger, Ray	90
Rank, Allen H.	*
Ransteat, Marian	106
Raugroth, William	78
Ray, Allen S.	*
Reader, Henry	12
Rebek, Frank	130*
Rebek, Polly	89
Reichold, Clarence	*
Reid, John	15
Reid, Rev. Walter	132
Reilly, Joseph	16,125,126
Reinhardt, Betty	84
Reinhold, W.J.	*
Reising, Mrs. Emma	122
Remic, Donald	134
Remec, Joe	93
Remmer, Otto	72
Repke, Rev. Paul E.	103
Reusch, Mamie (Sphecht)	63
Reuter, Herman	87
Rhode, Olive	89
Richards, Florence	121
Richards, H.	*
Richardson, Rebecca	31,80
Ricker, Joseph	134
Ricki, "Jay"	90
Richter, Werner	118
Rieger, William	88
Riener, C. Edward	64
Ringhaver, Marge	122
Robbins, Glen "Shine"	91
Robbins, Kenneth, "Little Shine"	92
Robbins, William A.	83
Robillard, Harrison H.	78,95,112,132
Rockwood, Frank	68,79,80
Rockwood, Fred	68,80
Rockwood, Harvey	80
Roe, Harry A.	*
Rohmeyer, Fred H.	60,78
Ronske, Edmund	87,91
Ronske, Frank "Cy"	91
Ronske, John	87
Rosback, "Buzz"	93
Rosdail, J. Hart	29,119
Rosback, Herbert G.	*
Rosche, George F.	55,68,72*
Rose, Lawrence C.	142
Rosenfeldt, William	87
Rothmeyer, (Jack)	104
Rowe, Viola	117
Ruby, Irvin	113,130,131
Rude, Wally	87
Rudolph, George	87
Ruebling, (Charles)	81
Ruebling, Louise	114
Rudolph, Arthur	86,87
Ruffan, Ray	91
Rumsey, George F.	16,80
Runge, Fred	106
Runge, Wilfred	88
Russell, Don	116,117,119
Russell, John Robert	119
Rusteberg, Wilbert	130
Ryburn, Glenn S.	*
Saint, Frederick	134
Sanford, William O.	*
Samuel, Wm.	134
Samuelson, James D.	140,144
Sanborn, Jack	141
Sanborn, Mary	141
Sandberg, Carl	23,63,101,115,124
Sandberg, Helga	116
Sandberg, Janet	116
Sandberg, Lillian Steichen (Mrs. Carl)	115,116,117
Sandberg, Margaret	116
Sandiland, Frank W.	106
Sater, Miles	69,116,122
Sater, Mrs. Miles (Gertrude Griffin)	121,122
Sawin, Carrie Rust (Mrs. George)	45
Sawin, George, jr.	45
Sawin, George	43,45,149 *
Sawin, Gertrude	45
Sawin, Robert	45
Sawyer, Dr. Robert Lee	132
Schaefer, Walter C.	*
Schaefer, Abram L.	69
Schafer, Mrs. A.L.	110
Schaper, William	50
Scheppach, Mrs. George	132,141
Schick, Rev. Herman J.	96
Schick, Mrs. Herman J.	114

Schiele, Dr. Richard	107
Schiffman, Rev. Merl	133
Schill, Robert	126
Schlener, John L.	142
Schmidt, Dick	45
Schmidt, Herman	72
Schmidt, "Dick" Richard	72
Schmitz, Gustav	89
Schnitzius, Woodrow D.	142
Schneider, Jack A.	142
Schoenbeider, Clara (Miller)	63
Schourek, Dan	144
Schradel, "Vern" O.	89
Schram, Ed	83
Schroeder, Fred	*
Schroerine, Fred	47
Schulke, Mildred	84
Schulke, Vera	84
Schultz, Albert T.	50
Schulze, David	142
Schultz, Dr. H.L.	106
Schumacher, Art. Jr.	87,91
Schumacher, Benjamin A.	*
Schumacher, Eugene J.	134
Schumacher, Heinrich	122
Schumacher, Henry C.	70,72,106,107,108,109,139*
Schumacher, Mrs. Henry C.	71
Schumacher, "Jack"	92
Schuttler, Erwin	125*
Schwab, Phyllis Bates	22
Schwarz, "Marty"	88
Schwass, Fred	77
Schween, Lucy (Mrs. Henry Glos)	44
Schweppe, "Ed"	88
Schwerin, "Bill"	89
Scott, Garfield J.	*
Scott, Stephen J.	12
Seabright, Laurence	119
Seavey, Harry L.	134
Seeck, Harold	87
Seeck, John	87
Seibert, Rev. L. Yarger	103
Seivers, Mrs. Ruby	106
Selden, Mrs. Carlyle	114
Sellergren, Willard	88
Semple, Mrs. William	125,126
Seton-Thompson, George	83
Setzer, Rev. W.H.	103
Shabbonah	6
Shiley, Donald H.	142
Shipeks,	81
Shynikevich, Dale	88
Sibley, Frederick J.	142
Sieloff, F.	88
Sieloff, "Ray"	93
Sievers, Arthur	50
Simmons, Bert	*
Simon, "Tex"	88
Sinn, Herbert C.	125
Skeele Family	16
Slavik, Max J.	*
Sloane, Wm. B.	120,121
Slocum, Mark M.	*
Smith, Miss Georgia (Bates, Mrs. Gerry)	15,19
Smith, Mason	12,20
Smith, Rollin C.	136
Smith, (Ruth) Mrs. Robert	119
Smotherman, James	92
Smotherman, Wm.	88,92
Snite, Frederick B.	36,80,107
Snow, Dorothea	117
Snow, Electra	20
Sommerschield, Rev. W.S.	74
Sorenson, A.W.	*
Sorrick, George A.	40, 41,122
Soukup, David	105
Soukup, Irwin	104,105
Soukup, Jack	105
Soukup, Philip J., Jr.	104,105,121
Soukup, Philip Jacob, Sr.	104
Soukup, Ray	104,105
Soukup, Rudolph	104
Soukup, Ted	105
Soukup, Vernon	105
Spaeth, Jerry	92
Speckmann, Kurt	134
Spratt, John	90
Stach, Rev. Edward	74
Stange, Otto H.	*
Stange, Mrs. Otto H.	81
Stanger, Christian C.	40,41,97
Stanger, Robert	93,97,126
Stanton, Dick	90
Staudt, Genevieve	96
Stavros, Chris	134
Stegen, "Art" Arthur	87
Steichen, Edward	23,115
Steichen, John	115
Steichen, Mary	115
Steingraber, Norm	93
Steinhebel, George	87
Steinhebel, Kenneth E.	142
Stellman, M.	91
Stender, Mrs. Arnold	131
Sterling, Rev. Chandler	73,118
Sterz, Rev. Ewald L.	133
Stevens, Byron F.	83,124*
Stevens, Chris	107,138
Stevens, Francis O.	95,121
Stevens, Fred	110
Stevens, Peter	138
Steward, Sanford H. Jr.	*
Steivart, Rev. Paul	73
Stickle, Ruth	126
Stolper, "Hub"	88
Stone, Bernadine	83
Stone, Geraldine	83
Stone, Ira A.	83,107
Stone, Mrs. Ira	84
Stone, Mrs.	120
Stoner, William	34
Stoop, Principal	55
Stopka, Jim	88
Storm, Dorothy	121
Story, Howard K.	125
Stott, "Don"	91

Index Of Individuals

Stoutmeyer, Rev. G.	133
Strand, Axel J.	*
Strand, Earl	83,126
Strand, Lucile	84
Strand, Ruth	84,124,125,126
Strane, Thomas M.	*
Strauschild, Otto	82
Stringer, Gerald	83
Stromberg, Louis	154
Struckman, Al	87
Struckmann, Deidrick	43
Struckmann, George	87
Struckmann, Henry G.	*
Stuart, Jeanne	*
Stuenkel, Martin	75
Stumpf, "Bob"	89
Sturges, Frank	16,61,80
Sturges, Lee	28,80,116,122,124
Sturges, Mrs. Lee	124
Sturges, Mary	28
Surges, Ronald L.	142
Sullivan, Mrs. Eugene C.	84
Sullivan, Philip M.	*
Sveinsson, Solveig	119
Swanson, Richard R.	144
Tallman, Rev. Clare E.	132
Tallman, David	12
Talmadge, George	58
Talmadge, John	12
Tarabilda, Victor	137
Tarbell, Harlan	112,119
Tarbell, Mrs. Harlan	84
Taylor, Benjamin Franklin	68
Taylor, Samuel G.	*
Teason, James	122
Tecumseh,	6
Tedrahn, Fred H.	49
Tedrahn, Henry	49,63
Tennyson, Alfred L.	89
Terwedo, Mrs. Robert	108
Thoen, Frieda	122
Thollander, "Bob"	88
Thoma, D.W.	82
Thoma, George W.	154
Thomas, Mrs. Frank	112
Thomason, Camella	64
Thompson, Edith	114
Thompson, Robert	93
Thorneycroft, Matthew R.	112
Thorpe, Mrs. George	84
Thorsen, John	121
Thrasher, John	13
Thurston, David	12
Tiberi, "Joe"	90
Tiedemann, Henry	92
Tilly, Charles O.	*
Tilly, Naneth R.	*
Timke, Catherine Glos (Mrs. August Glos)	14
Timmer, George	*
Timmer, Herman	33
Timrott, Ernest	93
Toeppen, Donald	136
Torode, Nicholas, Sr.	12
Torode, Peter	19,22
Traeger, Lawrence C.*	*
Trenkler, W.P.	75
Trenn, Herman	72
Trenn, William	100
Treptow, Walter	87
Trick, Peter A.	134
Tripp, Lester	131
Tripp, Mrs. Lester	131
Troost, Mrs. Frank	142
Turyna, "Joe"	92
Ugoveck, Albert	33
Uhlir, Wm. O.	134
Uhlhorn, B.H.G.	77
Uhlhorn, Henry	72
Uhlhorn, Henry R.	50
Ullman, Albert J.	124
Ullman, Albert I. (Mrs. Ida Emery)	55,73
Ullman, Stuart	83
Ulrich, William	49
Ulseth, Nels A.	*
Ungery, James	34
Unverzagt, George W. Jr.	140*
Urbik, Jerome A.	141
Utley, Edward	62
Valcarenghi, John	134
Vallette, Henry F.	33
Van Auken, Claude L.	99,111,112,157,158,159,160,161,162 *
Vandekerkhoff, Henry	*
Van Gorkom, J. Jr.	*
Van Mater, Bill	88
Van Norman, Joyce	118
Van, George	126
Van Plew, Rev. Wright	103
Van Slyke, Charles R.	*
Van Voorst, Jack	92,93
Vernon, John P.	*
Vertovec, Carl	89,92
Vertovec, "Ed"	92,93
Vertovec, Frank	92
Vinton, William	33
Voelz, "Ed"	92,93
Voelz, Marvin J. (Bud)	92*
Vogel, John W.	*
Wachenheim, Mrs. Lee	84
Wade, Caroline	17,69,70,122
Wade, Charles	43
Waddell, Donald W.	134
Wadhams, Dana	31
Wadhams, Seth	29,30,31,68,102,123
Wagstaff, Rev. Cecil F.	133
Wakeman, Bradford	33
Wakeman James	54,78
Wall, James M.	119
Wallen, Richard	142
Walsh, Harry	106
Walter, Rev. Carl H.	103
Wandschneider, Anna	77
Wandschneider, Fred	77
Warnecke, Hermann	50
Warren, Alexander C.	116*
Watson, Dr. Ernest S.	106

Watson, Mrs. John 121
Watts, Alfred E. 87*
Webb, H. Adair ....*
Weber, "Ernie" Ernest 90
Weber, Gottfried 72,75*
Weber, Johnny 89
Weber, Richard 125
Webster, "Bob" Robert 89
Weisse, C. 40
Weeks, Harry 136
Weigel, Charles Jr. 140,141*
Weinbauer, Herb 105
Weinert, Herman 87
Weiser, John F. 92,122
Weiser, Walter 83
Weldon, James ....*
Weller, Bert 137
Weller, Stan 91
Weller, Wm. S. 137*
Welsh, William 33
Welsher, Philip 134
Wendland, Herman C. 107
Wentworth, John 16
Wetzel, Dorothy Hobein 76
Whaley, Mrs. Twitty 114
Wheeler, George M. 16
Whitney, Everett A. 113*
Wiegrefe, Henry 50
Wiemanski, "Jerry" 92
Wiencek, Marilyn ....*
Wilcox, Ward H. 76
Wilder, Harold 95
Wilder, Thomas E. 36,71,80,120,123,125
Wilkins, Jack 90

Willis, Thomas 119
Williston, Charles S. ....*
Williston, Rev. Martin L. 55,59
Willman, Howard C. 136*
Wilson, Ervin F. 113,125,130*
Wilson, Ervin, Jr. 130
Wilson, May Reed (Mrs. Ervin Wilson) 125
Wilson, Nancy 125
Wilson, Scott 121
Wilson, Theodore 16
Winchester, Wilhelmena 68
Winchester, William 68
Windrich, August 122
Wirkus, August 72
Wittenberg, Jacob 49
Woeller, Theo. J. 87*
Wolf, Henry 100
Wolf, Lorenz ....*
Wolf, Peter A. 43,47,49*
Wolf, Theodore H. 83
Wood, Mrs. William H. 95
Woodruff, "Tenny" 87
Wright, Frank Lloyd 119
Wright, Katherine 93
Wykoff, James 55
Yates, Gov. Richard 21
Yeisley, Ralph L. ....*
Yeomans, Louisa (Mrs. Frances King) 36,37
Youngberg, Walter R. 112*
Zajac, "Ted" 92
Zilla, Rev. John 23
Zimmerman, Lois 124,125
Zink, Frank J. ....*

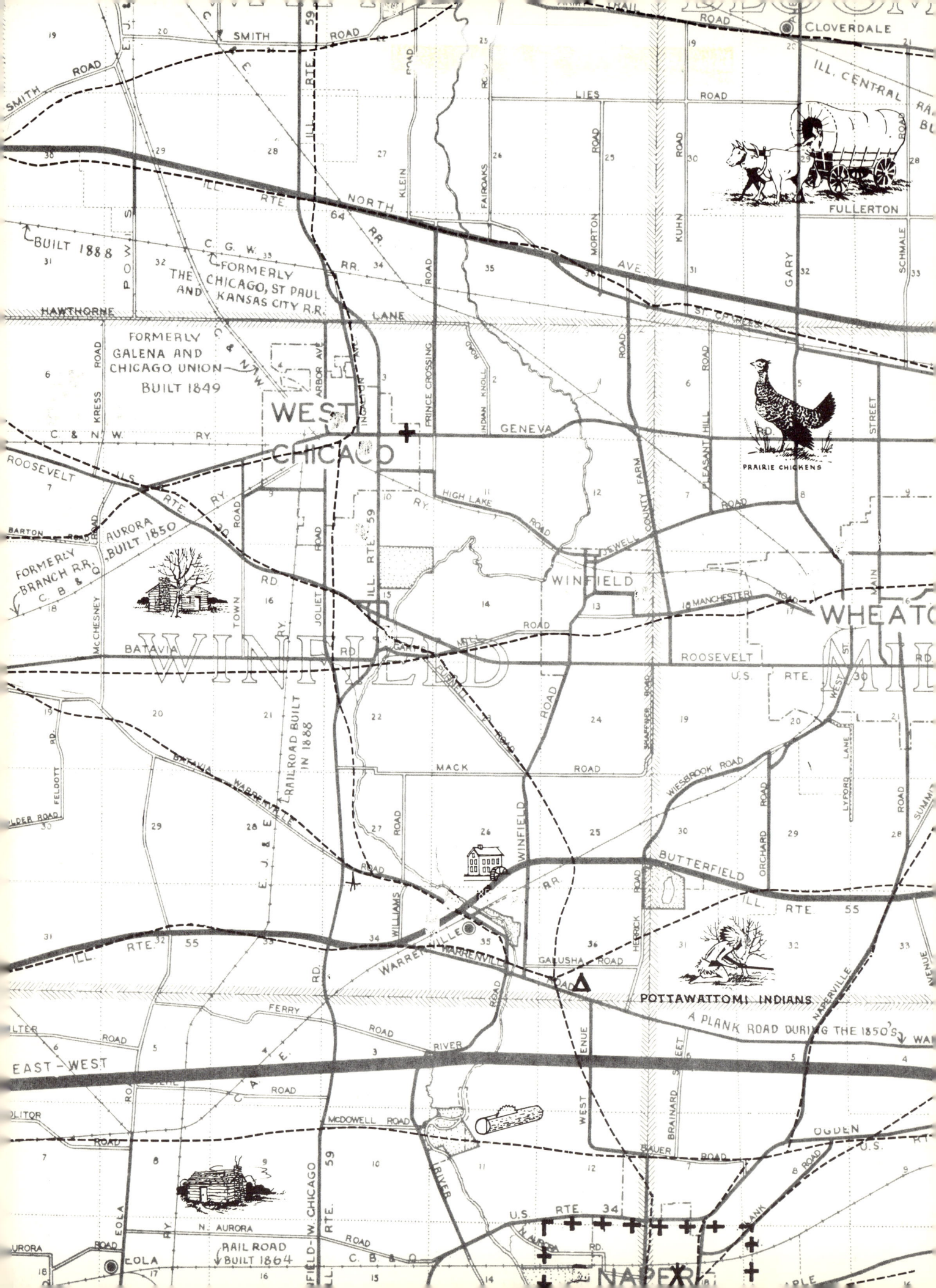